THE RATS OF RANGOON

Lionel Hudson was a working journalist in Melbourne, Australia, when he joined the RAAF in 1940. He was trained as a pilot in Southern Rhodesia and Kenya and flew Blenheim light bombers with the RAF in North Africa before flying to Ceylon with his squadron at the outbreak of the Pacific War. At the end of his first tour of operations he became one of the first Australians in the Empire Air Training Scheme to reach the rank of Wing Commander. After a stint on the staff at Air Command South-East Asia, New Delhi, he was given command of No. 82 RAF Mosquito Squadron.

As a correspondent after World War II he covered the Allied occupation of Japan, the Korean War, the Emergency in Malaya and the Vietnam War during the French involvement.

He won a Nieman Fellowship to Harvard in 1953 and studied Ancient Chinese History. Then he returned to Australia to be a television news executive and later produced and directed a number of wildlife documentary films. He now lives in Sydney where he is representative in the region for NBC News, New York.

THE RATS OF RANGOON

*The inside story of the
'fiasco' that took place
at the end of the
war in Burma*

Wg Cdr Lionel Hudson
RAAF (Retd)

ARROW BOOKS

Arrow Books Limited
62-65 Chandos Place, London WC2N 4NW

An imprint of Century Hutchinson Limited

London Melbourne Sydney Auckland
Johannesburg and agencies throughout
the world

First published by Leo Cooper 1987
Arrow edition 1989
Reprinted 1989

Printed and bound in Great Britain by
Courier International Ltd, Tiptree, Essex.

ISBN 0 09 960050 1

Dedication

For months after my release from Rangoon Gaol a noise outside in the middle of the night would have me scrambling out of bed and standing there braced at attention ready to bow to any Japanese guard who might appear out of the darkness. This book is for Audrey, the young bride who coaxed me back to bed.

Contents

Illustrations

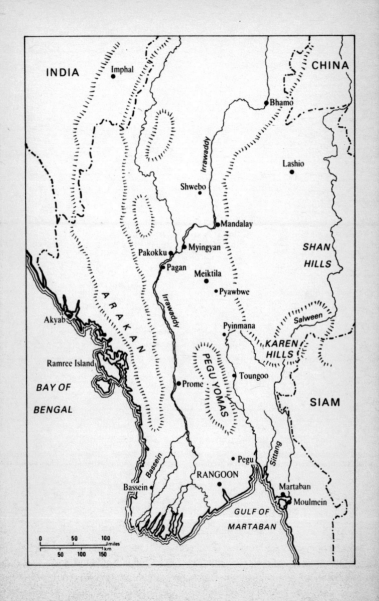

Dawn is breaking on a 'No Man's Rangoon'. The Japs have left (I think), the British have not arrived (as far as we know) and the Burmese must surely have taken to their heels. That deduction leaves me Emperor of Rangoon. I am free, too, but I don't feel a thing – except impatience at daylight being so long in coming.

The birds are beginning to squawk a little and soon I will not need the light of these five flickering candles that are spreading grease over the prison commandant's table. A Japanese doll is raising dainty hands in the centre of the table. Half a bottle of saki is on one side of her, a cactus in a pot on the other. The boys have just brought in a bucket of tea.

This day is a frightening one. Anything may be in store for us. All is still now after several hours of frightening explosions that came from a fire to the east of the gaol. Calm men sit about talking normally. One army Lt. just asked another browsing through an encyclopaedia to look up a bishop's salary. Never has there been a stranger situation.

Birds are noisier so daylight is not far off.

I have locked the prison gate from the inside but before I did I pulled it ajar and stood and looked out on freedom. It thrilled me, too. The moon was high in the sky and all was quiet . . .

It still amazes me that Japan's Burma Area Army gave up, without a fight, the strategically important port of Rangoon towards the end of

1

April, 1945, at a time when the order of the day for the Emperor's fighting men at Okinawa and elsewhere in the Pacific called for fanatical suicidal resistance. For we Allied prisoners-of-war, helpless behind high walls in Rangoon Gaol and fully expecting to be caught up in the battle for the city, the furtive withdrawal of the Japanese was a miracle we had not even dared to dream about. Their moonlight flit came as a complete surprise to Admiral Lord Louis Mountbatten, Supreme Commander, South-East Asia Command, and to Lt-General William Slim whose powerful 14th Army had been pushing south to Rangoon for eleven frustrating months. At first they refused to believe their luck even after decoded signals had indicated that the enemy headquarters had fled from Rangoon. They suspected trickery.

However, no one could have been more astonished than Emperor Hirohito himself. His Commander-in-Chief in Rangoon had been ordered to defend Rangoon at all costs. Despite this, the last of his devoted warriors sneaked out of the city on 29 April – his birthday.

As it happened, the south-west monsoon, which breaks regularly, year after year, in mid-May, turned up two weeks early that year and the tank-led British forces, so tantalisingly close to their objective, were bogged down in the mud and their supremacy in the air nullified to a large degree by the cyclonic conditions that ensued.

Operation Dracula, an amphibious assault launched by Mountbatten as a trump card, was always a gamble but, suddenly, it was in peril of being trumped by the monsoon. It is even conceivable that, in the changed circumstances, a determined Japanese defence of the area could have held out for months after the rains came and thwarted the British thrust to recapture Singapore. Remember, this was more than three months before the atom bomb was dropped on Hiroshima.

The last of the Japanese retreated from Rangoon four days before the first of the British forces finally arrived and, for those four long days, we emaciated gaol birds, now free, held sway in the beleaguered city. Believe me, we were not for a moment trying to be heroes. We were motivated solely by a desire to survive. We were both feeble and fearful, but determined not to be killed off now so close to going home. Our desperate efforts to convince the British that the enemy had abandoned Rangoon failed miserably. We were terrified that the fleeing Japanese might be cut off and pushed back into the city, so we disarmed the Indian 'Traitor' Army troops there and fortified our gaol. We also huffed and puffed to keep at bay the local Burmese opportunists, bent on independence.

Finally, we handed over Rangoon on a platter to the advance units of the seaborne expeditionary force.

'*What might have proved a difficult and costly undertaking thus ended in an atmosphere not far removed from* opera bouffe,' *Captain S. W. Roskill D.S.C., wrote in* The War At Sea, *Volume III of Britain's Official History of the Second World War.*

Another of his comments reads: 'The first intimation of the Japanese withdrawal, which actually took place on 23 April, was received on 1 May, when an aircraft flying low over Rangoon read in large letters on the gaol roof "Japs gone! Exdigitate!"* The ribaldry of the composers of the message (no doubt from the Royal Air Force) was perhaps a not inappropriate piece of sarcasm over the failure of our Intelligence organization to learn about this development.'

The farce in Rangoon was enacted in a week when:
– nearly a million Germans surrendered in Europe as prisoners-of-war;
– the war in Italy ended;
– the bodies of Mussolini and his mistress were strung up head downwards on meat-hooks at a petrol station in Milan;
– Adolf Hitler and Eva Braun committed suicide in a Berlin bunker;
– the battle for Okinawa was at its height and the British Pacific Battle Fleet, which had just joined the fray, was savagely attacked by self-sacrificing kamikaze pilots.
So the eyes of the world turned only briefly to the non-event in Rangoon.

It is not hard to imagine that the British Government preferred it this way with a General Election only weeks off. Burma was the first British territory to be re-occupied and it must have been hard to swallow that the ultimate prize, Rangoon, was actually handed back by a half-starved Australian pilot and his band, dressed in loin-cloths.

Until now the inside story of the Rangoon fiasco has not been told in full. A few months ago, forty years after I wrote it, I read for the first time the diary I had secretly written in prison. After that I felt driven to search out more facts from official records in London and to talk to people in Rangoon and Tokyo to enable me to tell all sides of this intriguing, if inconsequential, capsule of military history.

---

*Actually 'Extract Digit'. Slim got it wrong in his *Defeat into Victory*.

I

Into Captivity

19 December, 1944

The irony of it all is that sheer pilot error landed me and my navigator in Rangoon Gaol as prisoners of the Japanese. My flight into Burma from Assam that day was my own bright idea. It was a journey that was not really necessary. Group operations had no specific target to offer, but I was keen and wanted to test-fire my cannon. I should have stayed put and played poker.

The morning cloud over the southern spurs of the Himalayas was breaking up as our two jungle-green Mosquito Vl fighter bombers dropped quickly and flattened out just above the tree tops on what we called a low-level 'rhubarb' – seeking targets of opportunity.

My wingman was another Australian, Scotty McKenzie, from the goldfields town of Kalgoorlie. He kept his distance in loose formation.

We used to say no woman could be as sensitive as a Mosquito. You flew it with the tips of your fingers on the control column, delighting in the response. We were flirting with the earth a whisper above coconut-tree height, now lifting the wing to check a jungle village, now zooming down over glistening paddy fields, now swerving to miss a gleaming white Buddhist temple. I recall feeling inside me the reckless rhythm of a Viennese waltz. Perhaps I was fanning the palm tops too closely but that was the spirit of the dance. My partner and navigator, Jack Shortis, a Londoner, who had to share my moods, gave me a furtive, quizzical look or two but said nothing. Trusting birds, these navigators.

The air speed needle was steady at 250 knots. Nothing moved below. Nothing to shoot at. Anyway, it was a beautiful morning. The forest of temples of Pagan, the ancient capital, caught the sun over my starboard wingtip. I knew little about Burma, but at least I was aware that the name had nothing to do with pagan worship.

Jack gave me a new course – north to Mandalay. Before us was the Irrawaddy River, broad and smooth and lightly veiled in morning mist. It beckoned. I swished down and skimmed it. Then there was a jolting crash, a jarring note, and a freezing of the music inside my stomach.

Incredibly, we were still airborne and climbing, but my serene and purring Mosquito of a moment before was now vibrating madly. The tips of the port airscrew were curled back and the Merlin motor looked as though it would shake itself out of its bed. White coolant was streaming from it like smoke. I switched that motor off and it seemed to sigh in relief. The starboard motor was still running but it was a struggle to keep straight and level. Anger was my only emotion.

'You stupid bastard, Hudson,' I yelled.

Poor Jack had nothing to do but sit there.

'The port engine's on fire,' he shouted.

I knew it was the coolant but I could not tell him because my microphone was dangling. He swivelled around and pressed a fire-extinguisher button. I suppose it was the right one. Anyway, we were now dropping out of the sky like a falling leaf . . . stick forward or you'll stall . . . straight ahead . . . land it there . . . look for a tree in a wooden aircraft, that instructor in Rhodesia had told me three years before . . . put a wing into it . . . puts the brake on . . . and I'd laughed. A tree came up on cue, dead ahead, and I put the port wing into it.

When I came to I was standing there on drying mud in a tangle of control wires, with Jack, slumped a little, alongside me. He was still attached to the armour plating by his Sutton harness. I punched the release and we climbed out of the mess of wires. There was a smell of burning, but I have no idea what happened to the rest of the Mosquito. It seemed to have vanished.

There was cover over to the left.

'Can you make it?' I said to Jack.

He said he would try but then fell like a sack. Leaning on me, he was able to hop a few steps. Then the enemy came over the hill just like in the movies. Our hands went up with alacrity. The Japanese just stood and stared but a tall, turbaned Sikh among them dropped to his knee and aimed his .303 at us. He was shouting excitedly. Obviously he wanted to prove his hate for the British. We reached higher. This Sikh would belong to the Indian National Army, the 'traitor' army, men who had changed sides.

I suppose I breathed while all this was going on but when the little Japanese NCO pushed the Sikh's rifle away and yelled to us, my heart pumped wildly. He beckoned us and made signs that he wanted us to crawl towards him. We dropped to our knees and crawled. We were on our way to Rangoon. The date: December 19, 1944.

Whether I was too busy cursing myself or whether I was feeling too ashamed to look up I do not know, but I covered the first twenty yards with my head down. Then I had the ridiculous thought: Am I crawling too fast? Does one crawl quickly or slowly towards an enemy who is about to take you prisoner or, perhaps, behead you? I sneaked a look back at my navigator. He was making heavy weather of it because of his mangled leg. He also had his head down but he was dead on course. I slowed down and waited for him. This was one race I did not relish winning.

They must have walked to meet us because, without warning, a boot caught me in the midriff. I rolled away from a second kick and, instinctively, knew I should stand. The boot had been aimed at my crutch.

'Up quickly,' I said to Jack and helped him to his feet. We both neglected to put our hands above our heads and were prompted by prodding rifles. We were not searched. They just gaped at us. Both sides were face to face with the enemy for the first time.

There was a burst of excited chatter and then the little soldier who was calling the shots stood in front of me, tapped my shoulder and rattled out a question in Japanese. I shook my head, pretending not to understand, but I knew full well what it was all about. Stupid fool . . . I had forgotten to take off my wing-commander's stripes. Now I was in real trouble. It was a cardinal rule that senior officers put up junior rank while flying over enemy territory.

The open-handed blow caught me unawares. It seemed to come from nowhere. I scrambled to my feet again and shot my hands high. This, I decided, was the right drill.

Half-a-dozen soldiers went off at the double in the direction of our crashed Mosquito and I was relieved of the German Luger in my holster. It was brand new. I had never fired it because guns bored me. This was one of a cache we had found, still in their oily wrappings, near Tobruk in the Libyan Desert where the Germans were the enemy. I had given the others away.

'The boss,' as we labelled him, ordered us in Japanese and sign language to march. Jack took one step and crumpled to the ground in pain. The boots scuttled forward but I got there first and helped him to his feet.

The hissing Japanese NCO gestured along the path so we stumbled off. I was half-carrying Jack. His leg was a mess. Before long they let us pause for a rest and we sat down. My search for a handkerchief came up with the squadron 'Mayfly', a report on the aircraft situation in my squadron – how many were operational and so on. Hell. This was unpardonable. Before you took off on an operation you cleaned out your pockets, so as not to be carrying information which would be of use to the enemy if you happened to be captured. I felt sick in the stomach as I palmed the tell-tale document and prodded it into the soft earth. I looked up and caught the eye of one of the Burmese villagers who had gathered around us. Obviously he had seen what I had done. He just grinned.

The left leg of my trousers was torn, so I yanked it up to see what damage had been done. My kneecap grinned at me too. It was sliced to the bone, with the flesh puckered like lips. I was still staring at it when the shouted order came to move on. Jack was up like a shot but I was paralysed by the shock of seeing my mutilated kneecap. They slapped me, put the boot in and prodded me with their rifles, but, for the life of me, I could not get to my feet. Jack bent down and, with the help of one of the soldiers, pulled me up, but I could not even stand on my good leg. I fell to the ground.

The Japanese NCO was furious. A few minutes before I had been able to give Jack a hand. Now I could not even stand up. Finally he gave up and, after some more shouting, some Burmese appeared with two litters made from poles and vines. We finished our journey to the Japanese camp in style.

They put us on a bamboo sleeping platform in the open, tightly bound together, back to back. Concussion from the crash caught up with both of us and we were out for an hour or so at a time that afternoon. It was all a blur to me except that at one point I remember coming to and focusing on the barrel of my Luger near my face, but it was only one of our guards trying to puzzle out how to work it. I reached out with one of my hands that had worked loose and snapped on the safety catch.

'Ah,' he said and nodded. Then I passed out again.

Another time, when I was aware that Jack was conscious too, I touched his hand and he responded.

'Sorry, Jack, to have got you into this mess,' I whispered.

'What do you think they'll do to us?' he asked.

'I can't imagine,' I said.

However, my imagination had had some prompting in Calcutta only a week or so before in a conversation with an Intelligence Officer from RAF Headquarters there.

'Best advice I can offer,' he said with worried eyes, 'is to tell your crews not to get caught by the Japs. The scanty information we have at hand indicates that any prisoners they take get bloody rough treatment during interrogation and a lot lose their heads whether they talk or not . . . no future at all. If I got caught, and had the chance, I'd bump myself off before they did. At least they'd respect you for it and give you a decent burial.'

At first they just stood around and stared at us but as night approached we were ignored. No food, no water, no medical treatment. My head throbbed and my knee was agony.

'Did Mackenzie see us go in?' I asked Jack.

'No idea. We seemed to have lost him after we turned north. Anyway, what hit us?'

Surely Jack was being kind. 'Nothing. I hit the drink. Must have just touched it and bounced off . . . shit-arse flying.'

'Could it have been a trip wire?' Jack persisted. And he had seen tracer bullets coming from the high bank of the river. I, too, had wondered about a trip wire. I had lectured my pilots only a few days before about how the Japanese stretched wires across rivers from bank to bank to catch low-flying aircraft.

The truth was that I was a clot. I should have resisted flirting with the river. Every conscious moment that night I felt the burning fury inside me . . . you stupid bastard, Hudson.

This pitch of anger kept me going over the next five months. I just could not face up to coming to such an ignominious end.

Back at Delhi was an English Wren, Mary Hayhurst. We had been engaged to be married until I told her one night that I was going back to flying. I had no option. I had been offered the command of No 82 Squadron, RAF, the second Mosquito Squadron in India.

She gave me a choice: Mary or Mosquitos. I chose Mosquitos. That night she threw my diamond engagement ring into a pond.

That had been some months ago and there was no way of her even knowing that my squadron had moved to a forward base.

I learned later that around midnight on 19 December Mary knocked on the door of a mutual friend, John Galvin, a legendary figure who, at the time, was Admiral Mountbatten's political adviser on matters involving British territories occupied by the Japanese.

'Something's happened to Bill Hudson,' she blurted out. (My friends call me Bill.)

Mary said she had been fast asleep and woke in shock. 'It's Bill, I know. Something terrible . . .'

Nobody in Delhi had better access to secret information than John Galvin. He assured Mary that no word had come through about me. He sent her back to bed.

Next day the official message at Air Command South-East Asia headquarters in Delhi was that I was missing, believed killed.

Just on dusk I felt a strain on the rope that bound us together and turned to see Jack on his knees. I knew I was awake but it was like a nightmare. They were about to behead him. I waited for the sword to come crashing down on the back of his neck. I tried to cry out but no sound came.

Jack, still on his knees, turned and looked at me.

'What in the hell is happening?'

'I'm praying,' said Jack.

'You stupid bastard,' I snapped. 'It's too late for that now. Save your strength.'

On reflection that is the most brutal thing I have ever said to anybody.

Jack sank slowly back on to his side and rolled over turning his back on me. He stayed like that for a long time.

We were both too sick to eat but it began to worry me that we were not offered any food. It was dark now and I was beginning to think more clearly.

'Jack,' I whispered. 'Do you feel like talking?'

'What about?' He was still flattened. 'If they hear us they'll murder us.'

'Well, we both know we haven't much of a chance anyhow. I was just thinking we should hold out for as long as we can in the hope that something will turn up.'

Jack was silent.

'Look, Jack . . . I'm sorry I got you into this but there's no point in beating about the bush. They'll let us live only while they think we can give them useful information.'

I hesitated, but then it came out.

'They are going to kill us off eventually. We have to face up to that, don't we?'

Jack did not answer.

'So I feel we should give them number, rank and name only for as long as we can. When they get stuck into the torture we can spill out a story, but not the right one. We've got a chance now to concoct a story that will hold water . . . one that won't be any use to them.'

All I knew about Jack was that he was a Cockney, in that he had been born within the sound of Bow Bells, and that he was regarded as an ace navigator. It seemed strange to me that only now that we were in this desperate situation was I beginning to wonder what kind of a man I had chosen to fly with me.

Jack nodded, tight-lipped, showing the British pluck that was expected of him. Number, rank and name only, he agreed stoically.

The truth of the matter, however, was that my motive was more selfish than patriotic. Very little that Jack could tell the Japanese would have been of much use to them. Air supremacy had been won by the Allies in Burma shortly after the arrival of the Spitfire squadrons at the end of 1943. By now all the Japanese bombers were based outside Burma and came forward for sporadic raids. It was most unlikely they would try to penetrate into Assam to hit our base there.

It was most important for me, however, that we told the same story to the Japanese. Strictly, I should not have been flying over enemy territory. I knew too much.

For more than a year I had been a staff officer attached to Air Command South-East Asia, Delhi. As Squadron Leader Air Plans I had been involved in planning Operation Bullfrog, a combined operations invasion of Akyab Island. On a special mission to the North African theatre I had studied combined operations planning in Algiers, Sicily and Italy with General Dwight Eisenhower's staff. Until a few months ago I had been Wing-Commander Organization, Air Command South-East Asia, in full knowledge of a vast amount of top secret material.

So, I am afraid, this was the main reason I went over and over a cover story with Jack, making sure we had it off pat. I was afraid that, if the Japanese suspected my real background, I would be the target of special torture to disclose my secrets.

We had just flown out from England in our Mosquito, went our story. We had been serving in Coastal Command against the Germans. We were part of a squadron that was forming in the Calcutta area and had come to Burma to familiarize ourselves with flying over tropical jungle. We knew nothing about what was going on in the India-Burma theatre.

Neither Jack nor I remembered much of what happened over the next day or so. We were both unconscious for hours at a stretch. Concussion can be a mercy. I came to on one occasion to find that we were in a bullock cart passing through a village. Jack was stretched out alongside me. We were both bound tightly and my limbs ached. Burmese children were running alongside the cart staring at the hog-tied humans. Bystanders at the side of the road were more discreet. They merely turned their heads to follow our lurching progress.

The scene, to me, was too reminiscent of films I had seen of French noblemen on their way to the guillotine. I cursed again and lapsed back into unconsciousness.

The next sequence of events in my memory bank starts with a blur of marching legs. They were treading close to my head but the sound was strangely soft. As I instinctively moved my head away two odd-looking jungle boots came to a standstill and into focus. But only

12

for a moment. I saw the boot coming and rolled. It caught the back of my neck a glancing blow. Then there was a well-timed kick in the backside which hurt. I lost my temper.

'You bastard,' I screamed, swinging back to face my tormentor. The faces leered down and laughed. There was another half-hearted kick at my thigh from a soldier as he hurried away to join the column. I rolled over on to my side. It was not a bad dream.

Jack was still alongside me. In fact, we were bound together, stretched out in the middle of a narrow road that ran down to a wide, brown river. The Japanese troops were boarding a river barge moored at the point where the road disappeared into the river.

'Christ, what's going to happen to us?' There was despair in Jack's voice and it was understandable. Odd soldiers were breaking ranks to show their contempt for us. One tubby, little fellow trotted over, turned around and broke wind in our faces. Out of the uproar this noble act prompted, I heard 'Imphal, Imphal' being hissed.

I opened my eyes and looked straight into the angry face of a Japanese soldier. He was pointing to a circular scar on his left forearm, a healed bullet wound.

'Imphal, Imphal,' he said again and then reached down to slap my face with the back of his hand. He was not able to get much force into the blow so he stood up frustrated. His eyes darted to the gash in my left kneecap, a mess of dried blood and mud. My issue water bottle was on the ground beside me. He picked it up, raised it above his head in both hands and brought it crashing down towards my wounded knee. The bottle struck above the wound and hardly hurt at all but the Japanese thought he was right on target. When I stared back without flinching the expression on his face changed. There was something like awe in his look.

'You brave,' he almost whispered.

He hurried away with my water bottle and returned a few minutes later to give me a drink from it. He had filled it at the river. For the next hour or so the little corporal who had been wounded at Imphal fussed around us. He kept away the other troops and, as the sun grew hotter, he fixed a palm leaf in a way that shaded our faces. He talked at length with our guards who sat apart and with the use of his few English words he got across to us that a truck was on its way from Meiktila to pick us up.

13

I refused the cigarette he offered but Jack took one. Then he acted out a message to us that the barge was leaving and he would have to go but he had arranged for us to have our wounds dressed in half an hour.

'So sorry,' he said, backing away with an almost perceptible bow. It was unreal.

As the sun climbed higher in the sky the palm leaf was useless as an umbrella and our guards were not inclined to readjust it. All we could do in the way of self-protection was to turn our heads to get our eyes away from the burning sun.

After what appeared to be a couple of hours there was movement in a palm-roofed house at the side of the road nearby. An order was barked out from the front window and one of our guards scampered across at the double. He was back in a few minutes. He untied our legs and pointed to the house. With two good legs between us we somehow managed to get there. I remember the relief at being able to stand up and I recall no pain.

It was a Japanese casualty clearing post complete with a medical officer who looked us up and down from a distance and promptly donned a surgical mask. His aide gestured us to sit on a bench. The M.O. was strongly built, had an intelligent face and his uniform fitted. Here, I decided at once, was a doctor and a gentleman.

'Do you speak English?' I asked but he ignored me and started prodding Jack's swollen foot. He bound it meticulously with a crepe bandage and dabbed something pink out of a bottle on some of the lacerations on his face and legs.

'Thank you.' Jack was grateful. The doctor turned to me, ignoring his remark. Using the same piece of cotton wool, he scraped some of the muck out of the mouth-shaped wound on my kneecap and dabbed the lips that had formed with the same pink fluid. It was a dirty-looking bandage he put on it but I, too, was full of gratitude and said so. The doctor acted as though I had not spoken. His face was without expression as he waved his hand to the orderly indicating that we were to be bound again. Our hands were tied behind our back as we sat there.

The doctor stood squarely in front of Jack for a few seconds and then his right fist came up in an uppercut that clipped the side of his patient's jaw. Jack toppled off the bench. He was out cold. I was next

14

for the ananaesthetic. Rubbing the knuckles of his operating hand in a nonchalant manner he faced up to me. Our eyes met for a moment as he measured the distance. They told me nothing. Then all went black.

It was the open road again for us when we regained consciousness. The rope binding my wrists together was wet with blood.

'What happened?' Jack did not know what had hit him. I described the knockout. Jack shook his head incredulously and only then realized he had a sore jaw. They had been deftly scientific blows.

'The crazy bastard. What got into him?' asked Jack.

'I suppose as a doctor he felt he had to treat us . . . something to do with his Hippocratic oath . . . but there's nothing in the oath that says he has to like treating us.' For most of the next five months I was continually wrong in my judgments as to how the Japanese would react to certain developments.

Our bored guards spent most of the time scoffing down rice but we were not offered any. We were becoming interested in food again. It was now a day and a half since I had turned up my nose at the eggs swimming in fat back in the mess at base. I had taken off on an empty stomach.

In one respect I turned out to right – we were about to be handed over to the Japanese intelligence for expert interrogation. A car came down the road like a speeding tree. Branches had been lashed to a frame on the roof of the vehicle for camouflage. The guards yanked us to our feet as a smartly-dressed Japanese officer climbed out of the battered sedan. He introduced himself to us politely in fluent English, explaining that he was attached to the Kempei Tai. We were to go with him to his headquarters. His manner was casual as if this was every-day routine. I looked into the car, wondering where he intended to put us. The front seat was full. A Burmese youth, who looked about 14 to me, was at the wheel and an old man, who could have been his father, was in the front seat. The officer had been in the window seat. The back seat was piled to the roof with mattresses and supplies.

'Where do we ride?'

'On top.'

I felt like laughing when I looked at Jack. His mouth was wide open with disbelief, but it was no joke. Within minutes they had us lashed to the frame on top of the branches.

'Kick the roof if you are going to fall off,' the officer said as an afterthought and climbed into his seat.

The rope around my wrists had loosened after a few hundred yards and I pulled my hands free to get a firmer grip on the wooden frame. Then, as my confidence grew, I investigated a jute bag that had been thrown up with us. It was full of raw toddy sugar. I helped myself to a few handfuls and, psychologically, strength flowed back into my body. Jack ate some.

'What if they catch us?'

'What have we got to lose?'

Then, for the first time, I thought of escaping.

'You know, Jack, this is our last chance to get away.'

'And how in the hell would we do that?'

'There must be some way.'

'You're crazy. We can barely hop.'

I was agreeing with him that it looked hopeless when there was a clatter from underneath the car. By the time we had come to a standstill Jack and I had slipped our wrists back into our bonds and pulled them tight with our teeth.

The Kempei Tai man was a man of action. He wrenched away a five-foot length of exhaust pipe that had been rattling and lashed it to the frame alongside me. Then we were on our way again.

'This is it, Jack.'

'What?'

'Our chance to escape.'

'Not me . . . I can't even walk.' Jack turned away his face. He did not even want to discuss the idea.

'Listen to me, Jack . . . we are on our way to be tortured at best. Then they'll get rid of us. We'll lose our bloody heads. We haven't got a chance. Now, this is it. We can easily get free. We've got this exhaust pipe as a weapon. I'll just bang on the roof and they'll stop, thinking we are falling off. The Jap's on my side. As he gets out I'll clobber him with the pipe and fall on him. You drop on the kid driving. He won't want to fight. Then there's the old man. I'll have the Jap's gun by then.

'Anyway, how do we know the Burmese won't help us? We must

be near the river. Once we get to the other side we are not far from our troops. We could even lay up for a few days until we can walk. Jack, it's our last bloody chance.'

'This place is full of Japs. We wouldn't have a ghost of a chance.'

'We certainly won't once the Kempei Tai gets us. Look, there are lots of lonely stretches.'

We were passing through open country dotted with toddy palms and clumps of stunted acacia trees. Apart from the odd bullock cart as we passed through a village there had been no other vehicles on the road. Travelling in daylight was dangerous when the enemy has air supremacy.

'You are out of your mind. We wouldn't stand a chance. I won't be in it.' The blood rose to Jack's face.

I'm afraid I did not spare Jack for a moment as we raced towards the Kempei Tai headquarters. I reminded him that it was his duty to escape. I bullied him. I told him that I would try it alone but he would not budge from his stand.

I untied the knot holding the exhaust pipe and was actually shaking my legs free of rope when we ran into the outskirts of a town. Anger welled up in me. We had missed our chance. As I bound myself up again with some help from Jack I cursed him.

'You deserve everything that's coming to you,' I told him coldly.

When the car pulled up outside a house the rear doors of the car swung open and two Japanese soldiers climbed out with their rifles. They had been asleep on the back seat during the journey concealed by a mattress. My escape bid, as it turned out, would have been suicide.

'Wow, that was close,' I whispered to Jack, who smiled for the first time in two days.

The soldiers propped up their rifles on the bumper bar and then helped us to climb down. The first thing that caught my eye once inside the long, front room of the house was the pile of bamboo cages in the corner. I froze. What sort of torture would this be? I immediately pictured us like animals in cages with sharpened bamboo sticks piercing our flesh at the slightest movement. When it was my turn to sit at the table facing the interrogator I took a closer look at the cages. Stuck to the bamboo bars were tell-tale fowl feathers. They were not torture chambers at all. I was torturing myself.

'Get a grip of yourself, Hudson.'

But the Kempei Tai officer left nothing to my imagination. I told him that under the Geneva Convention all we had to tell him was number, rank and name. He narrowed his eyes as if trying to control himself. Then he rose and walked slowly around to my side of the table.

'Stand up,' he screamed. He started slapping my face when I was half way up. The stinging blow sent me reeling but I regained my balance and stood to attention. Sharp slaps punctuated the staccato sentences that followed.

'You are my prisoner . . . you will answer my questions . . . if you don't you will be put to death . . . tomorrow.' I was sure he meant it. Then he stamped out, shouting instructions as he went.

My knee was throbbing. I lowered myself to the floor next to Jack.

'The trouble is that he means it,' I said. Jack nodded, grim-faced.

Nothing happened for half an hour or so. It was getting dark when we were helped on to a bullock cart and taken to the town gaol. To us it was like finding a motel in the middle of the wilderness – immense relief. The security of being behind walls away from the slap-happy Japanese turned the cell into a refuge. We relaxed for the first time for two days free of ropes and the fear that we would be kicked awake.

There was no sign of food. Obviously they meant to starve us into submission.

Something woke me. I lay there listening.

'Hullo there.' It was a soft voice at the high side window of the cell.

"Hullo,' I whispered in reply, pressing close to the wall.

'Are you all right? Do you need anything?'

This was getting too like a second-class movie. I had heard a Japanese sentry coughing and spitting on the other side of the cell door before I fell asleep.

'What about the guard?'

'We're watching him. He is sleeping well. We don't like the Japanese. They are bad men. Have they given you any food?'

'No. We have not eaten for two days. They . . .'

'Shhh . . .' There was a faint sound of movement outside and then dead silence for a few minutes.

'Hsss . . . it's okay. He is still sleeping. Our people are getting you some food.'

'Please don't take so much risk. The Japs say they are going to kill us tomorrow anyway if we don't talk.'

'They always say that. You will be all right.'

'Your English is very good.'

'Yes, I'm a schoolteacher. My name is U Saw.'

It was a feast that came out of the night and in through the bars – curried chicken and rice wrapped in a banana leaf, succulent bamboo shoots, a sort of sago with jaggary sugar syrup and subtly-flavoured Burmese tea served in small bowls. There was a suppressed hilarity about the occasion. I sensed that the silent bearers of the dishes were relishing the danger and defiance as much as we were savouring the food and soothing tea. We licked the banana leaves clean and passed them back through the bars with the wooden tea bowls.

'Thank you,' I said, acutely aware of the inadequacy of what I was saying.

'Don't worry. We will pray for you.'

1 May, 1975

I am in Rangoon, Burma, on my way to search for U Saw. I owe him a meal. This man, capable of such calm, unselfish, unassuming courage, was really just a voice to me from the other side of the wall but I had thought of him so often over the thirty years that had swept by since that night that my mind had conjured up a face for him.

Some years before I had applied in Canberra for a visa to visit Burma, but nothing happened. The application was not granted and was not refused. It was just ignored. When I went to the Embassy to check the situation I was palmed off with a shrug and a smile. Of course, I wondered whether my reign in Rangoon in 1945 had anything to do with it all.

The urge to try again came to me while I was wallowing in the artificial atmosphere that is thick over Cannes, in the south of France, at film festival time. Life was good. I had sold the television rights to some of my wildlife films at the documentary supermarket there and had won money at the casino. Out of the blue came this desire for something sharp and real. Loud and clear came U Saw's whisper: 'Hullo there . . . are you all right? Do you need anything?'

19

Next day I was in London applying for a tourist visa for Burma. No, I had never been to Burma before, I lied. For years the socialist government of Burma had shut the door to tourists, but now it was ajar. I was in for seven days but there was a restriction on travel up-country. I could visit only Rangoon, Mandalay and Pagan and it was essential that I fly between these centres. The fact was that rebel forces virtually controlled large tracts of the country and the safety of overland travellers could not be guaranteed by the Burmese authorities.

I had only a vague idea as to where I might find U Saw. Jack had been able to pinpoint in his mind where we had crashed near the junction of the two rivers but we had been moved under cover of darkness by the Japanese and at times were in a semi-conscious state. The town gaol where the manna came through the cell window that night had to be on the eastern side of the Irrawaddy. More than likely it was Myingyan, just north of Pagan on the way to Mandalay.

What I knew of his name was not much of a clue. In Burma 'U' is a title of respect somewhat stronger than our 'Mr' and Saws are as common there as Smiths in Manchester. On the other hand I know he was a teacher and that he spoke fluent English. So, somehow, I had to get to Myingyan in an area in Central Burma forbidden to foreigners. Also, the country is under martial law.

First, I need to satisfy a compulsion to see again my gaol in Rangoon. Sheer masochism, but my return is in delightful contrast to the day, nearly thirty years before, when I had been put behind bars sick with anger and despair.

My companion this time is a prim lady, Ann, from the Australian Embassy, aloof and cool in pink floral. Her voice is small but it has a ring of authority. She stands back as though not to intrude. Inside the gate to the right is the old mango tree, home of the woodpecker family I had spied on through the bars of my upstairs cell window. These birds had been my proxy contact with the world on the other side of the high walls.

'It stopped being a gaol in 1968,' a Burmese woman carrying a baby tells us. She is one of the wives of privileged government servants who live in the squalid buildings around the main gate where, in my time, the Japanese commandant and his staff were quartered. Any roof is still a good roof in Rangoon.

The cell blocks have been turned into an army recruiting centre, except that one of the spokes in the wheel design of the gaol has vanished. This was the block which had been skip-bombed by an RAF Mosquito three days after we prisoners had taken over the city. It was this bombing that had prompted the painting of the 'Extract Digit' message on the roof of the gaol.

It turns out to be a happy visit. This place of anguish in my nightmares is exorcised.

Over dinner that night a smiling fellow guest writes for me in the Burmese language a letter explaining why I am searching for U Saw. It is my passport to the hinterland. I am warned, too, that I am not allowed to stay overnight in places like Myingyan, away from the major centres.

Minutes after I land in Mandalay I am adopted by U Bo Gyi, a fast-talking guide who, during the war, had been an interpreter for the Japanese. His solution to my problem is for me to go by river boat to Myingyan and by bus to Pagan. Would they take a foreigner on the boat? He smiles and pats his chest.

'The police will be still sleeping,' he said.

An hour before dawn he wakes me and produces breakfast of papaya and bananas. It is still dark as I board the Taung Tai, a two-decker with a squat black and red funnel, and am told to keep out of sight until the ship sails.

The swollen, brown mass of the Irrawaddy River is a mile wide here but the dawn does not come up 'like thunder outer China 'crost the Bay,' as Kipling had it. Instead, as usual, it comes out of the east with little more than a whimper. Tiny craft with palm-leaf sails use the morning breeze to edge their way up river. There is no sound of 'paddles chunkin'' as the modern counterpart of Kipling's 'old flotilla' hugs the eroded western bank heading south.

In ten hours or so I will be in Myingyan and, with the help of a miracle, asking U Saw what prompted him to risk certain death for two strangers who were doomed to die anyway.

One of my fellow passengers, an elderly Burmese, has brought with him his own life buoy, an inflated inner tube. All of them came aboard with their own mats and food snacks of rice, curried chicken and pickled green mangoes wrapped in banana leaves.

As I prepared to get off at the stop for Myingyan the old man with the inner tube becomes quite fatherly, grabs my arm, shakes his head and gives me a lecture in Burmese. Obviously, he is worried about me going off alone. I barely have time to shake free and jump down on to the jetty before the boat rattles on.

The only thing in sight is a pony cart. The driver stares at me incredulously for a moment and takes fright. I chase after the cart and fling my bag aboard, determined not to be abandoned out here on this mid-Burma moonscape.

The town, I discover, is three miles away. The Irrawaddy has changed its course in recent years.

I cannot communicate with the driver. He cannot even read my to-whom-it-may-concern letter in Burmese. He just drives on, stops the cart in the main street and points to a doorway. It is the surgery of Dr Sein Hlaing, the only man in Myingyan who speaks English. We are warm friends in no time. I produce a bottle of Scotch and we go off to drink it at a nearby restaurant with Myingyan's leading citizens, members of the Committee of the People. My comrades drink the whisky and all barriers are down. They are all keen to help me.

The trouble is that Dr Hlaing cannot quite place the gaol I describe to him. He is the official gaol doctor for the whole region and knows them all. It cannot have been the Myingyan Gaol, he says, too many cells. However, there is a small police lock-up on the outskirts of Pagan at a place called Naingoo, that fits my description.

They squeeze me into the front seat of an ancient bus alongside a saffron-robed Buddhist priest and we rumble south through the dry zone which is the heart of Burma. It is a forlorn, featureless landscape with, here and there, a prickly pear fence. The heat is like a blow lamp.

There is a bus change, a switch to a pony cart and then, at the end of the day, there it is, without a doubt, the two-cell gaol I am seeking.

The local police officer is using one of the cells as his office. He is away but his wife walks across from her house with a question mark on her delicately chiselled face. I hand her the letter.

'He is Thai,' I think she says.

'You mean he is not a Burmese?'

'No, he Thai . . . two years ago.' Her face is sad.

Then I realize what she was saying: U Saw had died two years ago.

'He was your schoolteacher?' I ask.

She nods.

'He tell me that story about the prisoners.'

22

'He was a good man.'
She nods again and her teapot brown eyes glisten.

On the night of 22 December, 1944, Jack and I were moved to Meiktila in the back of an open truck trussed like fowls. We wormed closer together when the evening air cooled off around midnight and, as would be expected of any good host, the Japanese officer with us peeled off his own topcoat and spread it over us. Now and again when he lifted his face to the light of the stars as we crawled along the darkened road I saw that he was shivering.

Soon after dawn, when we arrived at what we guessed was the Kempei Tai headquarters, our kindly host on the truck turned interrogator. Each refusal to answer a question brought a slap, a punch or a kick. Finally, our host lost his patience, harangued us in Japanese for five minutes or so and then we were told in English that we would be tortured until we talked.

'The Army of Nippon demands that you answer questions,' he yelled into my face. Obviously, the moment of truth, or lies, was fast approaching.

It was all very business-like. They took us to a spreading coral tree. Red flower spikes were bursting out of brown sheaths on the trees' bare branches. I recall wondering whether this was ominous.

A rope that tied Jack's hands together behind his back was tossed over a fork in the tree and pulled tight, yanking his hands up towards the back of his neck. When he lent forward and dropped his chin to relieve the pain his torturer was indignant. Now that was not sporting. He slapped Jack's face until he lifted it again.

When he could stand the agony no longer Jack screamed, 'Okay, okay, okay, okay . . .' They cut him down.

This was the cue for our little pre-arranged play.

'No, no Jack,' I pleaded. 'I forbid you to talk. No, no. In the name of our king . . .'

A guard brought my act to an end with a flurry of face-slapping.

'Sorry,' Jack said softly, head bowed.

'Coward,' I hissed. He knew I did not mean it.

Now it was my turn. I was sure my arms would be torn from their sockets. My body went numb with pain. The red spikes on the coral tree were blurred. I gave in.

'Yes, yes . . . okay, okay,' I croaked.

As the Japanese moved towards me the air-raid siren stopped them in their tracks. There was the sound of low-flying aircraft and our hosts vanished into their fox-holes leaving me strung up and Jack tied up on the ground. My shouts were ignored. I passed out and next thing I knew I was lying on the ground alongside Jack.

Our plan to take punishment before we talked worked beautifully. They interrogated us separately but we told the same stories about having just arrived in India. We did not even know the number of our squadron because it was just forming. We must have been fairly convincing because at the end my interrogating officer suddenly spat in my face, shouted something and then strutted out of the room. The interpreter stopped laughing long enough to tell me that the officer had said: 'It is no wonder you are losing the war if all senior British officers are as stupid as you are.'

My kneecap did not hurt any more. It was just an open mouth filled with pus and dirt and I was convinced it was becoming gangrenous. So I angrily demanded some treatment and, to my surprise, a medical orderly turned up a short time later with his first aid kit. He untied my hands and legs and left me on the ground while he went to the river to fill his steel helmet with water. It was the first time for four days that I had been able to move all my limbs freely and was by far the best part of the treatment. The wound was splashed with water and when I started to clean it out with a leaf he unexpectedly left me to my own devices. I went through his assortment of bottles but the only thing I could identify was some permanganate of potash. As a kid we called it Conde's Crystals and my mother used to dilute it with warm water in a bowl and bathe our wounds with it. I unscrewed the jar, spilled a heap of it into my wound and was packing it down when I heard a yell. The mild medical orderly standing over me suddenly turned into an angry monster. He hammered my head with his fists as he hissed abuse at me. He grabbed the jar from me and kneeling down, tried to scrape the crystals back into it but they were too mushy. He gave up and to teach me a lesson for stealing some of his meagre medical supplies he tied me up tighter than ever. That was to be the most sophisticated medical treatment I was to get in nearly five months as a prisoner.

For the next two nights we bumped our way to Rangoon in the

back of a truck. During the day the truck was concealed under trees out of sight of strafing aircraft.

The Warrant Officer in charge was a tough, swaggering character. He paid little attention to us. We were merely cattle on the way to slaughter. Also, he was fully occupied all night with a laughing Burmese woman on the other side of the truck. Jack and I were both too sick to be interested in the sexual activity a few feet away but at one time during the night I woke to find the woman's longyi had been tossed over me, whether as a kind or as an abandoned act I will never know. In the morning she was wearing it again.

We had been offered little to eat since our furtive feast in the town gaol and we were becoming interested in food again. Also, I needed to relieve myself. I called out to the sergeant and tried to get the message across by nodding vigorously and looking down over my stomach but he walked away and helped himself to some coffee. Then the woman's soft face was close to mine.

'Number one or number two?' she asked in a confidential whisper.

I closed my eyes and then opened them. The face was still there. So this was really happening. I think I laughed.

'Sorry,' I said. 'Thank you . . . I want to do both – number one *and* number two and so does my friend . . . badly.'

She bounced across to the sergeant as though bent on attacking him. He laughed and turned away, but she persisted with the tenacity of a fox terrier. She abused him and then she swiftly changed tactics and pulled his shirt out. Laughing, he pulled out his sword and menaced her with it. Clearly, from his gestures he then told her to handle the situation if she felt so badly about it. So she did. With nimble fingers she quickly untied the rope around our legs and, heckled by the small crowd of Japanese and Burmese who had gathered, she led us behind a bush a few yards away.

Once out of sight of the soldiers she was immediately the well-trained nanny, unbuttoning our clothes for us and looking away discreetly at the right moment. She earned a medal for bravery under fire that morning. So warm with gratitude towards her was I that when they mocked and ridiculed her on our return to the truck I felt shamed and angry with myself for not leaping to her support. I was wholly intimidated.

Then the Warrant Officer flared into anger. Whether it was

something she said or whether he suddenly felt that his authority had been undermined, I do not know, but he knocked her aside as she knelt down to bind my ankles together with the rope. Screaming out guttural orders, he yanked me to my feet and pushed me, stumbling, along a path leading away from the roadside camp. To my own surprise I was not hopping on my right leg as before but half-running. I was nothing more than a scared animal. Those few minutes have to be the bottom point of my life. I hated myself.

We came upon a small, unkempt Buddhist temple which had been painted white but now the stone was showing through. The bullying sergeant shouted an order in Japanese and pointed to a spot near the temple wall. I knelt. It seemed the thing to do. My hands were still tied behind my back. I looked up but his hand pushed my chin into my chest. There was a swish and I felt a rush of wind on the back of my neck.

'Shit . . . this is it,' was my sudden thought. Of course, I was in the classic beheading position.

Another swish. This time my right cheek felt the breeze. My eyes were pressed tight but I knew it was his sword that was slicing through the air. Accompanying each wild stroke was a belly grunt and something that sounded like an oath. I froze with fear. The hairs on the back of my neck tingled. The swishing stopped. There was a pause. Then my executioner exploded into laughter and slapped my backside with the flat of his sword. He helped me to my feet and gestured that we would now go back to the truck. He walked back alongside me and said something to me in Japanese in a soft voice, inhaling deeply every few words. I got the message that he thought I had been very brave. He was wrong.

Anyway, there was a new attitude towards Jack and me after that. They gave us a meal of curried chicken and rice, with coffee, and untied our hands so we could eat it. The sergeant had nothing to do with us but I felt his eyes on me once or twice. Once it was dark we started off again travelling south along the rutted road to Rangoon.

At dawn next day we were parked close to the boundary of what I later realized was Mingaladon Airfield, on the outskirts of the city. The brave Burmese lady had vanished overnight.

I was intrigued to hear the sound of an aircraft engine revving up. By half-sitting up I could see over the side of the truck into an open

26

aircraft bay where a single-engined plane with a rising sun for a roundel was being warmed up.

'Here's our chance,' I said to Jack. 'We'll bump off our guards, grab that aircraft and I'll fly you home.'

'Yes, we'd be back in time for the plum pudding.'

Until he said that I had not realized it was Christmas morning. As it happened there was anything but peace and goodwill at the next port of call.

Our guards were a slovenly lot but they spruced themselves up as best they could after a few brisk orders broke the morning air. They were all sitting straight-backed and alert as we turned into a complex of buildings that looked like a college. Here, without a doubt, was an area headquarters, a place where fates were decided. It was obvious to me now that none of my interrogators so far would have had the authority to dispense with me. They did not snare wing commanders every day and the order, it seemed, had been to bring me to Rangoon for high-level questioning. This would be the vital test. If the intelligence people here suspected for a moment that I had been involved in combined operations planning as a staff officer in New Delhi I could become a prize prisoner and be whisked off to Saigon or Singapore for intense interrogation, even the truth-drug treatment.

Having hit bottom in my self-respect the day before, I found I was facing up to my next round with less despair. A little fight was stirring up inside me. If I was lucky I might make it into the sanctuary of that gaol for prisoners-of-war the boy interpreter said was here in Rangoon.

There was a brisk, martial atmosphere about this place. Staff officers marched along the corridors. Everyone was taking themselves seriously.

It did not surprise me that their first move was to separate Jack and me. We were to be interrogated independently.

Say as little as possible, I told myself. The more you fabricate the more vulnerable you are to cross-examination.

Finally, my antagonist was there, looking fiercely into my eyes. His head was close-shaven and he was in full green uniform with high shiny boots. The interpreter who sat on my left had an American accent. He summed up the opening tirade in Japanese very smoothly: 'He says he doesn't believe the story you and your navigator are telling. It is all lies. You are a flying colonel and must know a lot more than you are pretending. He says you are his prisoner and will have to answer his questions.'

I tried to sound indignant as I lied that I had told nothing but the truth. This made him angry. He bashed the table with a round, black baton or ruler he had in his hand but his voice was cold and under control. He told the interpreter to free my hands and then showed me how to place them palms down on the table in front of me. It was a relief to get the rope off but I had only a few seconds to enjoy it. The baton crashed down on my outstretched knuckles as I shook my head in answer to a question about the number of fighter squadrons in the Imphal area. My reflex action was to pull my hands away. Without a word he bounced the baton on my head until I replaced my hands on the table.

This game went on for some time. It got to the point that I was not listening to the questions.

'I don't know, I don't know,' I was crying, eyes fixed on the black baton coming down on my fingers sticky with blood. I pressed down hard on the table with my hands to keep them there because I was sure my head would split open if he bashed it again. Then he stopped, carefully put down the baton and stood up. He said something quietly in Japanese as he left the room.

'He says you will lose your head if you don't answer his questions when he comes back.'

The interpreter could not take his eyes off my bloody hands. Suddenly he stood up and pushed the door closed.

'You stupid, goddam bastard,' he whispered. 'Why don't you answer his goddam questions? Tell him anything . . . just talk . . . only make it sound good. You don't have to spill the beans.'

I stared at him for a few seconds, wondering where the catch was.

'Where did you learn English?' I asked cautiously.

'I was at Yale. I was visiting Japan when war broke out and was caught there . . . Now, give yourself a break.'

When the interrogating officer came back I had my hands folded. I looked into his face and nodded.

'What do you want to know?' I asked. I divulged a mountain of misinformation in the next half-hour or so and he took a wad of notes. At one point he pulled out a map that showed Australia and asked me where the Australian navy was based. I picked up his baton and pointed to Melbourne. He pointed to Sydney with a question on his face. I shook my head.

'There's a secret base north of Sydney,' I told the interpreter. This whetted the officer's appetite. He wanted details.

'Harrington, at the mouth of the Manning River,' I said and pin-pointed its position on the map. 'American submarines,' I added for good measure. As a boy I went to Harrington for holidays. It was good fishing on the sandbanks but you used a rowing boat because the water was so shallow.

After I had written down the name in pencil my interrogator stood up, looked at me with what I read as contempt for a few seconds and left in a hurry.

Then the interpreter took a pin out of the collar of his shirt and handed it to me.

'You might find this useful in the gaol,' he said quickly. I barely had time to thread it into my collar before two of my guards arrived to take me away.

17 April, 1985

I am somewhere deep in the subway spider web under the city of Tokyo in Japan on my way to meet Major Maeda Hiroshi (retired) who had been a staff officer in intelligence at Burma Area Army Headquarters, Rangoon, in 1944. The appointment had been made on the spur of the moment only half an hour before, when a fellow Japanese major, another Burma veteran, had mentioned Major Maeda's name out of the blue at the end of our talk. My interpreter, Commander Sadao Seno, Japanese Marines Security Defence Force (retired), fixed the appointment by telephone within minutes. We bought a sponge cake because Japanese custom forbids you to visit somebody empty-handed. That cake was left behind by the Commander when he used a public telephone to cancel a previous appointment. We changed trains, bought a second sponge cake and hurried on.

A smiling Major Maeda watches us approach. He is a mild-looking, grey-haired man of about 70, smartly dressed in a blue sports coat and carrying an umbrella. We shake hands and he leads the way out of the station, obviously deep in thought. Suddenly, he stops in his tracks, turns to study my face intensely as he fires a few questions at Commander Sadao. Then he walks on saying something over his shoulder.

'*He says he interviewed a wing commander in Rangoon once. He remembers you were frightened.*'

My friend and interpreter grins.

'*I remember, too. I was more than frightened . . . I was terrified.*'

Neither of us talks as we walk to his home. We are both busy remembering.

Looking down on us from the mantlepiece as we talk is a small statue of a Japanese Imperial Army Officer flanked by two fluffy toy dogs, one yellow and one brown. There is no black baton in sight. He became a banker after the war, he tells me, but is now retired. I say my main interest is the Japanese retreat from Rangoon in April, 1945, and he assures me he is happy to tell everything he knows. In fact, he is surprisingly frank. Towards the end, he says, his Commander-in-Chief and his Chief-of-Staff quarrelled a lot over operations.

'*They were like a dog and a monkey,*' *he says.*

I purposely save the wartime encounter between the wing commander and the major for the end. I am smiling inside. I am savouring it. Yes, he recognized me at once when we met at the station. He smiles.

'*He says he got nothing out of you at the interview.*' *The interpreter is laughing at the incredible coincidence involved.*

'*This is a 120 million to one chance that you two should be talking together here today over tea and cake,*' *he says. We nod but I have to be absolutely sure.*

'*Did you interview me at the gaol?*' *I ask. It is a trick question. He shakes his head. The interview was at his headquarters. Right. Did he remember his interpreter? Yes, he spoke better English than Japanese. He was educated in America. At what university? Yale. What happened to the interpreter? He died after the war.*

Major Maeda makes the point that he had not been captured but had surrendered under orders at the end of the war. The British Army had put him behind bars in Rangoon Gaol. We both laugh. Then I am cruel. I use a psychological black baton. I tell him how his interpreter betrayed him at his headquarters on 25 December, 1944. He smiles but he fails to conceal the hurt look in his eyes.

Being locked up in Cell 6 in Rangoon Gaol was something of a relief. Our legs and hands were free of rope and there was no sadistic interrogator striving to get under your guard. Now I was one of a herd of a thousand, just a number. The thought brought with it the slighest glow of elation.

Across the corridor in Cell 35 a fellow inmate was pressed against the bars watching us.

'Hi there,' I called. His forefinger jerked to his lips and he shook his head. He concentrated on listening for a full ten seconds.

'No talking,' he whispered. 'They'll bash you up for it.'

'When do we eat?'

'Tomorrow.'

'No.' My yell of dismay was certainly no whisper and I was admonished for it. Supper had been served half-an-hour before and the next meal would be rice and tea for breakfast. It was late in the afternoon of Christmas Day and I was hungry, having had nothing to eat all day. I must have looked pretty desperate because my neighbour went to the rear of his cell and reappeared with a large bone which he poked through the bars.

'Here, have this,' he said kindly. It was a sordid looking shank, bare of meat as the iron bars I gripped. The light was dim but I thought I detected a look of sacrifice in his bearded face. This man was sick, sadistic. I waved away the offering and retreated to my bed board.

'And a Merry Christmas to you, too,' I muttered grimly.

Several weeks later the Japanese put me into a cell with my would-be benefactor across the way. His name was F/Lt Herb Ivens and he had been a Thunderbolt pilot shot down near Meiktila. He came from Saskatchewan, Canada, where his father was a sheriff. He was one of the few lucky ones to get a bone with his Christmas dinner that day and had been saving it up to suck out the marrow to flavour his rice next day. I had turned down a precious gift.

In fact, something of a Christmas miracle had happened to the inmates of the dreaded cell block. For more than a year the Japanese had singled out all airmen prisoners for especially harsh treatment. An edict had been issued at the top that all captured Allied airmen were to be treated as criminal prisoners, not prisoners-of-war. At a later date they were to be put on trial for 'murdering Burmese women and children'.

The British, Indian and Chinese army prisoners in Rangoon Gaol were confined in compounds inside the prison walls and were free to move around the yards, sit in the sun and yarn. They had their own doctors, cooked for themselves and the fit men could earn a modicum of spending money outside in working parties.

The fliers were locked away in cells day and night, some in solitary, except when it was their turn in the morning to empty the 'banjo', a lidless cartridge box used as a latrine, and for the very rare visit to the well to douse themselves with a bucket of water. As one RAF pilot put it: 'We're the bleeding villains, the whipping post.'

Somehow, the British brigadier in the army compound had persuaded the Japanese commander of the gaol to let up on the 'bad men' in the cells as a Yuletide gesture. The first the airmen knew about it was when one of the guards started singing something that resembled a carol and urged some of the prisoners in the downstairs cells to join in. They were afraid, thinking it was some fiendish trick, or that he was drunk. Then one or two started singing 'Silent Night' in low, tremulous voices and, as the guard kept smiling, others joined in. The haunting notes floated to the upstairs cells and in no time the singing swelled joyously. They sang with tears in their eyes, these half-starved, grimy men who had been silenced by decree. Some of them had wondered whether they would ever sing again out loud. Now and again at night they had risked the wrath of the Japanese with *sotto voce* renderings of the odd hymn, but this was euphoria. The cell block choir sang carols until sunset. Then the guards hissed it into silence once more.

With the rice on Christmas morning came a present from the army boys of five Burmese cheroots for each airman in the cells. This, too, was unprecedented and there were some agonizing minutes for the smokers while they wondered about the problem of no matches. Then the guards started passing their lighted cigarettes through the bars. Many of these emaciated men had not smoked for a year or more. They chain-smoked that day and as a result, most of them were physically ill. They were not really able to benefit fully from the extra ration of meat authorized by the Japanese.

Jack and I had missed out on all these festivities and did not hear the full story for some time. The optimists were whispering that surely this showed a change of heart by the Japanese and a more humane deal for airmen was on the way. Next morning, however, the guards were as repugnant as ever. It was bestial business as usual.

Four men died in our cell block in the week that followed. It was exasperating to watch the coffins being carried out by the Chinese and be absolutely in the dark as to how they died.

One morning, while standing in the queue to empty our 'banjo box', I whispered to an American in front of me: 'That bloke yesterday . . . what did he die of?'

Without turning his head the American said in a low voice: 'What's it matter? It was his turn. You'll be next if they catch you talking.'

On the way back along the corridor to my cell a prisoner signalled me with a slight movement of his fingers. I paused long enough to take in the tall, gaunt creature behind the bars stripped to a G-string. He smiled wanly as I nodded.

Back in the cell I stood wondering, holding the 'banjo box' in my upturned hands as if it was an offering. Jack was flat on his bed board. He raised himself on his elbow.

'You look as though you have seen a ghost,' he said quietly. I told him about our fellow prisoner along the corridor.

'I know that man. I've met him somewhere.'

Then it came. He was a pilot from another RAF squadron. I had played rugby against them.

'Of course, he was that huge front row forward. When he got the ball it took three or four of our chaps to pull him down. Jack, he's a mess. He can't be more than seven stone now.'

The front row forward was dead within a week. Somebody told me later he died of malnutrition and dysentery, while others survived on the same amount of food. Nobody really knows; except that he just faded away.

I suppose it was at that stage I seriously set about staying alive. Escape from this walled prison on the edge of the city of Rangoon would be next to impossible. At least I could keep as fit as possible and wait my chance. My survival programme kept me so busy I was exhausted at the end of the day. Our two bedboards took up most of the space in our cell so calisthenics were restricted to such simple exercises as clenching and unclenching each fist a hundred times morning and afternoon and pedalling on my back with my eyes closed while I recalled picnics out of the past. A shaft of sunlight angled through the barred window for ten minutes each morning. I soaked my angry-looking knee in it.

For mental exertion I wrote a novel in invisible shorthand, tracing the outlines on my bedboard with my forefinger. The exacting part of the exercise was to carry on next day just where I had stopped in the previous session. It was important not to cheat. The plot avoided sex and war.

All this was really a means of filling in the minutes between the feasts of rice – two heaped handfuls three times a day. Served with it at breakfast was a splash of 'nuka', a slightly bitter, brown porridge made from rice bran, sweepings from the mill where the rice was polished. It did nothing for my taste buds but I licked up every scrap of it. Midday a feeble vegetable soup was on the menu and once or twice a week a taste of some sort of meat pervaded the rice. The evening meal was just rice and tea. (At the War Crime Trials in Rangoon a year later the commander of the prison, Captain Motozo Tazumi, gave evidence that the 'aviators' were on short rations because he had orders from Burma Area Army Headquarters not to send them out with the working parties. Anyway, all they did was to sit in their cells all day.)

Meals for me were a deliberate affair. I chewed every mouthful exactly twenty times. I saved enough tea to wash the top half of my right forefinger and then massaged my gums for ten minutes or so. Then, if there were no guards close by, I produced with a flourish the pin presented to me by my friend the Yale graduate and used it as a toothpick and then to clean my finger nails. These I kept trim by grinding them on the stone window sill.

Jack was having problems. He just detested the rice and could not bear the 'nuka'. I pleaded with him to eat it. He would give it a go, then promptly sick it up. I was a proper bastard. Using every trick and threat in the book, I stood over him until he finally was able to keep it down. It did nothing for our relationship but the last thing I wanted was for him to die on me. Jack showed his toughness by going the distance. We have had some good times in London since.

A few grains of rice were the cause of my first beating in the cells. The Chinese who served our rice through the bars that day spilt a little in the corridor outside our cell. The fact that the concrete there was never washed did not enter my mind as I reached out and meticulously salvaged all I could. I was busily munching away on it when the Japanese sergeant flaunted through the block on an inspection. He spied the few grains of rice that I had not been able to reach and yelled for the guard, who came running. The sergeant was in a rage. He tongue-lashed the quivering soldier and then, in full view of the prisoners, slapped his face with blows that sent him reeling. The guard dropped to his knees and picked up the rice. His sergeant marched off.

Then the guard shouted something at me. I just stood there and bowed. He raced away, came back with the keys, unlocked our cell and threw himself at me in a fury. His fists were closed but only a few of his swings were on target and I managed to stay on my feet. My ears were ringing but there was no real damage. I slipped in a quick bow and said, 'Sorry, master,' which stopped his flailing arms. My punishment was terminated.

Only a few nights before, the Canadian opposite had schooled us in a few basics: Never, never look a Nip in the eye when he is slapping or punching you. Try to bow at every opportunity. When you hear a Nip coming, get on your feet and bow. Never be caught sitting or lying down unless you are very ill and they know it. Wear your boots day and night because when they come to take you out for anything they will not wait for you to put them on.

My trouble was that I used my left boot, which had been torn in the crash, for a pillow. I had to sleep wearing my right boot anyway because one of my socks was also torn, exposing my toes to the clouds of mosquitoes that buzzed all night.

The saki must have flowed in the gaol mess on New Year's Eve because there were more thrashings the next day than anyone could remember. I copped one for walking too close to one of the guards as I passed with our latrine box.

Jack and I were taken out for two more interrogations with the gaol interpreter, Weary Willie, and officers from outside, but they did not tax our imaginations too much. Our fabricated story seemed to be standing up.

There was a Royal Marine petty officer in the cells when we arrived. I glimpsed him once. He was red-haired and had a deathly pallor. Apparently, he had been captured at Akyab, on the Arakan coast, and the Kempei Tai were giving him a good going over. A fellow in a cell next to him passed the word that the Japanese were injecting the Marine with the 'truth' drug. They took him out one day and he never came back. Perhaps he ended up in Singapore.

Anyway, it was another warning for me. This Marine could easily have been caught while checking the beaches for landing craft in Operation Bullfrog. I had no future if my hosts ever found out that I had been involved in planning that operation.

While I wallowed in mere fears that week, a fellow airman from a cell along the corridor had his left arm amputated below the elbow. The word whispered from cell to cell was that the surgery was done without an anaesthetic and when the poor creature let out the odd cry of pain the Japanese doctor watching the operation cuffed him across the head for complaining. He was an American master sergeant. I watched him shuffle out with the guards. Two of his fellow officers carried him back to his cell.

'They won't even give him an aspirin,' Herb told me that night.

The American's name was Montgomery. A month or so later he told me the full story and I put it down in my diary. He was a legend. Although the Japanese guards did little or nothing to help him there were signs that they had a certain respect for Montgomery. An honourable war wound was involved here, not one of the tiresome maladies such as malnutrition, beri beri, jungle sores or dysentery.

The guards were a surly lot with one exception. We called him 'The Frisco Kid'. Apparently he had been a merchant seaman before the war and had been to San Francisco several times. He spoke a little English and took delight in boasting about his sexual conquests on the San Francisco waterfront. He pounced on me one day when I was in the yard emptying our banjo box.

'Calcutta?' he asked. I nodded.

'Jigajig Calcutta . . . goodka?' I nodded.

'Ah . . . No 1 flophouse Calcutta.' He handed me a pencil and a tattered notebook. Obviously he wanted an address so he would not have to waste time when he was posted there after the Japanese forces had invaded India and captured the place. I wrote '38 Chowringhee' across a page, looked up into his eager face and nodded again, this time with a man-to-man wink. As I walked back to my cell I chuckled at the thought that I may have given him the address of one of the churches.

The mood of our squalid cell block changed remarkably at dusk when our 'masters' locked us up for the night. First, for my part at least, there was a sense of relief when the big centre gates clanged shut that I had survived another day of barbaric treatment. Only at night could you really relax. For a few minutes while the guards marched away all was quiet except for the sounds of the birds in the roof settling down. Then came the 'all clear' stage whisper from the cockatoo, or look out, in one of the end cells upstairs and the prison came to life.

'Hey, check out King in 26 for me, will you? He didn't look too good today.'

'How's Monty?'

'Any war news?'

'The boys upstairs say they've had a message from the army compound that they're smuggling some boiled eggs to us tomorrow buried in the rice.'

'Christ, I hope I get one.'

'Who was that groaning last night up the row a bit? He sounded bad.'

'The Japs must be getting a bit edgy. They've had Oscars up on patrol at dawn and dusk for three days running.'

'What's the date? Does anybody know the date?'

'I got half rice and half gravel today. Broke my bloody tooth.'

'Have they given Monty a fresh bandage yet?'

'Better be careful with that new tall guard. He's a mean-looking bastard.'

'It's my birthday today.'

'Happy birthday.'

The hundred or so wretched souls in the cell block pressed against the bars of their cells, if they were fit enough, hungry to hear any scrap of news. You could only see the man in the cell opposite but conversations were held by relaying questions and answers through go-betweens. For a bunch of men forbidden to talk to each other at any time this was a blissful happy hour.

How we got news from the other compounds puzzled me at first until Herb illustrated to me the 'sky-writing' technique of communication. Using a home-made fly swatter or a finger, if you were sure the Japs were not looking, you outlined letters of words in the air right to left, mirror image. It was a great substitute for talking and, as far as I know, nobody was ever caught.

On my second night behind bars Herb hushed me to silence and put his hand to his ear. Straining my ears, I heard the words of a lesson from the New Testament coming from an upstairs cell. The chatter had stopped. It soon became clear to me that this was holy worship. An airman had died that day and now in defiance of the Japanese a low but stirring voice was praying for his soul. The service went on. In the dim light across the passage I could make out Herb, eyes closed, head tilted up a little and his hands clenching the bars. A second lesson was read and there was a prayer asking that the Japanese guards be forgiven . . .' for they know not what they do. O Lord.' The hundred men did not join the voice in saying the Lord's Prayer. The sound level would have been too loud. We just said it to ourselves.

'It's an American from a B 24 crew,' Herb told me later. 'He's got a Bible from somewhere.'

For nearly two months I took part silently in those forbidden services without being able to put a face to that voice. Any time the prisoners from the upstairs cells filed past my cell on their way out to the yard I scanned their bearded faces for a clue as to which of them was the voice. But none of them even dared to look sideways.

Apparently, the New Testament was shared with the prisoners in neighbouring cells. They read it furtively during the day and slid it back to the 'pastor' any time there was to be a service. One day a prisoner died reading it. He was alone in his cell and there seemed to be no way of retrieving the precious book. The guards were sure to confiscate it. Criminal airmen were not allowed reading material.

'Hey, looks like we've lost our Bible.' The word went from cell to cell.

It was a short service that night. The prayer asked the Lord to help get back the New Testament.

'Shindow,' the prisoner in the cell opposite told the guard next morning, pointing to the dead man on his bed board. The Japanese glanced at the body and marched off. An hour later two Chinese prisoners turned up to take the body away. One of them palmed the New Testament and, while the guard had his back turned, deftly passed it through the bars to an astonished American.

The Bible had a truly blessed existence. A month or more went by before I gathered the full story.

Two years before, Lt Grant W. Erwin Jnr, a navigator from

Milwaukee, Wisconsin, was the sole survivor of a B 24 crew of ten. The bomber was attacked by Oscars over the target and caught fire. Erwin baled out at a mere 300 feet and, miraculously, got away with it. He and two other American fliers ended up in a bamboo hut prison at Bassein, in southern Burma, with a bunch of thieves, a prostitute and an English-speaking Burmese who had been caught helping Allied airmen. The Burmese lent Erwin his New Testament and refused to take it back when they were being separated.

'Keep it,' he said. 'You will have need of it.'

Erwin's next gaol were the infamous cells attached to the New Law Courts in Rangoon. He and the other airmen were searched by the Japanese on arrival but they missed the Bible because it was slipped from one to the other in a sleight-of-hand operation.

Never was a Bible so coveted. These shattered airmen took turns to read it avidly every minute during daylight. It was a single book circulating library until tension went so high that the New Testament was broken into five parts. Lookouts were posted to warn of the approach of the Japanese guards. Every time a man died a lesson was read in a whispered secret service at night. The indication was that most of the Japanese were anti-Christian. One particularly mean guard knocked down a tiny bamboo cross that had been hanging on the wall of a cell and then bashed its occupant with a club until he was unconscious.

On two occasions careless airmen were caught reading the Bible and, by extreme coincidence, the guards turned out to be religiously tolerant. Perhaps they were Christians themselves, because all they did was to advise the prisoners to keep the good book out of sight of the other Japanese.

They lost an Old Testament to the Japanese. It had been quietly handed over to one of the prisoners by an interpreter who had been educated in the United States but was found one day in a surprise search of the cells and confiscated. Was this the same interpreter who presented me with my precious pin?

In July, 1944, when the victimized airmen were moved from the Law Courts cells to the main Rangoon Prison they took the Bible with them. At the new gaol they had to strip and hold their hands high while the guards searched their clothes. But the Bible got through again. One of the prisoners stood on it.

The battered New Testament survived the war and was taken to the United States by the navigator who borrowed it in that bamboo gaol in Bassein.

'Huddison . . . Huddison.' An impatient Japanese was at the door of our cell hissing my name while he rattled the butt of his rifle against the bars. My reflex action was to spring to attention and bow. This, I had quickly learned, was the survival drill. Fear knotted my stomach. What now? The guard unlocked the door and waved Jack away. They only wanted 'Huddison'.

I was marched to the water tower, the hub where the various compounds of the gaol converged like spokes in a wheel. This could be it, I told myself. I could be on my way to Tokyo. Then again, it could be something fatuous like the big malaria quiz a few days before when some of us were pulled out of our cells and asked: Why are you not sick with malaria when many Nippon soldiers in Burma very sick with it? It was obvious, of course. We were all yellow from taking prophylactic Atabrin but perhaps these people thought this was our natural colouring. Anyway, as a matter of principle none of us divulged the big 'secret'. I took great pains to describe in detail the regulation back in the squadron of rolling our sleeves down at sunset and the mosquito net inspection each night. If they caught on to the fact that I was sending them up they did not show it. Today was different. This was something important. The 'Big Tai-i' was there which meant that the soldiers were noisier and brisker than usual.

I joined three other Australians standing there at attention. This was unprecedented. What was going on? The Tai-i stepped forward, said a few words and paused for the interpreter.

'Australians goodka . . . goodka . . .'

Then, as we started to breathe again, the story unfolded. The Japanese Imperial Navy had attacked Sydney Harbour. The crews of midget submarines which took part in the onslaught had died bravely during the battle. The Australian Navy had recovered their bodies and buried them with full military honours.

'Australians goodka . . .' The Tai-i nodded his approval. Then it was back to the cells.

They took Herb Ivens away first. Since the black-bearded Canadian alone in the opposite cell had offered me that precious, bare bone on Christmas Day we had developed a warm 'sympatico' from a distance. We were in constant communication across the corridor. In the daylight hours Herb and I would 'air write' to each another at every opportunity. At night we had brief whispering sessions when we were sure there was no guard about. With looks and gestures we conveyed our anger and frustrations and showed sympathy. We had struck up a friendship.

Herb had reached the prison only ten days before we did but he was well drilled on how to survive and he was at once our tutor in the art.

The guards were unlocking the door of Herb's cell before I knew they were there. In an instant I was on my feet bowing to their backs and wondering, with growing fear, what was going on. This was a departure from routine. One of the Japanese grunted something and pointed to the mess tins on the bed board. Herb gathered them up and left the cell with his guards, raising his eyebrows imperceptibly when I caught his eye, then a slight shrug of his shoulders that told me he had no idea what was going on. The whispered word that night was that Herb had been shifted into Cell 6 with a Texan pilot.

Next morning it was my turn. 'Huddison,' the guard called as he unlocked our cell. I grabbed my mess tins and was marched upstairs to Cell 41 to join Herb and the Texan.

'What is going on, for Christ's sake?' I asked after the guards had gone.

'Search me,' said Herb shaking his head. Then he formally introduced me to Lt Aaron L. Bearden, from Houston, Texas, a P38 pilot who had baled out after his aircraft had collided with another P38 while dive bombing a bridge near Mandalay.

I was a trained journalist, so naturally I started asking questions. Herb was strangely uncommunicative. He just shrugged his shoulders. The Texan offered no theory.

'After you've been in here a while,' he said, 'you'll give up trying to work out why the Nips do things.'

Then I caught a furtive look in Herb's eyes that promptly shut me up. I switched to more mundane questions. What happened to you? How did you 'buy it'? Herb said he was doing a low-level strafe at 400 miles an hour in his P47 at Meiktila when the ack ack hit him. He lost consciousness for a brief period but managed to crash-land his aircraft. He had head and leg injuries. The Burmese captured him and handed him over to the Japanese.

The Texan said the Burmese had also handed him over. The Kempei Tai had given him a rough time for four days before he woke up to himself and told them a heap of bullshit. That was nearly five months ago. He stretched out on his bedboard and closed his eyes. Without taking his eyes off him Herb sketched a three-legged stool in the air with his finger and fluttered his hands. I nodded. The message was loud and clear. The Texan was a stool pigeon. He certainly had not lost any weight during his five months in captivity and it was hard to imagine any other reason why he should suddenly be put into a cell with two new arrivals.

We had other warnings. The fellow in the cell opposite wrote a 'take care' message in the air to us and half-a-dozen of our fellow prisoners touched their closed lips at various times during the next few days.

The Texan must have been aware of all these warnings. He did not seem to care and spent most of the day and night on his back while Herb and I kept busy exercising and discussing every subject under the sun except matters that might be of interest to our enemy. I should record that not once did the Texan ask a leading question. He did not ferret for information.

All you saw through the barred window of Cell 6 was a grey wall, but from the window of upstairs Cell 35 you could see over a wall into the yard of the adjoining compound where prisoners were free to move about the yard.

On the first day there I was savouring the joy of looking out onto the outside world when I became aware of something familiar about a tall, olive-skinned prisoner dangling from the top of a doorway doing chin-ups. He dropped to the ground and looked up. There was no doubt at all. It was F/Sgt Harvey Besley, a pilot from No 11 Squadron, RAF.

On 5 April, 1943, just on twenty-one months ago, Harvey and I had been flying Blenheim light bombers in a formation that bombed Japanese bombers dispersed on Meiktila airfield. We were attacked by fighters and when the formation tightened up for greater firepower two of the Blenheims collided in midair. We saw two parachutes blossom before both aircraft crashed in flames. Obviously Harvey had been one of the survivors. He was from Texas, too. Texas, Queensland, Australia.

42

It was after that raid that I became flight commander with the rank of squadron leader. You only needed to stay operational those days to get promotion. In fact, at the time, I was the sole surviving officer among those who had flown with the squadron against the Germans in North Africa.

The Texan left us after four or five days. 'Weary Willy', the Japanese interpreter, took him away one morning. I thought he looked slightly self-conscious as he left the cell. We did not wish him good luck. The whispered story from one of his fellow Americans in the cell opposite that night was that Bearden lived in a house outside the walls of the gaol and that he was plentifully supplied with food, cigars and Burmese women.

What worried me at the time was that it was all too blatant. There had to be something more to it. No way could I imagine anyone with an iota of intelligence thinking he could get away with something like this. Perhaps he had a plan . . . perhaps he was, for some reason, playing a game with the Japanese and thought he could double-cross them at a critical stage and do something for the prisoners or for our war effort. Perhaps I was being too generous . . . perhaps he was a man who would do anything for a belly-full of rice and his belly on a woman. At any rate, his fellow Americans made no secret of their shame in his actions.

With the third man out of our cell Herb and I felt we could talk more freely. In fact, we never stopped. Both of us were obsessed with how lucky we were just to be alive.

'We're on borrowed time,' Herb said.

'You smack the Irrawaddy in your three-ply Mossie at 300 miles an hour and I run into some flack at 400 miles an hour right down on the deck and here we are with one sore knee each. It's fucking incredible.'

He did not say anything but I had a feeling Herb did not believe my string of survival stories since joining the air force four years ago, but they were all true.

My first life had been a mid-air collision between two Tiger Moths during elementary flying training in Southern Rhodesia.

'Put this down sweetly,' my instructor had said, 'and you can go solo.'

I knew I was overshooting a bit but there was plenty of airfield. At fifty feet I landed on another Tiger that was taking off directly underneath. One of my wheels jammed in the empty front cockpit and we span in, locked together, the wings taking most of the impact. My instructor escaped with bruises, my nose was scratched but the pilot of the other aircraft was knocked unconscious. I pulled him out of the wreckage. It was my best friend, Tommy Kelsall, from Wagga Wagga, Australia.

I managed to survive to fly north to Egypt in June, 1941, for operational training at Ismailia on the Suez Canal but we were bombed out after a few weeks and I found myself in a formation of three Airspeed Oxfords on a delivery flight to Kenya. We ran into bad weather and became hopelessly lost. Eventually, with fuel tanks showing empty, we let down through the cloud and found a railway line which led us to an airfield where we landed. The trouble was that we did not know whether we were in the Sudan, Uganda, Ethiopia or Kenya. It turned out to be Uganda.

Then, near the end of my operational training in Nakuru, Kenya, I flew a Blenheim into two masts erected on the bombing range to simulate a ship for skip-bombing runs. On one engine and with a large gash in the leading edge of the wing I barely made it back to the airfield and had to crash land. More skin off my nose.

Back to Cairo where I learned that before joining a squadron in the Western Desert I had to ferry an aircraft to Gaza, in Palestine.

'Take your pick of any of those kites outside,' said the tough-talking flight commander at Kilo 17. 'They need them up in Syria in a hurry.' The only aircraft there were Hurricane fighters. I had never even seen one before except in *Flight* Magazine. Here, to a bomber pilot, was an exciting aeroplane. I drooled over it for a few minutes and went back into the flight office.

'There are only fighters out there,' I said. 'I've been trained on twin-engines.'

'You've got your fucking wings, haven't you,' he bawled. (Obviously, the film *Dawn Patrol* had left its mark on him.) 'Get someone to show you the cockpit.'

A few of the pilots refused to fly the Hurricanes but Charlie Adcock, a South African, and I, could not resist them.

A sergeant fitter checked me out on the cockpit controls and within twenty minutes I was in the air over the Pyramids.

Christ . . . the cockpit canopy . . . I should have opened it for take off. So, I opened it now and the map on my lap was plucked away by a rush of wind. Getting into the air had been my big worry. I had left the navigation side of things until after I was airborne. There was a dust storm below which cloaked the airfield. All I could recognize were the Pyramids and the Nile. No alternative but to press on. My school geography stood me in good stead. I went up the Nile to the Mediterranean, turned right and followed the coast around.

'Gaza is the next airfield after Tel Aviv,' the flight commander had said. I found it but the wheels of the Hurricane would not come down for landing. In my panic at losing the map I had neglected to return the lever to neutral after selecting for 'wheels up' and now it was jammed. There was no option. I had to crash-land this beautiful Hurricane. I stooged around burning up surplus fuel and struggling with the jammed lever. On the last landing leg I was crying with anger at myself. 'You stupid bastard,' I yelled. The strip was dead ahead.

Then I did an incredibly foolish thing. I punched the button of my safety harness, stood up and kicked the lever back savagely with my right heel. It came away and the wheels locked down ten seconds or so before we kissed the grass. An irate duty officer blasted me for being 'split arse' and putting my wheels down at the last moment. I was laughing with relief so much that I could not tell him why.

(Herb's face showed he did not quite believe that story.)

Next day twenty of us crowded into an ancient Vickers Valencia to be flown back to Cairo but one of its engines burst into flames on take-off and the pilot turned against the sick engine, which is frequently fatal, and put it down in a hurry downwind. Incredibly, we also walked away from that one.

Luck was again my co-pilot on my first raid. I took off from a salt pan inland from Mersah Matruh around midnight just before Desert Air Force Headquarters grounded all aircraft because of bad weather. Our radio was not working so we did not receive the recall signal. It turned out that we were the only Allied aircraft operating in North Africa that night.

We pressed on through the storm to the target only because we knew we had little hope of finding our home base before dawn. I must have flown some erratic courses that night dodging cloud masses but Ged Moore, my navigator, a grazier from Winton in the Queensland outback, somehow got it right and we bombed our primary target, Derna, on schedule. I was enjoying the fire our bombs had started until a searchlight hit us and then we saw an ME110 night fighter just ahead on our level, obviously searching for us. Its headlight was catching the clouds now and again. I throttled right back so the German pilot would not see the flame from my motors and dived. We were easy meat for an ME110 but somehow he missed us.

Our first landfall was Tobruk but the trigger-happy gunners there threw everything at us so we had to go to sea again. The fuel gauge needles were showing empty for twenty minutes before I landed at Maaten Bagush. Both motors cut at the end of the runway. There was not enough petrol left to get us to a dispersal point.

Our fourth operation was a daylight attack on a German-held airstrip at Gasr-el-arid. The ack-ack fire was thick and the port wing of our Blenheim was holed but we landed back intact.

Not so on our ninth raid when we bombed Bardia. The starboard wing was holed fourteen times and the hydraulic system shot to pieces which meant no wheels, no flaps and a messy crash landing.

Herb was showing signs of dwindling interest in my death-cheating stories until I came to raid number 13. On this one we took along for the ride Damien Parer, an official war cameraman from Australia, who later made a name for himself in the Pacific. Damien had been at school in Bathurst with my rear gunner/radio operator, Leo Hore, from Shellharbour, N.S.W. The night before he had shared our foxhole alongside the airfield at Zauiet Msus, inland from Tobruk. We were all snug in our sleeping bags when he realized he had not said his prayers – he never missed. In getting to his knees he dislodged the precarious ground sheet roof and we were half-buried in sand.

The formation bombed a petrol dump at Antelat, south of Benghazi, and as we turned for home, a force of ME109s and Macchi 202s appeared above us. We tucked tightly into a defensive pattern but there was no attack. This happened now and again when the pilots were Italians. They did a few brilliant aerobatics and flew off.

Not the German pilots, however. They always showed aggression.

We had an escort of Kittyhawks from No 3 Squadron, RAAF, and there was a moment of comic relief when the irrepressible Bobby Gibbes mocked the bomber pilots by coming in close formation with the Blenheims.

'Look at Gibbesee,' said Ged.

I whisked my eyes away from the port wing of the C.O.'s aircraft for a split second and saw Bobby just a few feet away thumbing his nose at me. I was not amused. I was all keyed up waiting for the tracer bullets.

'Shit. What's going on?' I yelled over the inter-com. 'Leo, can you still see the bandits?'

'I can't see a thing,' said Leo. 'I'm not in the turret.'

'For Christ sake, why not?'

'Damien's up there with his camera. He wants to get a shot of the Messerschmitts coming through.'

'Get back up there . . . now.'

He did and was just in time to welcome the ME109s with his twin Brownings as they dived through the formation. We lost four of our escort Kittyhawks. Bobby Gibbes got away with it.

On the next operation I landed in personal strife. The squadron commander, W/Cdr Tony Smyth, lent me his own Blenheim and I promptly bogged it in a soft patch of Benina airfield, outside Benghazi, and bent the tips of the port airscrew.

We took over another aircraft to lead a sweep over the sea searching for the Italian fleet which eluded us. Next day when we flew back to base at Sidi Bu Amud the C.O. was not pleased and ordered me and my crew straight back to Benina to retrieve his aircraft. General Rommel was on the move and looked like recapturing Benghazi any day. The sergeant fitter came along with the tools necessary to straighten the airscrew. On landing, a British Army officer raced up in a jeep, shouted to us to take off immediately because the Germans were on the outskirts of the airfield and disappeared in a cloud of dust. The C.O.'s aircraft had been towed out of the pot hole. It would be a pity to leave it there, I thought, so we set to with hammers trying to take the curls out of the airscrew. The fitter was not happy, pointing out that this was a precision job.

The sounds of the battle for Benghazi were getting very close so I decided to abandon the bent aircraft and go back in the Blenheim that had flown us to Benina. There was talk of blowing up the damaged Blenheim before we left but at that point a gun fight broke out on the far side of the airfield. It was too close for comfort.

In retrospect, the rest was pure comedy. The seven of us climbed back into the Blenheim that had brought us there but the port motor would not start. The pilot persisted without avail. We tumbled out and raced to the C.O.'s stricken aircraft. So far the army rearguard action was holding the Germans on the edge of the airfield. The battle was so close we could smell it.

This time the fitter was not so fussy. He gave the blades a few more sharp blows and followed us into the aircraft.

'She'll vibrate like hell,' he yelled, 'but let's give her a go.'

Then Ged, who was not a man to waste words, pointed to the bomb bay.

'What about the bombs?'

There were four 1,000 lb bombs in the belly. They still had their safety pins intact but it was risky dropping them to the ground. The armourers always said it was not a healthy thing to do.

The other pilot, who had been watching the battle for the airfield from the top of the Blenheim, had news for us.

'Shit . . . our blokes are pulling out. Let's go, let's go.'

I cut the normal warm-up time by half, held her on her brakes until I was close to full throttle and let her go. We had seven aboard instead of the usual three, plus the bomb load and a bent airscrew which was vibrating violently. We were barely airborne as the wall at the end of the airstrip loomed up so I bounced us over and, miraculously, we stayed in the air. With wheels and flaps up I was able to coax her to 600 feet or so. This was too low to safely drop bombs but we were approaching some hills so I motioned to Ged to drop the bombs and held my breath. At least one of them went off. We felt the blast. From the rear turret Leo saw German tanks roll on to the airfield as we flew away.

'What do you think,' I asked Herb at the end of this story. 'Should I accept the blame for the loss of the Blenheim we left behind as a gift for the Germans?'

'Why not? It was the result of your stupidity.'

★

Our cell by this time was bristling with irritation. Jack and I had made out fairly well in Cell 6. At least, to me it was an agreeable relationship. Granted, we were both stunned and very sorry for ourselves. We needed each other.

At first, when we were thrown together like fowls to be plucked, Herb and I seemed to be kindred souls. We had a lively rapport and sparked off each other. We were a team, too. It was us against the Texan. A day or so after he left for better pastures Herb and I clashed over some trivial remark or incident. I forget just what it was. Then, on 12 January, all the airmen in the cell block, except Herb and me, and one or two others, were moved to No 8 compound. There were nearly 100 altogether and it was great for them. They were free to talk and walk about the yard. They could sit in the sun.

Why were Herb and I left to rot in the cell? We were angry, exasperated and frightened. We were like caged lions. The other few prisoners left in the cell block were, as far as we could ascertain, recent arrivals. It was becoming obvious that we had been selected for special treatment. The Texan had told us a handful of prize prisoners had been shipped off to Singapore, even to Tokyo. Was this to be our fate? Jack Shortis had gone to the compound as well as others who had been captured around the same time as us.

The Japanese offered no explanation as to why we had been left behind in this near empty cell block. We were neglected, too. Now and again they missed out feeding us and that is serious when you are on survival rations only.

Tension built up in the cell. I took it out on Herb and he retaliated with a vengeance. We were really starting to detest each other. More intense, however, was Herb's growing hatred of our Japanese 'masters'. He simply loathed them.

14 February, 1978
I am in the lobby of the Hotel Vancouver looking for Herb Ivens. It has been thirty-three years since we shared Cell 41 in Rangoon and now we are to dine together in the old world splendour of this spacious hotel.

Soon after the war ended Herb had written saying he was in tow with a nightclub singer and was finding it hard to settle down but I did not get around to answering that letter. Now I am in North America for the National Audubon Society on a lecture tour with one of my wildlife films. There is one other man in the lobby with a searching look but he is huge, built like a house. As I look away this dominating figure takes aim with an outstretched forefinger pointed at me.

'Wing Commander Hudson,' *he bellows. It is Herb. He has tripled in weight. We take stock of each other. He has grown in more ways than one. His personality has blossomed and leaves no doubt at all that he is now an important man.*

Herb's fist glances softly off my shoulder.

'Hey,' *he says,* 'you haven't met my wife.'

I take a quick look. There is nobody there. Then from behind Herb's back emerges a wisp of a woman smiling shyly. She is Japanese.

'Machiko,' *says Herb,* 'this is the Aussie bastard I've been telling you about.'

Herb savours my surprise and roars with laughter. I recover to introduce my niece, Beverley, who lives in Vancouver and we go in to dinner.

'I said to myself a few years ago: You don't want to die hating the Japanese,' *says Herb telling the story.* 'So I went off to Japan to get it out of my system.'

He became involved with a Japanese wartime pilot and flew around the country with him. He was taken to the pilot's home town and there he met Machiko and they fell in love.

My adversary in Cell 41, I find out, is now a leading barrister and heads up the firm of Ivens, McGuire, Souch and Ottho.

Next day we are fishing for spring salmon off a luxury cruiser in the bleak waters between Vancouver, the city, and Vancouver Island. I am the only one to catch fish.

'You kept telling me in the gaol about your luck,' *remembers Herb. He asks about the girl I married and when I tell him that Audrey is at the moment visiting my daughter, Jane, in the country, he wants to know the telephone number and disappears into the cabin. Soon there is a yell to come below.*

'I'm talking to your Audrey in Australia ship-to-shore,' *he says. I hear him tell her that he will be introducing me to a friend who is a big diamond merchant.*

'So expect a precious present,' *he chortles.*

We are warming to each other again. Salmon fishing has a slight edge on sharing a cell.

(Herb Ivens died of cancer in 1980.)

Our Japanese tormenters kept Herb and me isolated, for no apparent reason, in Cell 41 until the end of January. We were barely talking to each other but I carried on telling Herb the saga of my lucky escapes. No XI Squadron was moved from Egypt to Ceylon after Pearl Harbor and we had a month of high living in Colombo before the Japanese bombed the port on Easter Sunday, 1942. Our job was to follow the Japanese planes back to their aircraft carriers and bomb them. We could not find the carriers, thank goodness. Taking on the zeros with our lumbering Blenheims would have been suicide.

Four days later, our mission was to attack the battle fleet which had turned up off Trincomalee on the east coast of the island. I could not get off the ground. My port engine would not start. The other eleven Blenheims found the Jap carriers this time and five of them were shot down. The crews, numbering fifteen, and two naval observers were lost. Two other Blenheims crash-landed back on the island but the crews escaped. I felt cheated that I had missed out on the mission, but at least I was still alive.

Later that year I flew a Blenheim from Madras to Colombo but, instead of going straight into land, I made a couple of runs over the Australian Army Hospital there to alert a nurse that I was back in town. A motor cut while I was in the landing circuit because I had neglected to check my fuel and switch to the outer tanks. I managed to get the aircraft on to the runway but was heading for a row of Hurricane fighters out of control so I yanked up the undercarriage. The Blenheim was a write-off.

'Christ,' Herb had said. 'Not only Hitler should give you a medal but the bloody Emperor too.'

Finally, the contrary Japanese excelled themselves by putting me into a cell on ground level by myself and marched Herb off to the comparative paradise of the aircrew compound. Why? By this time I was becoming philosophical about the whole affair and, in fact, felt relieved at being alone for a while.

Herb never did hear the last of my 'survival' stories.

14 January, 1943, engine failure over the target, Akyab, bombs

jettisoned, just made it to our nearest airfield at Chittagong for a forced landing. Abandoned it there.

13 May, 1943, having lunch in District Officer's bungalow at Feni, in Bengal, when air raid sirens screamed.

'Another blasted false alarm,' said the D.O., 'but seeing I'm the Chief Air Raid Warden I suppose I should show up.'

I went to the lavatory, which was a separate structure away from the house, and was sitting there when I heard the sound of aircraft motors. I knew they were not ours so I raced to the nearest foxhole yanking up my shorts. As my face hit the dirt the bomb hit the bungalow and I was covered by debris and mud. When I lifted my head the lonely lavatory had vanished and there was not much left of the bungalow.

At the end of my first tour of operations I was assigned to Air Plans, Combined Operations, in New Delhi and soon found myself on my way to North Africa to study with General Eisenhower's planners. I flew to Sicily on the eve of the invasion of Italy and was able to organize myself aboard an LCM in the first wave as an observer. This was the only way to study amphibious operations, I reckoned.

It was not until we were half-way across the Straits of Messina on the way to the toe of Italy that I asked myself what in the devil I was doing there. Two Focke Wulf fighters screamed down and wildly tossed some bombs at us. They missed by a mile but then the LCM was warned to expect opposition on its assigned beach at Reggio di Calabria. We ran into a smoke screen and there shells started to scream. Frankly, I was frightened. Here I was going into battle with nothing more to do than just look. On my hip was a Luger I had never fired. I confessed this to a Canadian corporal whose job was to drive a truck up the beach. He offered me his sten gun and said the healthy thing to do was to get off the LCM as soon as possible.

'We're the target,' he said.

'Whatever they've got there, they'll throw at us.'

As we touched bottom the ramp splashed down and I was first off, running for dear life through the shallows, knees high like a Bondi lifesaver in a surf race. There was cover up the slope and I headed for it, thinking of bullets. I felt like a black ant on a white tablecloth and flung myself under the nearest bush.

A figure approached and my fingers searched frantically to switch off the safety catch – without success. It was just as well because the enemy turned out to be an old Italian woman in black carrying a basket. She stumbled towards me through the sand with her hands outstretched as if in a blessing.

'Liberator . . . liberator . . . liberator,' she cried. She was smiling through her tears and just had to be genuine. I stood up and, still suspicious, looked into her basket for hand grenades. It was full of ripe figs. She offered me some. I dropped my Sten in the sand to free my fingers for peeling them. With hands and sound effects I was able to ask her the direction of the airfield.

'Germans?' I asked.

She pursed her lips, shook her head and waved away towards the north. I learned later that the nearest Germans were miles away on their way to defend Anzio. However, the place was thick with Italian soldiers trying to surrender to me with their hands held high.

'POW camp, POW camp. Where POW camp?' I waved them towards the beach. I walked to the airfield, observed the situation there for my report, had a meal with the engineers and was back on the beach waiting for a lift back to Sicily when a bunch of war correspondents and photographers swarmed down to the water's edge. It was General Bernard Montgomery, Montgomery of Alamein, doing a General Macarthur by getting his feet wet.

The other story Herb did not have to suffer was about the Mosquito I wrecked at Kanchrapara, India, three months before I was captured. The port engine failed near the end of my take-off run. I aborted and was careering across the airfield out of control when a crowd of Indian labourers loomed up dead ahead. I yanked up the undercarriage and we screamed to a sudden stop in a cloud of dust only yards short of where the Indians were working on a new runway. Only the all-embracing Sutton Harness, snug safety belts, had saved me from being flung forward through the windscreen. Then, sitting there thankful for yet another life, I shivered with the strangest feeling. Who had put me into my harness? I never wore one.

In Bengal eighteen months before I had raced out to a Blenheim that had crash-landed on its return from a bombing raid. As I approached in the Jeep the aircraft had burst into flames and I had watched agonizingly while the pilot struggled to free himself from his harness. He was still held tight when the flames enveloped him. From that point on I had always flown without the safety harness. For the life of me I could not recollect having made an exception for this take-off. Somehow I had unconsciously anticipated my fate or was there an invisible hand in it? Down-to-earth Herb would have scoffed at that idea.

After a couple of days in solitary I woke up hungry. I had missed out on a meal the day before and was consumed with the idea that my captors had some diabolical plan to slowly starve me into submission. Somehow they must have found out that I had been involved with combined operations planning at the New Delhi headquarters of Air Command, South-East Asia. Why else would I be singled out for this special treatment? Or were they about to send me to Singapore or Tokyo?

I was suspended in one of those long, lonely moments one experiences at dawn when there was a soft thud on the stone sill of my gaping cell window. Now I was wide awake and I got there just in time to thrust my hand through the bars and grab a featherless squab pigeon which, obviously, had fallen from a nest under the eaves of the roof above. It lay still in the palm of my hand for a few seconds. I pinched its neck and then ate it. The blood was warm.

Later in the morning a Japanese guard came for me. Here comes the big inquisition, I thought.

'Huddison, come,' he grunted and marched me out of the cell block to my fate.

*   *   *

As a youngster in Sydney I was a reluctant tap dancer. I had no talent whatsoever, but, for some obscure reason, my mother insisted that I take lessons from a Miss Robinson. Once a year Miss Robinson staged a grand concert and all her pupils had to perform. I was on the programme to do my waltz clog just before the interval and I vividly remember standing petrified in the wings when my music cue came up. A shove in the back from Miss Robinson sent me stumbling on to the stage and into the glare of the footlights. The Blue Danube Waltz was well under way before I recovered from my stage shock.

It was a strangely similar experience that morning in Rangoon Gaol. Fearing the worst, I was stiff with fright as I left my cell and walked in front of the guard in the shadow of the wall. Then, suddenly, we were at the gate of No 8 compound. It was open. That was my cue but I just froze. The guard gave me a shove in the back and I stumbled into the glare of the sunlight, the cynosure of all eyes. I faltered. It was all so unexpected that I did not know what to do. There were cheerful grins and warm handshakes from my fellow airmen and within seconds I was dancing on air. I had been liberated, just another prisoner, and felt the security of being in the flock again.

A few weeks out in the open air had done wonders for most of them. They had lost their despairing, anxious looks. In the cells they had been nothing more than creatures. Now they were people.

Compared with the wretched cell block, life in the compound seemed to me that day to be close to heaven. No more sleeping with your latrine box and you could talk and walk at will day and night. You could sit in the sun, stand in the rain and watch the birds. Our own fellows cooked and served the food. We had our own hospital, of sorts, as well as a rumour-mongering factory.

I had been inside the gate only a matter of minutes when somebody volunteered the fact that we were winning the war.

'It won't be long now,' he said reassuringly.

'Why, what's the news?'

'A drunken Jap was talking to us through the fence yesterday. Do you know what he said? He said: "War no good."'

The enemy, silly with saki, was our sole tenuous link with what was going on beyond the grey walls. My jubilant informant was stripped to a G-string. His face was thin but his legs were bloated with beri beri and angry with ulcers.

'This is living,' he called back over his shoulder as he pressed on with his perambulations around the narrow yard.

Of course, there were still rules. Every Japanese had to be bowed to and called 'master'. Prisoners were forbidden to congregate in groups and we were not allowed to communicate in any way with the prisoners in other compounds. The doctors in the British Army and Indian compounds were still not permitted to treat us.

We aircrew were still the pariahs of the prison. The other inmates went out in working parties, to the docks and other places of work, and returned with tobacco leaf and cheroots given to them by the local Burmese. The fit ones among us envied them. Also, they were paid some sort of a pittance. They had money to buy the odd egg.

I should make it clear here for those not familiar with this phenomenon during the Second World War that Allied fliers on squadrons usually regarded rank lightly. The important demarcation was being aircrew. Once in the air a sergeant pilot or navigator could be as equally effective against the enemy as a group captain. I happened to be a wing commander because I commanded a squadron of twin-engined aircraft. The C.O. of, say, a Spitfire squadron carried only the rank of squadron leader.

It was fairly easy to get rank those days as long as you stayed alive and your crimes were undetected. Frankly, I never considered myself as genuine 'officer material'. I had passed out of flying school as a sergeant pilot and was not commissioned until I had a swag of operations under my belt in North Africa. Sent back to Cairo to get my uniforms and pilot officer's cap I promptly went astray in Alexandria and spent my first two weeks as an officer AWOL. I got away with that by using my imagination.

Not so long after that I was a squadron leader and acting C.O. of No 11 Squadron RAF in Colombo, Ceylon. A slap-up 'bullshit' parade was organized for a visiting dignitary and I was expected to lead it. All my time in the air force had been spent in the field. I had never even seen a parade of this nature and had no idea what to do. So, I went sick for a day and one of my junior officers took the parade.

Alongside the airstrip in Assam from where I had taken off for what was to be my last operation was a sign that read: 'No Saluting On This Base'. It summed up my sentiments with regard to authority and discipline.

For someone who did not relish command it was quite a blow for me to discover that I was the ranking officer in No 8 compound. There was another wing commander, John Hill, an RAF Beaufighter pilot who had been shot down by Oscar fighters four months before. He claimed he was junior to me and, anyway, was weak from dysentery and beri beri. Among the Americans there was no one above the rank of captain.

When I hesitated about taking on a multi-national command I was told that there was little in the job except to take the dawn and dusk parades, called 'tenko'. So I did a crash course in Japanese commands and reluctantly took over. I felt there was no alternative.

Second-in-command of this air force compound was Captain Cornelius C. Meyer, an old-time flier with more than 5,000 hours up. (I had less than a thousand hours.) Meyer had worked with Wiley Post in the early days of flying in Oklahoma. He had a Silver Star which he wore above his wings. When the Japanese asked him what the star indicated he said glibly, 'Just an expensive pair of wings.'

No hard war news had reached the compound. We were cut off as though in another world. Japanese fighters, Zekes and Oscars, patrolled over Rangoon at dawn and dusk and a few Sally bombers passed overhead, but they were the only signs that there was a war on.

In the dry rice ration one morning there was a pamphlet in Burmese. Our unknown agent had translated it in pencil: 'Japanese fighting hard both east and west. Burmese not co-operating sufficiently. If you do not co-operate more we will evacuate and leave you to your fate with the British, Americans and Burmese.' The pamphlet was one of thousands dropped over Rangoon from an Army 97 plane with spats over its fixed wheels. Of course, this gave us food for thought. The main query in our minds was: What about us? What is in store for we prisoners-of-war if the Japanese evacuate?

There were some sixty Americans and forty English, Australian, Canadian and New Zealand aircrew in No 8. We slept hip to hip on the bare wooden floors of the king-sized cells in the shell of a building that practically filled the compound. Here, to a degree, we were allowed to structure our own existence.

I bedded down with two other Australians, Hank Wilson, of Sydney, a pilot from my own squadron freshly shot down, and Wally Trigwell, a Beaufighter pilot from Western Australia, who was shot down by a USAAF P-38 Lightning while he, himself, was strafing Japanese road transport on the Taungup Pass. Despite this, Triggy kept his sense of humour.

'The RAF was behind it,' he said one day. 'Just because I had been instrumental in destroying five of their aircraft while flying with them they organized the Americans to rub me out.'

It was not long before I got straight the story behind the victimization of Allied fliers by the Japanese in Rangoon. Apparently, aircrew had been treated as criminal prisoners since the first heavy bombing of Rangoon in November, 1943. The Japanese told us it was a reprisal because we had bombed Burmese women and children. As it happened the special treatment for aircrew also coincided with the loss by the Japanese of air supremacy over Burma. Obviously, they were taking it out on us because they could not compete in the air.

The Japanese army in Burma, stretched to the limit, was poorly supplied, virtually cut off by our navies and without air support. The British 14th Army in Burma had dubbed itself the 'Forgotten Army'. The truly neglected Japanese there surely had a greater claim to that title.

Sydney, Australia,
10 September, 1985

This is tricky but, after all, I am dealing here in home truths. I recall that, at the time, we were all indignant and angry at being branded as war criminals by the Japanese. No doubt there had been women and children killed in the course of the war in Burma but whose fault was that? It was well known that the Japanese regularly used local villages as cover for their operations. Many a grass-roofed hut exploded when hit by bombs or bullets. Anyway, none of the airmen in the gaol felt any guilt.

However, I have come across just now one entry in my pilot's log book that calls for an airing. It is dated 15 June, 1943, after I took over command of 'A' flight. I was flying Blenheim N6183. The duty column reads: 'RAID – Bombed Burmese village of Sikaung Myauk, Myittha River. Reprisal for massacre of W/C Pennington-Legh, F/Lt Ingram, F/Lt Burnley on June 1.'

Two weeks before, our Commanding Officer, Pennington-Legh, RAF, and his Australian crew, Ingram and Burnley, had crash-landed in the jungle south of Kalemyo after their Blenheim lost a propeller over the target. Then we had a report from an army unit operating in the area that their bodies had been found slashed with Burmese swords. Next day we had orders from Group Headquarters to bomb the particular village which was reported to have been responsible. Half-a-dozen aircraft took part in the raid. We dropped our bombs without the slightest qualms.

Forty of the hundred men around me were survivors of the infamous New Law Courts cell block which they dubbed the Rangoon Ritz.

Aircrew captured before November, 1943, had been put in with the army prisoners in Rangoon Gaol but then the new edict was issued by the Burma Area High Command that airmen were to be treated as criminal prisoners.

The Rangoon Ritz, a single-storied structure in the centre of a courtyard surrounded by high buildings, was a place of horror. Captured fliers were flung into the dark cells with dacoits, murderers, spies and lepers. From five to nine people were crowded into each cell measuring nine feet by twelve feet. They saw no sun and, despite the sweltering heat, they were given barely enough liquid to keep them alive. The food was scanty and medical treatment practically non-existent. Of the fifty-seven airmen incarcerated in the Rangoon Ritz in the first six months, twenty-three died from disease and bashings.

At the end of July, 1944, the survivors were moved to Rangoon Gaol where many of them spent up to five months' solitary confinement in the cell block. Men continued to die from malnutrition, beri beri and tropical ulcers and it was just before I reached the gaol that the first regular medical treatment of sorts was meted out to these aircrew prisoners.

Then, in January, 1945, with time fast running out for the boys from the Ritz, someone up there in Japanese High Command inexplicably had a change of heart and these damaged bodies were emptied out into the compound with access to open air and sunshine and were even permitted to talk to each other.

For weeks after I was let out into the compound I watched these wretched creatures moving about in slow motion or just sitting and staring into space. Gradually they started to talk again and I spent hours listening in awe to their stories.

'You can't imagine the pleasure I get out of this,' one of them told me as he sat in the sun leaning against a wall. 'In the cells at the Ritz, you know, we had to sit up straight, not allowed to lean against the walls. We were punished if caught talking. Some guards would make you stand for an hour or two with your arms outstretched, others had you place three fingers of each hand on the cell door crossbar while they crashed down on them with a teakwood club.'

They told how Captain Bill Wright died. He was outside his cell emptying a latrine box when he stopped to pick up a cigar butt lying on a window sill. One of the Burmese flunkies saw him pick up the butt and pointed him out to a Japanese guard who beat him on the back and shoulders for five minutes with a solid hickory club four feet long and 1½ inches in diameter. Two days later the Captain was furtively reading the New Testament in his cell when he keeled over and died. Presumably he died from a blood clot on the brain caused by the beating. That guard was promptly knicknamed 'The Killer'.

One airman died from malnutrition and beri beri and his body was left in the cell for twenty-four hours. The night before they took it away a rat chewed away part of one of his feet.

'Then there was that bastard who threw three bananas on the floor,' cut in another Ritz old boy. 'When I tried to pick one up he stamped on my hand. Finally, he forced me to eat them, skin and all, without using my hands.'

One statistic about the cells at the Ritz I will never forget: An American pilot once counted fifty lice in two square inches of his blanket.

There was one desperate attempt to escape from the Ritz. At midnight on 5 July, 1944, the inmates of a cell, jam-packed with thirteen men, broke the lock on the door and rushed the guards. One Japanese was knocked unconscious but a Burmese on duty escaped and raised the alarm. Also the civilian prisoners in the cells for some reason yelled their heads off. When seven of the escapees headed for the outer gate they were confronted with machine guns. They gave up.

The offenders were stripped of all clothing and beaten with clubs and whips. For nearly three days they were forced to sit nude, cross-legged, in their cells and were given nothing to eat. Then they were placed on one-third rations and twice a day a guard came into the cell and beat each prisoner with a club. One American bombardier lost the use of his limbs and could not eat. Then his mind went. He died two weeks after the transfer of all air crew from the Ritz to Rangoon Gaol.

The emaciated survivors of the Ritz were a quiet force in the aircrew compound when I got there. They stood a plane above many of us new boys who were still wondering whether or not we could take it.

Today, forty years later, three of them stand out among the men I have known. One, John McCloskey, a B 25 pilot from Pittsburgh, Pennsylvania, who took part in the attempted escape, had a soul-stirring singing voice that did wonders in shutting out the hate and the ugliness that engulfed us.

Gostaf ('Gus') Johnson, a bombardier from Miami, Florida, had been in captivity longer than anyone else in the compound but was invariably in good spirits. He shared the cell with us Australians.

Another who kept me going was Arthur Sharpe, a Beaufighter pilot from Weybridge, Surrey, who awed me with his serenity. It was Arthur who told me the incredible story of Major Hugh Seagrim, of the Burma Rifles, who had been a fellow-prisoner in the Ritz.

'This strange-looking fellow was brought into the cells at the New Law Courts at the end of March, 1944,' said Sharpe. 'He towered over the little Japs. He had long hair, a heavy dark brown beard and was bare-footed. He wore a black longyi with a red, smocked shirt hanging loose. His cheerful face was a joy.

'We were intrigued with this mystery man. He was interrogated continually and guarded all night. He was put into Cell 5 with a Chinese. There was something aristocratic about this man. Even when taking out his latrine box in the morning he walked tall and winked at us as he passed our cell. He refused to call the Japs "master" and persisted in making cheeky remarks to them. He had us laughing all the time. When the Japs said "No talking" he would ignore them. They would hit him on the head with their clubs and he'd start talking again. He laughed a lot, kept very fit with exercise and was never sick.'

Piece by piece, Sharpe put together his story from forbidden, whispered scraps of conversations. Major Seagrim had been a Captain in the British Army when the Japanese forces had pushed the British out of Burma early in 1942. He stayed behind in the mountains north-east of Rangoon to organize the Karen tribes as a resistance force against the Japanese. They hid him in their jungle huts away from the villages and he kept in touch with India with a portable radio transmitter. The Karens are Christians and there has never been any love lost between them and the Buddhist Burmese. So, when the Japanese occupied Burma and started pushing Buddhism, the outcome was inevitable.

For the first year Seagrim worked alone, quietly organizing the

Karens. He rarely left his hut in the jungle by day and spent much of his time reading and re-reading a Bible and a Shakespeare the Karens had smuggled to him. He told of eating bush rats and catching Rhesus monkeys, slitting their throats and drinking the blood while it was still hot. (In my notes jotted down in prison there is a line: 'Looked after by elephant . . .' I wish I could remember the full story.)

In the second year RAF Hudsons started dropping men and arms and radios in the Karen Hills but the guerrilla forces were betrayed and finally hunted down by the Japanese.

Seagrim escaped but the Japanese started savage reprisals against the Karens. In a bid to put a stop to this Major Seagrim (he had been promoted by radio) gave himself up to the Japanese.

One night in mid-June the roof leaked in Cell 3 and Sharpe was shifted temporarily into Cell 5 with Seagrim. He confided in Sharpe that the Japanese were trying to get him to organize the Karens to switch to the side of the Japanese.

He intimated that he was willing to pretend to do this because he was confident that he could secretly keep them faithful to the British. He knew the Karens loathed the Japanese because of the things they were doing to their families but they would be prepared to go along with the idea. Anything to play for time. The Major was convinced that it was the Japanese intention not to let anybody out alive. In the event of an invasion, he said, those still in the cells would be killed.

A navigator from Sharpe's squadron died in the cells from dysentery and beri beri while Seagrim was there. The major conducted a brief service from his cell and ended it with the words: 'Lord, forgive them, for they know not what they do.' The Japanese guards on duty were not aware that they had been brought into the prayers.

Major Seagrim was taken away in July just before the aircrew were moved to Rangoon Gaol.

'He's an exceptional man,' said Sharpe. 'I wonder what's happened to him?'

Early August, 1950
Korea . . . I am here covering the war for AAP-Reuter. The onrushing North Korean communist forces are launching an all-out offensive against

the Naktong River defence line which protects the last foothold South Korean and United Nations forces have on the Korean peninsula.

I am outside the headquarters of the U.S. 24th Division trying to hitch a ride to the front. With me is Ian Morrison, correspondent for The Times, London.

My trips to the front line to get the 'I was there' stories are rare because Reuters want the overall war situation, but Ian spends a lot of time under fire. Some of the other war correspondents say he seems to have a death wish. He certainly does not look the part of the rash adventurer with his Shan bag hanging from his shoulder. It contains his notebook, pencils and a fan.

'Did you get the Shan bag in Burma?' I ask.

'Yes. You were in gaol there during the war, weren't you?'

'Only for the last five months.'

Ian turns and fixes me with his piercing, pale-blue eyes.

'Did you happen to be in the same gaol with Major Seagrim at any stage?'

'No, but I knew all about him.'

I start to tell Ian what Arthur Sharpe had told me about Seagrim.

'That was Flying Officer Sharpe. Yes, I use him in my book.'

It turns out that Ian has written a book about Seagrim and his Karens.

'Well,' I ask. 'What happened to him? Did Seagrim get away with it?'

A Jeep pulls up raising the dust.

'You guys want a ride?' asks an American corporal.

As we bump our way to where the action is Ian tells me how the Major and those of his Karen followers who had been captured had been transferred to the Kempei Tai gaol at Insein, outside Rangoon.

On 2 September, 1944, Major Seagrim and seven of his devoted Karens were blindfolded and shot by a Japanese firing squad. They were buried in a common grave.

Ian is shaking his head sadly. 'Right to the end,' he says, 'Major Seagrim was pleading to the Japanese that he alone was to blame and the Karens should not be punished. He begged that his friends be set free. But it was to no avail. The War Office in Tokyo had confirmed their death sentences.'

I am tempted to end my Ian Morrison story there but it would be untidy if I did.

To appreciate these events fully you should know that Ian's father was Dr George Morrison, an Australian, also known as 'China Morrison', *who was special correspondent in Peking for* The Times, *London, for five years before resigning in 1912 to become political adviser to Yuan Shih-K'ai, President of the newly-formed Chinese Republic.*

The People's Army of North Korea marched across the 38th parallel at dawn on 25 June, 1950.

Next morning Ian, Denis Warner (London Telegraph) *and I, all based in Singapore, were on our way to the war on the same BOAC aircraft. We needed to stay overnight in Hong Kong to await our connection to Tokyo and so arranged to share a taxi from the airport to a hotel.*

However, Ian Morrison disappeared at the airport and we did not see him again until we boarded our plane for Tokyo. We learned later that he had been whisked away by Dr Han Suyin, Peking-born, whose mother was half-Dutch, half-Flemish and her father Chinese. She was a beautiful woman. I met her several times afterwards when she went to work as a doctor in Johore, Malaya.

Han Suyin eventually wrote a best-selling novel about a British correspondent who had a rendezvous in Hong Kong with a girl on his way to cover the war in Korea and was killed there. It was called A Many-Splendoured Thing. *In the film of the same name the war correspondent is an American. William Holden played the role.*

It must have been Taegu in September. . . . Ian and I were chatting in the sun and I was saying how I was aching to get back to my wife and children in Singapore. His wife and children were there, too.

'You're so lucky,' he said quietly. 'You know what you want for the future. I wish I did.'

The next day I got wind of the capture of a Russian tank and I told Ian about it. We organized some transport to go out next morning to get a story on it. Christopher Buckley, the London Telegraph's *veteran correspondent, was coming with us. That night there was a report that an American airfield had been surrounded by the North Koreans away to the east. It sounded like a better story so I flew off at dawn leaving a note for Ian saying* The Times *and* The Telegraph *could have the Red tank exclusively.*

Ian and Christopher went off on schedule. Their Jeep was blown up in a minefield and they were both killed.

We could see the antiquated Army 97 circling but it was a mile or so away from the gaol and chances of our getting any of the leaflets it was dropping appeared slim. Just then the wind picked up and, after an agonizing four or five minutes, the odd one fluttered to earth in the compound. The leaflet was in Burmese but the 'underground' gaol interpretation service went into action and within minutes the message was being signalled from compound to compound: 'British are close. Stay where you are. Don't leave Rangoon. You will be looked after.'

The air was suddenly tense. Was this the beginning of the end? The poker-faced guards remained inscrutable but this official news was in line with a series of incidents over the past week or so.

As February got under way the storage of food inside the gaol walls was stepped up and the old timers said it was obvious the guards had been instructed to tighten up on discipline. If our troops are really getting close they must be afraid we would make a break.

We had news from the British Army compound that when the Brigadier complained about the food he did not get the usual answer. The interpreter said he was complaining too much, considering how poorly the Japanese soldiers were faring up north.

Two days later a working party which had been in the city came back with the news that the Japanese were raising a Burmese Navy. Our guess was that they were gathering boats in readiness for a Dunkirk.

On 11 February, B 29s and B 24s made a large-scale raid on Rangoon, north of the city. We counted 134 bombers and quite a few glistening escorting fighters. Morale soared. Was this the pre-invasion softening up?

About this time I made contact with Pinky. He was British Army, I gathered, and had something to do with the food store on the other side of the wall at the far end of our compound. We had whispered conversations through the wall, but I never knew just what he really looked like. Whenever I glimpsed him it was from a distance from the top of our steps into the upstairs cell. Just the same, a close bond developed between Pinky and me over the next two months.

On 27 February, 1945, Pinky tossed a tiny notebook over the wall and whispered it was for me. It was 3¼" by 2½" and had thirty pages. It had been made from pages of a school exercise book and was hand-stitched. There was also a piece of indelible pencil with it. The extraordinary thing about it was that there was no way Pinky could have known it was my birthday. I was 29. Nobody knew but me. It gave me a funny feeling. Afterwards I told him.

'I must be psychic,' he said.

My prison diary started that day and I kept it going for the next two months writing on any scraps of paper Pinky could borrow or steal. As I filled up each piece I stuffed it into an empty chutney bottle and buried it in the wall of one of our foxholes. My big fear was that the Japanese would find it and that I would be bashed for breaking the rules but after a few days I found I was getting deep satisfaction out of my act of defiance. What the hell! It might help to keep me sane.

The main thing was not to involve anybody else. I resolved to keep it free of names but, I am afraid, it did not quite work out that way.

The first entry was in note form. It read:

February 27

Strange probe. Weary Willie and interpreter quiz chaps as to what war news we know. Played dumb. What will we do if British come? Foxholes. Our treatment? Cliff's beat up, number, rank and name . . . Japs worried: 'Dear Mum . . . stop spending my insurance . . . Be Home soon.' Chopsticks craze. Old-timers singing 'PPM'.

This first entry calls for some amplification: We were surprised just before dusk when Weary Willie, the Jap interpreter, walked into our compound and started asking questions as to what war news we had received. Of course, we played dumb and told him we only knew that we were losing the war. Weary Willie also asked one chap what he would do if the British neared Rangoon. He was so surprised that he nearly blurted out, 'Kick you in the face', but recovered sufficiently to say that he would remain in the gaol where it was safe. This probe was very heartening. Morale sky high.

Flight-Lieutenant Cliff Emeny, New Zealand Mosquito pilot, was bashed unmercifully today for handing a cap to a sick prisoner who had been braced in the sun for not bowing. The prisoner was so ill that he was practically in a coma but the Jap would not heed this and kept him out in the blazing sun for two hours. Cliff just could not bear it. For his good deed Cliff was punched and kicked until his face was pulp. He could not see or hear or eat for a day or two.

Spirits are high in the compound because the guards are starting to look worried. Gus said he would dearly love to get a telegram off to the States: 'Dear Mum . . . stop spending my insurance . . . be home soon.'

We are becoming more civilized, too. Instead of eating with our fingers many of us are using chopsticks made from pieces of wood ripped from the ceiling and ground into shape on the stonework.

Top of the charts in the aircrew compound at the moment is the song 'Pistol Packin' Momma, Pistol Packin' Momma . . .' One of the newly shot-down crews brought it with them into the gaol and taught it to some of the song-starved old-timers who relish it. They are getting weary of 'We're going to hang out the washing on the Siegfried Line.'

My diary is printed here exactly as written in the gaol. Even the misspelt words are left there.

Frankly, it is embarrassing for me today to read some of the entries, let alone have them published, but I feel it is important for the diary to remain intact and not to be rewritten in the light of how things turned out. It stands as a frank report on what went through the mind of one prisoner of the Japanese during two traumatic months when his fate was in the balance.

Also, this diary tells something of the animal survival qualities of men cornered like rats and how rays of human unselfishness struggle through. It sets the scene for the fateful days when Rangoon became a no-man's city.

The commander of the Rangoon Gaol is described by me as the 'Ti' and the 'big Ti'. The correct spelling for a captain in the Japanese forces is 'Thai-i'.

II
The Diary

3 March, 1945

During last week increasing number of bullock carts loaded with firewood into gaol. Our estimate is that sufficient firewood in gaol at this date to last this place 2–3 months at present rate of fires. At first-light daily carts start streaming in. Counted 50 carts in first two hours today. Alarm spreading. Do Japs intend to attempt to hold out in this gaol? Hospital during seige? Putting dumps here where will not be bombed? Lorry loads of rice, too.

Thank Christ we have these odd changes of weather. Day after day clear and sunny mornings followed by hot afternoons and starry nights. Only variety provided by moon.

But today dawned with heavy mist veiling ragged-edged, three-quarter moon. Foggy morning. Good break. Others probably appreciated it, too, but no emotion. It may be that they getting nothing out of nature anymore. Finer feelings worn away.

There is certainly excessive selfishness and greed in compound. I expected this communal life to straighten people up a bit, but apparently not.

I was surprised this morning when W/Cdr Hill admitted he had purposely refrained from going to fence yesterday to Q.M. because he is emphasising his beri beri in case Japs have in mind taking senior officers. He is well able to walk better than I but he allows me to answer these calls . . . summons to the fence. I don't care. I have learned that everything is for the good. I, too, could lay low and pass unnoticed but this compound needs a C.O.

As I write I hear, among other bird noises, the jerky call of the woodpecker. I have often seen him and his mate pecking a home in the mango tree, the upper branches of which reach up to the southern barred window of our cell. His crest is the warmest red I've seen.

4 March

Watched for sunrise this morning. It came out as a shimmering blob from behind Christian church steeples. Cross silhouetted. Not visible other times. (Mary Marlowe please copy for your dawn collection). I wish I had the space to describe it as seen from prison in such company as teeming bird life here. It awakens me just before dawn.

Last night I went from cell to cell and gave out the policy for when the British get nearer. I explained how I had sent a message to Brig. Hobson asking for orders. He had replied 'Stand fast.' So we will. Just how we'd like it. No trouble with the Japs. Peace at most costs. I told the entire compound that except for really sick boys we had to take 'stand still' beatings from Japs without protest as long as they only use hands or fists . . . and nobody is being seriously injured. BUT if some drunken or fanatical Jap or Japs used club or rifle and somebody looks like being badly hurt I will give the order to arrest the offending Jap. This will be done by 10/20 strong-arm men who will hold the Jap, take away club or rifle and take care not to hurt him. The sgt of guard or commandant will be summoned and culprit handed over. No crowd which will give impression of mob riot.

Then again, if Japs run amok before committing hari kari, plan is to close all steel windows, doors and get everybody upstairs, sick and all. Up through floor if necessary. On way up chaps are to grab axe, knives and other weapons, bricks. We then lock doors, pull up catwalk and sit tight until rescued by other compounds or army. Keep away from windows and stave off Japs with bricks etc. Other compounds better able to fight – greater numbers, fitter, more organization, weapons. This plan is definitely last resort instead of being killed. Impressed that all this is not so fantastic either as Japs so bloody unpredictable. Not a sign yet which way they will jump except that they appear to be worrying about our welfare more.

Anyway, I'm happier now that I have outlined a clear policy – just in case. Also, told everybody to conceal their homemade knives in case Japs make a surprise search for weapons. They seem scared that we are planning a break in order to join British troops.

About a week ago news was that our troops were at Prome,

Pyinmana, Taudy and Bassein. Morale soared. But today is third without news. Sceptics busy. I am purposely behaving over-optimistic and riding the pessimists hard. The chaps need news badly. Actually, I am surprisingly content here . . . a little anxious about how our sick boys are going to last out but looking forward to the excitement – whatever.

At present I am having a blitz on those who have a food complex and can talk of nothing else. I feel I am shutting them up somewhat. My attitude is that I personally don't give a damn and, surprisingly enough, I don't.

This prison diet is frugal, but I like it. The boys think I'm a freak.

I am organizing a party which will be ready the moment we are free to go to Mingaladon airfield and prepare it for use by aircraft. Army will demine it, of course, but my party of three RAF and three Yanks will form drome control. I think this might be instrumental in getting Dakotas here faster to cart away our sick. Even days might help some. The more constructive thinking I can incite the better, anyhow.

Ray of hope last night from two big flashes in sky to north. We have seen lots of flashes to south-east but I think that was lightning below horizon. I want both flash and sound effects.

Fresh fish for rations yesterday for first time. Just thing for our sick boys.

Prisoners in the other compounds are, all of a sudden, shying at the sight of us in the air force compound and are very reluctant to talk through fence. That is strictly forbidden, of course, but has been our only means of communication. I think they are playing safe since one of their men was flung into solitary for taking a cigarette from Burmese while out working.

Later: News of large-scale landings at Bassein. Lots of aircraft talk today. It makes me ache to fly a Mosquito again. I'm afraid I'll take a squadron rather than trip to Australia if I get the chance. A fool and his aircraft are hard to part.

Just before dusk today two Sally bombers flew separately high over Rangoon from west to east. Puzzling!

5 March

A calm, workaday atmosphere about the prison. Scores of bullock carts laden with wood flow in again. Piles rising high.

Japs attitude same as though they were storing wood for the winter. They give no outward sign that an enemy is bearing down on them. There is more wood now than we could use in six months.

Of course, wood is as valuable as water to Japs because, unlike us, they have to cook their staple food. It seems more than a coincidence that this storing followed close on a visit a fortnight ago to gaol of the Japanese Quartermaster for Rangoon area.

Day's end: I need a thunder storm ever so badly . . . something, anything, to relieve the tension. Compound filled with ragged tempers and sceptics. Morale running out. Skin disease rampant. Up till now old boys only had these running sores but now my contemporaries are stricken with them . . . mostly in the crutch and on the penis but they spread like wildfire . . . a number of bad cases. So, even fresh prisoners are disgusted with their lot. I am free of disease but I'm afraid of this epidemic. The rotten part of it is the helplessness you feel. Diseased and dying men and I can do so little. I have given orders that the dysentery and beri beri boys have as much food as is good for them at the expense of us fit men but their ghost bodies don't show any benefit. Their faces retain the desperate, yellow look. They are still greedy.

120 Indians were taken out of the compounds today, paraded, inspected by C.O. and a few Indian officers and a chap dressed like a maharajah on an elephant hunt. Then they were marched off – a ragged lot – to glory as I.N.A. A band led them away. Some Indians still left. If these are volunteers hard to understand at this stage of the war. They must know that the balloon's up (I hope). Another enigma! (Indian doctor's news good).

Nine Oscars came out of the NW this afternoon and seen to go east.

6 March

I feel fine this morning. My leg much better. Started exercises again.

7 March

Increased air activity yesterday and today. Three Oscars in the north at medium height. This morning Oscar over Rangoon. Otherwise things are humdrum. I organized Rs 1,000 sweepstake on the freedom date. Drew it yesterday. One hundred men at Rs 10 each payable within a fortnight of them reaching civilization. Some of the old boys reminded of the sweeps run by the Japs when fellows were dying in the cells. Nice people.

No lunch. They would not give us any water – and water is food in this country. No boiling water for bathing sores. Skin diseases are running riot over thin bodies. No medical treatment for three days. My knee wound is smelling badly. The chaps with the bad wounds are looking glum but saying nothing. Aha! An air raid siren.

The working parties have returned to the prison. They went out at dawn today and returned at lunch time. Weather is hotter. Is that it?

(Five minutes later . . . I'll start a new paragraph.)

A tense atmosphere has developed – all the Japs are out sporting rifles, strapping on extra cartridge cases. Some are carrying shiny-headed bamboo spears *á la* Burmese. Our little enemies appear a little excited. They are posted at regular intervals around the spiked fence. Nobody knows why. I could tell them we don't intend to make a break. That would only put us into the fire (out of the frying pan). The Japs are now collecting in little groups and they have something to talk about too. The knot below my window are jabbering about a map outline that one of them has drawn in the dust. A bag of extra cartridge cases and, I think, hand grenades are alongside them. There is one strange thing. The Japs never look in at us on these occasions. It seems they are ashamed to meet our looks. We are happy they are sad. All clear! But it shows us that the Allies are close enough to worry them.

One hour later: Another alert. Japs jump to it again. I lay full length on my piece of floor. My body is gluey with sweat and dirt. My knee wound also smells. A pleasant cool breeze from the east.

Two Oscars are patrolling low down over the prison in their circuit. As I prop myself up to catch a glimpse of them through the bars I sweep my eyes over two skin-rotten bodies belonging to two of my fellow officers. They are stretched on the floor beside me. Their conversation centres around 'when we were sweating out the expected invasion in the cells this time last year.' All clear. No sign of our aircraft. They must be operating close by. Working parties out again this afternoon. No wood today.

8 March

Back to normal again this morning. From the way everybody accepts this existence as an every day occurrence one would not imagine for a moment that we are a body of men, 100 strong, at the mercy of the Japanese who have discriminated against us so unjustly and obviously despise us for being air force. And what is more these Japs are in peril themselves. Our armies are bearing down on them and our air forces have supremacy. They are a proud race, steeped in nationality, and have been told they are invincible from their cradles on. Surely their reaction will be one of anger. They are taught to die first before surrender. So what is our fate? Do we accompany them to their heaven in the sun? Will they try to kill us out of spite? Their faces tell us nothing – or are meant to. But we have detected a trace of something in their make-up of recent months which says they are having a change of heart. Anyway, that's what we are pinning our faith to. We see them carrying on with the big self-bluff. We still call them 'master' and bow meticulously to even the most lowly private. We still quake when they bark at us because they still wield the club. But I sense that they are resigned and will gladly give in when the time comes. Of course, that decision may be influenced by wishful thinking. Anyway, we should know soon. Until then the day is routine . . . 'Izyu arimasen.'

There are 102 of us left. We never step outside our compound which is the size of a suburban garden. We are not allowed even to recognize the other 600 white men or the 500 Chinese, Indians, Gurkhas also in the prison. We are in Coventry for our sins. The compound building, bricked and red-roofed is colandered with 50 barred windows on either side and is two-storied. Downstairs the hospital patients and the other ranks sleep on bamboo platforms teeming with bugs. Upstairs the officers sleep on wooden floor. Some people have started sleeping on the ground outside for the first hot part of the night, coming indoors before it gets cold and damp.

At first light we have 'tenko'. I take the parade using Japanese commands and the sergeant of the guard counts us. Then breakfast of rice and 'nuka' – the bran from the rice cooked into a porridge. Also tea . . . but the meal is totally without milk or sugar except on the rare days when we have some of our home-made chutney made out of God knows what. 'Nuka' is bitter to taste at first but most of us love it. It is our only source of vitamin B and prevents beri beri. Mornings we are busy cleaning, sweeping, wearing down chopsticks

74

on the brick walls and pulling off wood from the building illicitly for firewood.

Meat ration days are full of interest with the chaps following the pigs down to the slaughter yard with their eyes and waiting until Chinese return to throw our meagre portion through the fence on to ground. Lunch is rice with greens. Afternoons are hot and people try to sleep. Dinner is rice and soup. Another 'tenko' at dusk and there you have another day.

Some of the boys are working on an idea of making a simple wireless set so as we can listen in to Rangoon radio news using a big diamond ring that belonged to one of the dead Americans as a crystal.

Rumour just came through the fence that European war was over five days ago and that Burma war has only 14 days to do. I won't allow myself to be swayed by these berserk rumours. Must keep this diary free of such nonsense. Just this: The above news came from Pinky. He said a Jap corporal told it to an Indian then pulled out photo of his wife and children and burst out crying. Now that's something to work on isn't it? The boys in the other compound have no idea just where our troops are. Japs are wary about us learning anything so we don't.

Big storm came out of the south so we stripped in the open for our first wash in eight days. But it only sprinkled, so we are still begrimed. Not so hot since storm passed.

One Tony with long-range tanks came out of the south soon afterwards and two Oscars followed it north-east. Another alert later but we saw nothing except a display of rifles and spears.

I have not washed my hands for eight days except for the two fingers I use to scrape my pans but I reminded myself that this is a ten times better life than in the cells.

9 March

Heard that working parties are toiling at unloading rice which is pouring into Rangoon. They are working long hours.

Excitement at 'tenko' last night. Jap Q.M. took inspection. He appeared anxious about our well-being. Then guard with him said to one of the officers: 'Free man soon.' Some who heard it said it was: 'three months old' referring to Yank's beard but we prefer to believe the former version. Anyway, Japs are uncommonly friendly of a sudden.

I must boil this diary down. No more paper.

Train whistles galore this morning. Yesterday's alert: Four of our fighters straffed road at Mingaladon . . . For some reason medical orderly Jap three-star very attentive to me . . .

Happy as hell. Soon after lunch three or four formations of B 24s and B 29s came over high in the glare with pairs of fighters showing up now and again. Their bombing was real music to our ears but we restrained ourselves from cheering because there was a dozen Japs on the other side of the fence – interested but emotionless. They ring a bell and insist that we stay near our trenches. Large scale raid – between 50–70 bombers . . . target around Insein 10 miles away . . . bluey-black smoke. Then came thunderstorm. Had a rain bath. Clean again. Index finger clean enough to clean my teeth. Then crowning joy – some of us found traces of beef in our soup. Jubilation. But it's amazing how many chaps in here can't believe they will ever see outside the wall. They just can't picture it in their minds.

No Jap fighters today and ack ack negligible. About 40 bursts in all.

At 'tenko' the Jap sergeant-major, young, good looking, swash-buckling, caught a sergeant looking at him and not ahead. He flared up, mighty face slap. I watched him go up to sergeant, eyes cast downwards as if afraid to look him in the eyes. They are certainly ashamed and hate being looked at. On edge, too. This poet-type Jap used to be so aloof.

10 March

Blokes are whistling and singing a lot this morning but yesterday's excitement already dead. The war is a thousand miles away. I play the part of the most optimistic fellow in the prison . . . purposely. Somebody has to offset these bloody sceptics. But my chance of freedom is perhaps less than everybodys. My rank might easily make me a prize worth Japs keeping. But what the hell . . . I'm off to play ball with some baseballers . . .

Japs had a saki party last night and some of the chaps report there was some commotion in the Chinese compound where some of the Japs live . . . News through fence that 500 gliders with 400 tanks have been landed 180 km away from here. Also Indian rumour that our troops are only 140 miles from here. Mechanics working party were ¼ mile from bombing on way to work. They saw Jap steel factory advertising for men. On way back all there was left was one chimney stack. They saw plenty of Japs laid out on roadside. Target area was 15 square miles. Heavy damage to factories and stores dumps. Japs say 140 bombers and 100 fighters. Day before 40 fighters.

Anthony signalled that an innocent-looking Chinese was stabbed in thigh last night by Jap using dagger or bayonet. A drunken Jap is really nasty. We must be more cautious not to provoke them. Tony flying high this morning and three Oscars this afternoon. We want more raids . . .

We need our hospitals more than anything else. The big wounds are just about holding their own with dressings every two or three days but there are two cases of septic throats or tonsilitis. Blokes in great pain, can't eat and have foul smell. Hell of it is we don't know what it is, whether it is dangerous or not. I just stood out at the fence for half an hour and finally pestered a sodden guard to get the medical orderly. He sent Chinese boy who painted throats with Iodine through fence. Skin diseases worst. Flt Lt Emeny, in charge of sick bay, spends day cleaning tracts of rotting body – disgusting sights. Emeny is earning a medal. Nearly the entire compound has sores of varying magnitude. The dysentery and beri beri is being held at bay by diets. Food is sufficient but everyone is hungry the moment they put down their chopsticks.

Latest report is that the Chinese incident last night was the stabbing of the O.C. of the compound, Major-General She. He was stabbed in belly and thigh by another Chinese – not a Jap and is in a bad way.

Big supply of cigars in today. The smokers in our compound who stood in pain watching them being unloaded from wheelbarrow say 10,000 cigars. The other compounds receive an issue. We don't. It is part of our punishment for being air force – Burmese baby-killers. Yes, we are the 'rough end' kids. We get the rough end of the deal.

Hot weather is driving many to have their beards shaved off. This is done with a little water and a sharpened table knife or piece of waste steel. My beard does not itch so it still curls. I had a hair trim with knife. Oldest inhabitant 2/Lt Gus Johnson sleeps on floor near me – eighteen months down. I have a bet with him that we had Prome by the end of February – a gallon of egg custard for winner.

11 March

By gaol wireless (air writing) that the Chinese general was operated on today by English colonel doctor and is in a serious condition. I glimpsed him on the balcony of his compound the night he was stabbed. He looked a benign little fellow and quite young. He was wearing a natty woollen cap.

The ring with a curse came to light again today. It is an ugly gold ring stuck with a big diamond and is reputed to be worth $500 U.S. In November last year three American airmen had collected in a Jap cell in Shwebo – a B 25 navigator, his pilot and a P 47 pilot. The navigator was wearing two rings – family heirlooms. He was ill with fever and the fact that he could not eat rice . . . 'garbage.' The P 47 pilot bribed Japs to provide medical treatment to keep the nav. alive by giving them the smaller ring. But the navigator died so his pilot took the big ring off his finger as they were burying him. The two pilots came here to Rangoon Prison where the B 25 pilot soon died. The P 47 pilot told the Japs about the ring. They robbed the body in its coffin but surprisingly enough gave the ring to the P 47 pilot who had told them. He wanted to give it to the nav's mother back in U.S.A. That was 2–3 months ago. Today I was asked for the ring. I disowned any knowledge of it. They checked up and asked the P 47 pilot for it. He produced the ring and the interrogator was about to take it for himself when the sgt. of the guard appeared. So the interr. gave it back to the P 47 pilot, who still wears it, the diamond flashing against the background of his dirty finger as he eats his rice with bamboo chopsticks. All the time the P 47 pilot has been wearing the ring he has been ill with beri beri and running sores. Perhaps he won't die. Perhaps the curse is wearing off.

Indian doctor in next compound threw me a note this evening. It contained some 'pot chloras' for gargling the septic throats and some other medical advice. He said he had a limited supply of drugs and will help us as much as possible. Things are looking up. We now have a consulting medico.

Lovely doll! There were explosions for 30 minutes after aircraft over. We counted about 80 bombers. There were more we did not see. Our hosts came out and looked but did not appear to be frightfully concerned. We waited while the nine new prisoners came out of the cells and were questioned and then we were returned to our cage.

Again I forgot to look through the main gate to see the red flowers growing in the outside world.

There were Oscars up both before and after the raid playing at dog-fighting but we saw no sign of them when raid was on.

News today is that troops are 95 miles north. Also pork in today. Cheers!

12 March

Great joy – today is Yakamisi Day (pork rice to you). Also, there was an air raid alert last night just to round off an eventful day.

I feel greatly relieved today about the medical liaison with the Indian compound. This means we will have real medical advice if anybody gets seriously ill or if an epidemic develops, instead of relying on these indifferent Japs. Except for the little three-star medical orderly who does his best the Jap medical staff pays little interest. I really believe that fat Jap doctor is pleased when one of us dies of natural (or is it unnatural?) causes. They refuse to allow the English army doctor to treat us.

Perhaps the most popular pastime in the compound apart from eating and discussing military and invasion tactics is watching the Japs' activities – always looking for an indication that the troops are approaching. Just outside our southern fence is the prison chapel, an austere, dirty building. The Japs use it as their mess and we can watch their comings and goings and their food supplies either by looking through the fence or from our balcony. One day one of these bastards will lose his serenity.

I had a mess meeting this morning and it was decided to spend the whole of our cash balance this week on rice and peas after allowing sufficient to buy eggs at one rupee each for building up the very sick. This money is what is left of the R565 I collected from those who were given back by the Japs last month the money taken from them when they came to prison. Each man was allowed to keep up to Rs 40 for private spending but gave the rest to pool. It was mostly money-belt cash.

We were told that a/c which raided on 9/3/45 dropped pamphlets telling Burmese that Germany was finished and that Burmese were to keep within 20 miles of Rangoon. If that is true interpretation I cannot understand it.

No bath for 12 days except for that inadequate thunderstorm. Everyone is filthy and itchy. The other compounds are allowed to carry their own water and look as though they have the odd bath but being the 'rough end' kids we are not allowed outside our cage. Chinese carry for us. We get only four barrels of water daily for everything. That is for 102 men.

Two Oscars up this morning patrolling high up. A bloody annoying sight.

13 March

These Japs are the most inexplicable people. Yesterday Weary Willie (Jap interr.) and Jap sergeant came into compound and asked me if we needed any buildings repairs done . . . just like any good landlord at home.

I said 'No' in an attempt to keep them out of the building which we had stripped for firewood but they came and looked and did not seem to notice that cross beams were missing from the roof. I pestered W. W. about water explaining that everybody was filthy and itchy. He nodded but I don't expect extra water.

I am a poor specimen to represent 102 men with dirty body, barefooted, loincloth, bearded and unsoldierly. No wonder they don't recognize my rank.

Apparently, these newspapers printed in Rangoon at times neglect to mention Burma fighting news.

A few unpleasant facts:

Of 57 airmen who fell into Jap hands in first six mths of reign of terror only 34 still alive. They are broken reeds.

More doldrums today. No apparent progress towards liberty. There was a high flying a/c over this morning but did not see it.

Saw a woman today . . . Burmese with a long green sarong and white blouse. Black shiny hair. She was just outside our fence knocking beans off a tree with a long bamboo pole. None of the Japs spoke to her. Perhaps she is the Big Ti's (Gaol commander) Burmese wife. It is allowed under Shinto ideas. Provided domestic touch to a lazy weekday atmosphere. I suppose the war is still on.

Two Oscars did a patrol at 2,000 ft and under for an hour or so this afternoon. Earlier heard a high-flying aircraft overhead but unidentified.

This has been longest day in captivity for me. I am thoroughly brassed off. I must occupy myself more.

Fence news that Japs had asked Burmese in newspaper whether they want independence or British rule. What magnamity!

Some of the fellows in my dormitory have made a tin table for meals but I prefer to sit on the floor – surely a decadent sign. I don't seem to mind my feet being dirty now either – just so long as my skin remains clear of sores as it is now. I am waiting daily for an outbreak. So many of fresh prisoners have sores. I think it is a blood condition.

14 March

I think the Chinese General must be either dead or dying. Yesterday I saw Indian doctor coming out of compound next door with equipment for blood transfusion. Then last night, just before lights-out, the Chinese started wailing and crying. It was like a crowd of sobbing women.

There was commotion at end of the compound where Chinese general has had a night light since stabbing. A Jap was seen moving about with a lantern but Chinese still cried. If it had been for something trivial the Japs would have stopped them. I took my bag outside and lay down in the dirt because it was too hot indoors and the wailing Chinese sung me to sleep. I'm sorry if the general is dead. He looked such a nice little fellow. We will find out later.

Some of the fellows say they heard two rifle shots close by last night. Maybe the Allies took the city last night. We would not know the difference behind these prison walls . . . or would we?

We have a unique dressing routine in here. During the day we dress in something akin to a loin cloth made out of torn-out pockets from our flying suits. We go barefooted and mostly hatless. But we dress up to go to sleep at night in the most weird ensembles. The object is to wrap your whole person away from the mosquitoes which have unchallenged air supremacy. Mostly chaps swathe their heads and arms in undershirts and underpants or even pieces of burlap. Those lucky enough to have socks or stockings without too many holes use them to cover their feet. The rest sleep in their boots or wrap burlap around each foot. It is a good thing not to have to wear boots because you then have a pillow.

I have complained to every Jap I could get within hearing of that we have not had a wash for two weeks. Last night I told Jap Q.M. so we might get a wash today.

A Sally just passed over low down heading S.E. Yesterday some Japs were seen doing some manual labour – first thing of its kind – they were digging air raid trenches.

Rations in yesterday. All items par or above par. They are obviously trying to fatten us up before British get here. I am feeling fit and to keep that way I do morning P.T. and walk miles daily and more at night. In some of the cells one could walk from corner to corner diagonally in four steps. It was practice for two men to walk this way for hours.

Scores more bullock carts laden with wood.

Further discrimination – when compound C.O.'s are called together by Japs for conference various topics we are left out. Not recognised. C.O.'s conference yesterday.

Beautiful morning. Pastel tints at sunrise. We are a strange crew in here – most of us are as touchy as hell and arguments spring up at slightest thing but next moment everybody will be laughing at something quite unfunny. We are certainly on edge. There are a few personal feuds – mostly among men who were in cells together for long periods before coming to compound but the camaraderie about the place is very pleasing generally.

News flash by gaol wireless that Chinese general is dead. Sorry. The General died at dusk! I would have liked to have met him.

Last night after dark half of us sat around near cookhouse and sang songs . . . *sotto voce* . . . so Jap guards could not hear. But happy spirit. Illicit, furtive singing . . . Against rules.

Chinese boy who brought in vegetables today was a sad man. Looked miserable. London boy squeezed his arm in sorrow. Nice gesture.

Fence whisper that newspaper 'Greater Asia' published . . . 'Allies 70 miles away, Germany finished, Russia marching on Manchuria.' Happy!

Learned today that man taken away from No 6 compound last evening was Bombardier Lt. Goad (B 24). He took all his possessions and his fantastic Japanese bank account was closed. Goad is a pilot. He was shot down on a Rangoon raid on October 14, 1943, belonged to No 7 Bomber Group. Two S/Sgts B 24 engineers also taken with him. Compound don't expect him back. Mystery!

More pork today – the largest lump ever. This is too much. Our troops must be coming fast. Pinky in the store is taking great risks to get eggs and onions through to us. If these Japs only knew how they are being fooled! These extras are a boon to our sick. Considering the effort by the Japs to segregate us it is amazing how much we liaise with other compounds.

There was no gun carriage or rifle salute for the Chinese general but his funeral this afternoon was a surprising event to me. I did not think the Japs would allow such a show.

The following observations were gained by a sneak glance through a crack in the gate and from what I could see of the top of the funeral from my balcony. A Jap orderly sgt went into the Chinese compound and saluted the casket. Then the procession emerged thru gate led by a Chinese spraying rice before him from a dish. Alongside him was another soldier displaying a white board bearing Chinese characters. Now and again it was sprayed with rice. The coffin, draped with a blue, pink material was borne by six countrymen. At the front was a big, brown rooster, alive and tied down, looking from side to side. Black tail. A mass of red-purple flowers (Bougainvillea) emblazoned the coffin. A man-sized horseshoe wreath of the same flowers and framing some sort of flag or emblem followed the coffin carried by two men, then mourners wearing scanty prison clothes and a black arm band. The Jap guards outside our fence presented arms smartly when procession appeared. The funeral party saluted. Sgt guard with black armband led procession down to main gate. Sentry brought up rear. Truck waited outside. We don't know the burial ground. Oh these unpredictable Japs. The old boys say that our dead were respected by Japs to extent of a flag-draped coffin and the odd salute but I can't believe. It does not fit in with their demeanour when chaps are dying.

Three Oscars up this afternoon.

15 March

I was lying on my bag outside in the dirt last night thinking how much better it is to think with eyes open looking at the stars when there was a sudden uproar of terror and jabbering from across the wall in the Chinese compound. It had a hysterical note. Then it simmered down and I heard the guard investigating. A few weeks ago the dead of night was shattered by similar shrieks of terror and the Chinese explained that one of them had seen a ghost. This time the guard was apparently not annoyed. In fact, he was apparently sympathetic.

Always before last night I had closed my eyes to shut off outside world when I wanted to think but I discovered the star-gazing more natural background for thoughts. To shut eyes is mechanical but to look into remoteness of dark sky for detachment is natural. When I stop making discoveries like that I want to stop living. This is a lovely world. So much in it which is sweet or pleasant or stirring or worthwhile. There is so much that I can get out of life.

Next thing to interrupt my thoughts was clanging that was time signal. It was nine o'clock Burmese time. Soon afterwards two searchlights pointed across the sky intercepting at a point above Mingaladon. They remained inert for about half an hour – could have been a beacon or a signal for the next hour I heard heavy rumblings of heavy transports or tanks moving. Also thought I heard sound of aircraft but none came overhead.

I was thinking it amazing how little we knew of drama being enacted in city outside walls – perhaps these were sounds of a desperate last-minute evacuation – when I dropped off to sleep. For all we know Rangoon may be bare of Japs.

Talked with Herb last night and he seriously told me of the type of book he was going to write about all this. It was all I had told him when we were in the cells together. I really think he thought it was his original idea. We were blessed with sufficient water yesterday for a basin wash for everybody. Morale at high tide. I managed only one foot. Washing the other foot tomorrow, I hope.

Long alert today without incident. Two Oscars on patrol at the moment about 1,000 ft SSE Rangoon.

Two Chinese caught fighting on stairs of their compound. Guard has stood them out in hot afternoon sun with arms held high.

Hank and Gus have carved a fine chess set out of some wood pulled off the roof. A game is now in progress using the floor as a board.

The chant of prayers is coming from the room below. It is the R.C. community of the compound saying rosaries for Lent. That room downstairs is used in the morning for ball-dancing lessons and for maths, music and accountancy lectures. The talk club has fizzled out since the Allies took Prome and the alphabetic knowledge session at night has given way to discussion on post-war jobs and freedom dinner.

The weather is unbearably hot by day and we sit around or walk in the shade with only scanty clothing. Exercise generally in morning. Clothes bake in sun all day but when we put them on for tenko they have unpleasant biscuit smell of sun-dried sweat. As soon as you don them – sticky.

16 March

Japs staged a vaudeville last evening. We heard raucous singing from near the main gate. It was a sight to laugh at. There were our fierce guards walking around in a circle, arms swinging, singing at the top of their voices. Children at play. The song was a chant-type repeated over and over. Around and around they went. They apparently did not know the song because they had papers in their hands to read from. It reminded me somehow of tune 'All the King's horses and all the King's men'. We peeped at them through the cracks making sure they did not see us because we felt they must be feeling self-conscious. It was a hilarious show. The boys watching were like a 'Hell's-apoppin' audience. After half an hour the merry-go-round suddenly stopped. They saluted and dispersed. I had heard the song while I was at Meiktila. There were twenty in the circle and three in the centre.

No water ration last night because a bitch of a guard saw some of the boys bathing their sores in hot sterile water. No breakfast. I stood at the fence and pestered until we had enough water for early lunch.

Weary Willie, pathetic interrogator, called through fence today for two typists. Then he had a typewriter carried in with our records in a file. He indicated he wanted particulars of everybody typed on to a parole form. It read: 'I, the undersigned, solemnly swear on my honour that I will not attempt to escape under any circumstances.' Also, some Jap. Another puzzle! Why this? Are we going to be told to sign this too? Already we have been forced to sign a parole under duress, several of chaps being starved for two days until they did. Of course, the topic for talk now is whether we will sign the parole if they ask us again. The old boys are unanimous they will sign anything put in front of them so long as they can keep the Japs unruffled. Lots of beatings and food-craving bodies dictate that policy. Anyway, they say it means nothing. But some of the boys have different views. They say they have an irrevocable order that they must not sign such a document. Personally, there is one thing certain, I will not order anyone to either sign or not to sign it. I will sign it myself because I feel it is the wise thing to do. This compound can ill-afford to be punished or suffer any of the few existing 'privileges' taken from it. We are just existing now and that's all. We can't hold sickness and disease at bay now, let alone with less food and more hardships. Anyway, nothing can be gained at moment by not signing it. I don't consider it worthwhile to try to escape at this stage. Rangoon Japs outside prison must be on their toes. We would not stand a chance outside. This prison is a real sanctuary. We are protected against irate Japs and also the Japs have to feed and guard us. So it is a serious commitment with Rangoon in peril and hard to supply.

I can't for the life of me see that our army needs our feeble help to take Burma. More likely we would hinder. Better that we try to keep ourselves alive to be rescued. Also, we know full well what the reaction would be against those who could not escape because they are too weak. The Japs would take it out on them as they have done before. I consider there must be 50% who would have to stay behind and suffer. I was told once that 27 deaths resulted from treatment after an attempted escape. The escapee was beheaded after recapture.

I will be firm on one thing: No half measures! I am dead against a move not to sign up making the Japs more suspicious of us and then finally giving in. The damage will be done as far as irritating the

Japs is concerned and they will also have our signatures. My only direction will be – stick by your decision. Anyway, I think everybody will sign.

Only two meals today but morale high since 782 cigars in the rice from the canteen. They are red hot so I have had them distributed so as there will be no chance of Japs finding loot in one lump. Great joy and much smoke. These fellows outside who take such risks to get us a few extras are certainly worth a 'mention'. Some of the chaps are cutting up cigars and making up to 15 cigarettes out of each by supplementing tobacco and used tea leaves.

While the Jap records were here I took chance of checking on my list the names of those who have died in this prison since July, 1944. Air force, I mean. There have been 16 since July 27. Two only died from wounds (contributory factor). Remainder disease and malnutrition. Today I bet four of the old boys Rs. 100 each we would be out of here, free, within one month. No new news at all.

Today has been very quiet and humdrum. There is not a sign that our troops are within 1,000 miles of here. Only sign that civilization is still alive outside is dogs giving tongue at night – and someone must be feeding them. No Jap aircraft today.

Jap language:	Sticky rice – pudi meshi	Bamboo fencing – kindo
	Captain – Ti	Shinto – army religion
	Bushido – Army code	Doughy pastry – moochi
	Colonel – Tusa	

17 March

I wonder who really killed the Chinese general?

Last night due south there were flashes in the sky and some thumps. They lasted for a minute. It may have been infernal tropical lightning again but one day they will be genuine gun flashes and I suppose we will say 'only lightning', roll over on our bags and sleep.

It was reported to me this morning that some of the people in this compound were bartering their clothes with Indians next door for tobacco. I told everybody at 'tenko' that this must stop and that I would confiscate any clothes or tobacco concerned in such negotiations. There are chaps in this place who are dressed in rags and need clothes to keep mosquitoes off at night. Anybody with spare clothes should give them away amongst his countrymen – not to the Indians for tobacco leaf. I told them that. I also told parade to be smarter towards me in front of Japs to show them there was someone in control in this compound.

At 'tenko' last night I handed to the orderly sergeant a letter from me to the Big Ti – the prison captain C.O. – requesting permission for this compound to carry its own water. I complained about the present system with Chinese carrying it and pointed out we had missed meals through lack of water. The sergeant took the letter away but there is no guarantee that the captain will read it. If we get any action it will be the first move towards relaxing our solitary state. It is a test issue. That is why it is important to show the Japs that the compound is controlled. Otherwise they certainly will not trust us outside our gate. My next step will be to endeavour to get permission to collect our own rations. . . and then, perhaps, a light working party outside our compound but in the prison. If we are ever to get these privileges and break our solitary it should be now. Just the same I have the feeling that the policy direction as to how we hated hundred are to be treated or maltreated comes from a higher level outside the gaol. Anyway, the campaign for recognition as normal Ps.O.W is in full swing. Wish us luck. Next page for a sad setback . . .

12 or 16 Oscars just roared out of the east and at the moment are parading over Rangoon – tangible evidence that J.A.F. has still a kick left. I felt sick in the stomach as I watched those vicious little fighters with a round spot of blood under each wing whipping across the morning sky playing at follow-the-leader. Our hearts sank as one. Here were another dozen a/c that our pals have yet to shoot out of our path to freedom. And we thought J.A.F. was extinct. They are obviously reinforcements from east somewhere. All aircraft camouflaged and leader had white band around belly of fuselage and another in front of tail. Looks as though they landed at Mingaladon. Every man here is willing our air forces in this direction to take a crack at these. I know some Spitfire and Thunderbolt pilots who would give up their best girl for such an opportunity.

At 'tenko' I also told everybody that No 3 Compound had signed parole without demur after Brigadier had told them that he would take full responsibility. I said that I, personally, would not take that responsibility but I intended to sign parole myself as I did not consider it worth trouble that would result if I refused . . . especially as I had already signed one parole. I did not direct them to do either. It was up to each man to decide for himself.

Then this morning the Brig's message came over that we were to sign the parole as he did not consider it meant anything. Last time they refused the Japs threatened to lock up the officers and starve the sick. They signed. Ten mins. later Wearie Willie came in with the pack of paroles. Everybody signed and put a thumb print of a blonde's lipstick red alongside. Weary Willie was in good humour and the mere sight of that funny little man who wears his cap like a comedian who depends on his dress to amuse. When he said to me that all the boys looked happy I could not deny it. But I was at loss to give him a reason because we are not supposed to know the news of troops. We should believe Japs still winning war.

W.W. asked me about the midget sub. raid on Sydney Harbour and said that Jap newspapers had published story of ceremony in Sydney for dead Japs. I told him about how Aust always respected brave men and then whipped in a query as to how war was going. He was on his guard and pointed to his three stars.

'I don't know,' he said. 'I'm only a lowly soldier.' When I said how long war last he said '100 yrs.' Quite impassive. I think he was surprised we all signed his parole so meekly.

In our hospital W/C Hill played up his beri beri to him. Hill is playing a crafty game leaving me to carry the baby and take on responsibility of this wild compound. But that's what I want. So what? I realise that I am publicising myself as a W/Cdr by pushing into the limelight. But I believe that if anything is going to happen to me this will make no difference. And in the meantime I may be able to do some good among this rabble.

There is surprising thing here: The sgts here behave like officers and vice versa. Being as cosmopolitan lot as they are does not make it easier. There are bitter men, bad-tempered men and just plain bad men all mixed up with a crowd of just men whose minds are not yet warped by long captivity and suppression. Of course, some of the old boys are unaffected but everybody is hungry and I have to be as careful as hell to see that everybody gets his share of everything and that's all. That does not include the extra food for the sick.

Nobody minds that but there have been cases of men sharing food unfairly.

(I type this diary in Sydney, Australia, on an electronic portable typewriter using a magnifying glass to read the minute, pencilled printing on the tattered pieces of yellowing paper. The incongruity of the contrasting situations appeals to me. Here I am on a sunny morning in my studio overlooking the Pacific Ocean typing away, but with one eye on Georgia, my nine-month-old grand daughter. I'm the minder today. My daughter, Jane, and her other children are shopping in the city. My wife, Audrey, is playing golf. Georgia has explored the studio thoroughly, yanked out files and scattered my shell collection over the rug but she is not too busy to reassure me with a fleeting wisp of a smile now and again. I type about men in gaol. Georgia revels in the joy of not being confined by her cot, playing pen or people's arms.)

Things are running a lot more smoothly now. There has been increasing activity in compound life. Apart from the chess (two more sets nearly finished) there are two bridge schools going all day with home-made cards. Principal pastime at the moment is making cigarettes out of broken-up cigars and leaves. Some of the blends are really distinctive. In my room we have made two rope quoits and play deck tennis outside. People are taking more exercise walking miles daily up and down the yard and a few do weight-lifting with a dumb bell made of bamboo and house bricks. Also, some fling an overgrown iron cannon ball about. Many still sleep all day.

There are another 200 cigars coming in to us. The 1,000 cigars are a present from officers of Nos. 3 and 6 compounds. It would have been a poor life here if we were actually (and not only officially) segregated from those people. The life the Japs think we lead is one for a dog. I thank God for the secret aid. Otherwise we would be cutting each other's throats.

Pinky told me through the bars today that when he first came into prison three years ago cigars were 100 for 8 annas. Today they are rupees 46 for 100 and the cigars bigger then. Eggs were 20 for rupee, now rupee each. There's inflation for you!

Air raid!! Back out of the foxhole after watching wave after wave of big bombers moving surely across hot afternoon hazy sky. The bombing lasted for an hour. There were well over 100 B 24s and B 29s. We could not keep count. Fighters, too. The bombers were straggly today with invariably one or two lagging behind formation. Same target area. No enemy fighters seen. A/A slight. Never more than 23 bursts at each formation. B 29s out of west. B 24s out of N.W. We hope this morning's Oscars were caught in their holes. The B 29s white against sky and moving as though drawn across by invisible ropes. Our hearts cheered by every crumpff. Big Ti sat immobile on his chair with face turned upwards. These are most proud moments of the war for me as I watch the might of our air power at work. We wonder what the target can be to warrant such a weight of bombs.

Apart from the raid we had another phenomenon to amaze us: As the first bombs fell there was a smallish wispy piece of cumulus cloud over area to north. With the first clouds of slate grey smoke rising beneath it that white cloud began to grow. We were all eyes for the formations and looking back at the Japs in their holes. The next time we noticed the cloud it had grown into a mountain of crunchy, tumbling cumulus cloud faced with billowing grey smoke. It kept growing until it filled the northern sector of the sky – trouble – great cloud at the bottom and hard-packed white at the top. Here was a man-made nimbo cumulus . . . nature at the tropics shows anger at the bombing.

Siren went about six minutes before a/c over Rangoon. Said Yank: 'I wonder whether bathing beauties will be out tomorrow?' (B.B. sit out on the beach and play but never swim. He was referring to the Oscars that only come out to play.) The warning for most of the recent raids has been negligible. The siren mingles with the steady roar of a/c engines.

18 March

It was the third night of the new moon last night. I slept out in yard of the compound. Serene, starry evening but it is not quite the same as a boy scouts' outing because one has to wrap one's head in an undershirt away from the swarms of mosquitoes and also sleep with trousers inside socks. The hole has become so big in my socks that I have to wear my boots while I sleep. My shirt is rotting and tears with every deep breath.

I stole a face and hands wash for everybody this morning – 10 men using same water. My feet are black – my socks sticky – even my umbilicus is dirty.

Good morning! Early air raid alarm. Big Ti out on his chair looking very pensive, spears glistening. But no sign of a/c.

Just watched unpleasant interlude from balcony: Two coolies wheeled in big barrow. Pinkie walked over nonchalantly from his seat in the sun. He lifted the bamboo strip lid and fish leaped out. The action that followed was over in few seconds. Pinkie whipped up 4 live fish and flashed around the corner to hide them. At that moment a Jap sgt – 'Banjo Eyes' – turned corner from main gate. He saw Pinkie, looked at barrel of fish and then called 3-star Q.M.'s stooge who had appeared on the scene. Pinkie was told to return the fish he had taken. He brought back two. Hot words, face slapping, but Pinkie just stood there perhaps a shade pinker. We stood there on the balcony praying. We recoiled at every slap. Then the Jap turned to normal behaviour and, apparently, the incident was finished. I had idea that Pinkie intended to give fish to us for our sick boys. I signalled him if he got away with it O.K. and he gave us thumbs up. He is lucky he did not get solitary cells. Perhaps he is too valuable to Japs. We are now sweating on fresh fish ration.

It won't be our fault if even our real sick boys don't hold out. The two most desperate cases in our hospital are fed 50% of our egg, onion and sugar (jagari) supplies. The other 50% is shared . . . eaten by 100 men. In addition, the sick get their share of all compounds' bones which all go to sick bay and the bottom of the soup pot, thick with vegetables, which goes to the sick bay. The fit and near-fit men sacrifice all this without much apparent effect except that most people are breaking out in running sores because of bad blood. Diet is only way to remedy that.

Today is Sunday. It is early afternoon now and I am aware of the only real Sunday atmosphere since I left Delhi eight months ago. Despite two air raid alarms and the faint sound of our recce a/c high up, today has had a stillness unlike other days. Breakfast was late and mid-morning we had a forbidden church service. Half our population sat around the edge of my bare room and did not see the bars across the doors and windows. Service started with the very English son of a British Army officer reciting Kipling's *If*.

Then an American navigator read the lesson – 25th chapter of Matthew. A B 29 pilot and a B 24 Northampton butcher gunner sang 'Jerusalem,' after which B 29 pilot (who stood head and shoulders over little English) gave a talk about preparing yourself for Easter. Simple and unforced talk. One of the best sermons I've heard. B 29 pilot from Duluth, Minnesota led strange congregation dressed scantily, bearded, tousled hair, in prayer. Rags around loins. Emaciated, diseased bodies. Cage. Unwashed. Chirping of birds in the short spell of silence that followed the Lord's Prayer. One line out of prayer asked God to bless our enemies and guide them in what is right.

After service people sat around and wanted to gossip. I've seen similar congregations outside a church. We trickled downstairs so as not to arouse suspicions of Japs. Rest of morning spent sprawled over floor playing or watching chess or playing deck tennis on the court in the yard . . . vine for net. Big lunch of rice and spinach and now everybody is taking afternoon nap. Remarkable that we can feel such a Sunday atmosphere because Jap's equivalent is Wednesday. Today is normal day.

100 cigs addressed to me from outside yesterday. Thank God I don't smoke. I shared them among Austs. who handed them around. Great industry in compound making cigarettes. Acute paper shortage but some of the chaps are rolling cigs now in fresh green leaves from our tree.

All is lost! My palate has gone haywire now. All my life I have been a confirmed spinach hater. I cannot remember eating it once outside this gaol. But here I eat spinach because it is important to keep alive. I eat it but I shudder at every mouthful. I still hated it until today when an amazing thing happened. For lunch everybody was served with sufficient spinach for a family of eight. One mess tin overflowing with dark green abomination.

'Toxon,' cried Gus joyfully. He loves spinach. The man alongside him tipped half his helping into Gus's pan. It was heaped high. Gus looked at it with a dubious face. Then he was promptly sick – physically. He, a spinach lover, could not face this mountain of weed. What chance had I?

I started eating with temerity but I soon found out that I was enjoying it. My palate had changed face. This was delicious food. I loved that meal . . . and then I came to the stalks of the spinach . . . light green, generally wooden. But I did not push them aside. I ate them. They were tender and succulent and, God help me, they had a distinctive flavour of asparagus. This is the end. I'll be liking red-headed women next.

Moved the sick bay to the end downstairs room today because of the bug invasion in the bamboo sleeping platform. The sick men could not sleep and were sitting out in the passage way to eat their meals and gossip. New room is bare and the chaps sleep on the tarred floor. At 'tenko' the genial Jap Q.M. was orderly sergeant so I poured forth complaints and bugs, buckets and lack of clothes. He was surprisingly sympathetic and promised all. He was interested in our deck tennis court so I staged a game for him to watch. It amused him. That man is at least human.

19 March

I have been in captivity three months today. When I crashed I sliced my knee badly along with other wounds . . . lacerations. My knee has not yet healed. I am perfectly fit otherwise. I thrive on this frugal living but I would dearly like to be free soon because I have so much to do. I'm getting old, too.

It rained yesterday evening so everybody took a bath. At 10 o'clock last night there was sound of cheering, British style, outside the prison. We soon found out the reason: The water was flowing once more. This morning our trough was brim full as a result of taps being left on accidentally and everybody spent morning washing clothes and having baths. It seemed fitting that day that followed yesterday should be washing day.

I received message through fence this morning that English colonel doctor instructs us to eat our 'nuka' because beri beri is breaking out in other compounds since rations of bean sprouts stopped. Unnecessary advice here as people eat all the 'nuka' they can get.

Worrying case in our sick bay. An English sgt who has been on his back for five months with acute beri beri, diarrhoea and an abscess in his groin. He is very weak and keeps having relapses in the evenings despite the rich diet he is on. He is refusing to eat at times, despite threats, and is very weak although pulse and breathing is normal at present. Now he has started to pass white mucus. I sent a note over the wall to Indian doctor giving case history and asking for advice.

Another alert this morning. Last night there was a rifle shot inside the prison. Birds shrieked their alarm from their trees but nothing else untoward happened.

This is amusing: Pinky was paraded before Japs for his misdemeanour in stealing the fish from wheelbarrow. 'They were very nice to me,' he said, 'and told me there was no need to steal. If he wanted anything all he had to do was ask.' O boy! The old order changeth yielding place to new.

The sgt in a bad way showed signs of giving up the ghost today. He refused to eat precious food and when Emeny reasoned with him he said he realized that he needed food to live but he did not care. He said he was tired of hanging on. Curious thing. He said he would drink a glass of milk and nothing else. None of us have seen milk in this prison.

U.S. navigator here has been allergic to eggs all his life – acutely. Could not even eat cake made with eggs. Allergic injection tests proved it not mental condition. First year in gaol absolutely eggless food. Then, about four months ago the English compounds sent over pieces of egg in 'nuka' for bad beri beri boys. He ate the egg fragments with fear in heart but surprised no convulsions like he had as child after eggs or welt-like hives on lips which was effect as youth. After that he was given three boiled eggs. He ate them with gusto. The first was first whole egg ever eaten in his life. No reaction. He is aged 26. Since then eaten all he could get of the raw eggs in rice which we came by once a month. He has spent months collecting names of dishes and recipes where possible from everybody in compound seeking dishes distinctive in certain countries represented here. His collection numbers 400 now. Many of them are egg dishes . . . Two Oscars up today.

20 March

Answer to my note to Indian doctor over wall after dark last night. He sent some vit.B powder and confirmed our ideas as to sgt's diet we have been feeding.

Doc says that from my description he is in serious condition. He could be put right with a course of vit.B injections but that next to

95

impossible here. He had had consultation with other docs. King bit improved today. I hope he hangs out.

Doc says Bassein is ours and Germany is finished. I'm putting a lot of faith in this moon period.

Had a session with NCOs last night and reminded them they were still in army and that compound was being run by officers. They are mostly sound lot but a few have been stepping out of line abusing free and easy atmosphere I have purposely allowed to develop. I warned them to use a bit more common sense and am happy now that things will remain serene. This is certainly the most difficult job I have ever tackled – a motley crowd internationally, all with different ideas of discipline and behaviour and on top of that a hundred men living on nerves day to day with from three months to eighteen months of prison life between them and last respectable living. Men with weak bodies, hungry for wholesome food, and warped minds hungry for freedom. Yes, a difficult crowd to administer but I am satisfied that spirit here is remarkable considering the circumstances.

This morning I talked to officers and impressed upon them need to set example to sgts and to inculcate community spirit to improve compound despite likelihood of early release. My idea is to keep everybody from brooding too much. I am encouraging everybody to exercise more; play more games. Calisthenics class as start on weightlifting course attended this morning by about 30. We have made a smart-looking set of bar-bells out of wheels off iron doors and piece of piping. Good thing. I have been approached on an escape idea.

21 March

Patched my socks yes'day with pocket of my shirt to stop mosquitoes biting my ankles. Hands are protected while I sleep by gauntlets made from shirt sleeves. I now sleep in flying suit top. I am presenting my now sleeveless shirt to a chap who has a rag for shirt. I'm sleeping like a baby nowadays. Not one a/c in sky y'day.

'Christ, isn't it peaceful,' complained Gus.

Yesterday afternoon was for me most pleasant I have spent in captivity. It was unbearably hot outside but cool breeze wafted thru bars upstairs. I sat and sewed. A knot of people on the floor nearby sat cross-legged around chessmen. Others just sat and talked about apples, walnuts, the yield of potatoes in Ireland, U. States, Australia and Prince Edward Island, French toast, surfing and egg custard. The evening rice was ready before I thought the afternoon was half over.

More than a month ago a pair of socks disappeared. There was a wide search because socks here are valuable beyond the dreams of avarice. Yesterday some of the boys were pulling down the bamboo sleeping platform in the vacated sick bay so as to put bugs out in the sun when the socks were found concealed in the bamboo tubing.

The owner of the socks said his suspicions as to who stole them were now confirmed. That man is now dead. He used to sleep on that part of the platform where socks found. It's libelling a dead man but there seems no doubt he was culprit. Story told against him today was that while he was in cells, quite fit, he was caught stealing meat from out of the mess tin of his cellmate who was very ill. He was caught by the third cell member. He was American officer with five confirmed in the air and two on the ground. P 51 pilot who wore air medal, D.F.C., silver star. That shows what this life does to some. His death assured the authority of our sick bay.

Soon after the crowd moved over to compound from cells Cliff Emeny, using commonsense and concensus of advice from the old boys, put all the beri beri cases in a bad way on a diet – minimum of liquid and no salt (this treatment has now been confirmed by doc.). Beri beri improved and then there was a turn for the worse. Joints went up like balloons and, after a day or two, Emeny discovered why. The beri beri boys were cheating. They were drinking draughts of tea outside. All the offenders apologised and promised to adhere to diet henceforth, but one, the officer now dead, said the diet was a stupid business and if he wanted tea he would drink tea.

'Then you must be too fit to remain in hospital and have people waiting on you,' was Emeny's reply. So the hot-headed one moved upstairs and continued to eat and drink unrestricted. He was back in hospital a fortnight later but would not rest properly and was soon dead. The hospital word was law after that and it has done Trojan job. Stocked with one depleted tube of Gentian Violet and what pieces of cotton wool, carbolic soft soap (Salve), iodine that could be stolen by the boys from the medical orderly's tray (Jap) it has held skin disease at bay mostly by using sterilised boiling water and sun and restraint in scratching.

The diets of reduced servings of soft rice but more of the vegetables from the bottom of soup pot have worked wonders with the patients . . . and the authority and energy and patience that has brought results has been provided by F/Lt Emeny, a New Zealand farmer.

King is still holding out and appeared little more cheerful today. He needs that vitamin B course.

The M.O. told W/Cdr Hill yesterday that he had permission from the Big Master to give him a beri beri injection. But not to anybody else. Hill has only slight beri beri but the Japs appear keen to get him fit. What for? Are senior officers going to be held by Japs. Until now all W/Cdrs and S/Ldrs have been shifted.

Although Rangoon should be taken soon by Allies I still have doubts that I will be here to greet them. There is a feeling in my bones that I still have to face a lot before I feel free. One lives day to day here – always in doubt as to what tomorrow will bring. The Japs are masters at holding you in doubt as to your fate. They tell you nothing and leave the rest to your imagination which is fed by the Jap reputation for being uncivilized.

My knee seems to be healing at last but the muscles in the thigh and leg have sagged and my left limb is about two-thirds size of right leg. I'm exercising more now. It won't be long before I'm back to normal. I'm walking one hour nightly.

Another uneventful alarm has just been sounded. No Jap a/c sighted today either.

I had a roasted sparrow for lunch. Capt. Hunt caught it first . . . presented it to me . . . but it escaped and I had to catch it again. I had to screw its neck, pluck and roast it. Very tasty. Somebody said like sweetbreads. It went well with lunch of rice and spinach and 'nuka.' Another chap had similar lunch.

None of us 100 special prisoners know whether our kinfolk are aware that we are alive . . . not even the old boys who have been down for a year or eighteen months. It makes it harder for some to picture their future lives. Some have had children born since they were captured.

The Nippon Q.M. appeared this morning in very amiable

manner. He called for an English pilot and a U.S. radar sgt. after I had whipped in a few complaints. He asked to be left alone with this pair. Speculation rife for ten minutes until pilot re-appeared in yard – the Q.M. was acting for the Commandant – the Big Master, and wanted to buy the watch the pilot had given up to Japs on entering prison. (They took away all our valuables and gave receipts which surprised us and we all mocked.). The Q.M. emphasized that the pilot did not have to sell the watch. It was purely voluntary. But Q.M. reminded him that some Jap soldiers just take away such valuables without hesitation or qualms. Also, it was possible that the watch might still be confiscated. The pilot questioned Q.M. on this and he explained that men in this compound were special prisoners and were awaiting a law officer who would judge whether they were to be punished. If the law officer decided that we were to be punished our valuables would be confiscated. The other two compounds with European prisoners had already been cleared and their valuables returned.

Then the pilot parried with: 'Surely the people in this compound have already been punished by the long spell in solitary. Look at the sick and diseased in the hospital.'

The Q.M. said: 'You will not be punished here. You will be taken away in a big ship.'

This may have been salesmanship but, anyway, it is first hint as to our fate we have ever been given.

In the conversation Q.M. admitted we are special prisoners and felt concerned at our lot.

At first he asked pilot for a price. Pilot said Rs. 300. He said Rs 100. Pilot held out. Pilot left him but Q.M. recalled him. Pilot said he had thought it over and now wanted Rs. 500. Jap started bargaining. No shame. Price got back to Rs. 300. Then pilot said O.K.

Soon afterwards pilot sent for. He was taken right outside compound to main gate building. Great thrill . . . further than any man in compound (except one man who has not returned). Pilot was handed Rs. 300 in office . . . signed gilt-edged receipt . . . bowed to Big Ti who was present . . . said, 'Hope it works well' and then back to cage.

Speculation as to why Big Ti wants watch. Is he buying up possessions realizing Jap currency valueless? Why was he so meticulous about buying watch when it quite simple for him to just take it? Personally, I have found that a lot of Japs are scrupulously honest. Jap race generally takes poor view of stealing.

Q.M. said 'raw' officer, of course, not 'law.' They cannot say 'L' (moroney, lice, wifu, knifu, speedo, O.K. – ka? All words in Jap seem to end in vowels. Can't cope with words ending consonant.)

Pilot came back with wad of notes and handed lot to me to buy extra food for compound . . . commendable gesture . . . typical of these RAF types here. I had talk with Suji and we have decided to buy bag of sticky rice, cow peas and tomatoes and take out Rs. 10 for sick boys egg fund.

I have asked Suji, to give him a sense of power. He has little individual personality. His way of staring intently without speaking is only a trick to cover a slow, calculating mind. Once or twice in sick bay he's relaxed his pose of being a strong, silent master. He squatted on floor, his little body doubled up, and his face creased in a sort of laugh. He looked just another mousey man to me. I stand head and shoulders over him. I imagine he must be self-conscious in the presence of the mighty brigadier – tall and gaunt-faced and heavy shouldered, who stands erect like a soldier.

The Ti is sloppy in his slacks and white shirt.

Most evenings now we have bible reading and prayers outside at dusk sitting alongside the water trough. Just at that time, too, the Indians next door sound their cow horn call to prayers.

Those who were beaten up last night say they were most frightened of the bayoneted rifles that the guards held in front of them while they punched. As they swung their fists from low down, putting all their body swing into it, the points of bayonets scraped passed their faces.

Some of the fellows had to stand up to six or seven mighty hits, others just fell down after first punch and were kicked up for more. A stock-taking this morning revealed that no serious damage was done even to the sick boys.

High flying a/c up today on couple occasions – big ones.

22 March

King, sick sgt, is in critical condition. His heart seems weaker and he had a touch of lock-jaw last evening. Would not eat his dinner last night. We had a ration of beef so two of the bad boys had beef tea, eggs, potatoes, tick vegetables – all the good things of life that everybody in this place is yearning for but still they deteriorate. The sacrifice by 100 men should be enough to keep them alive.

At 'tenko' last night I gave sgt of guard note to C.O. – Big Ti. It said that we had number of men here in serious condition and names three worst cases. Requested that at least King be transferred to No 6 compound hospital where proper medical aid constantly available. Pointed out we have neither knowledge or facilities. Hope this plea is answered because King would then be under British colonel doctor.

The sgt took note quite willingly. This experiment seems to have worked. It is best way to get things done. After the water note we had excellent water service from the guards.

The P.T. class each morning is a bracing success. An American NCO had control of it and class now numbers around 30. The weight lifting in the afternoon also popular. Just thing for this compound. Everybody is scratching a bingo on to back of mess tin this morning in readiness for bingo games which start today with little food tit-bits as prizes.

The last hour has been the fullest 60 mins that I've ever experienced. I was out walking in sun awaiting breakfast/lunch with the bandage off my knee for first time in three months. Then I saw the Indians next door scampering downstairs. At the same moment I heard the faint roar of bombers. I looked up and saw the formation out to the north going W to E. After about 10 secs the Jap panic gong rang out. The second wave was close on the heels of first who had already dropped their bombs. Dozen B 29s in each formation in nice pattern except for odd straggler. They kept coming, beautiful to watch. A/A was light – about 12 puffs to each formation. After 3 or 4 waves the passes started coming from the north. One formation made a bombing run right bang over prison and two others just off. We hit the foxholes for these occasions and it was noticed that the Big Ti's chair was empty. We were all puzzled by fact that we did not hear many explosions. We heard some bomb 'rushes' but no 'crumpffs'. They could have been either incendiaries or delayed action. Our count was 86 a/c. No fighters. We left yard to have lunch – yakimishi (fried rice) – a real treat. Also, 'toxon' spinach.

Then cooks brought up a special dish I had had prepared for the Rs

300 pilot – two eggs sunny side up, French fried potatoes and a slice of grilled steak.

When cooks handed me the dish to present to pilot there was gleam of achievement in eyes. Here was a masterpiece. No great painter ever handed over a completed canvas with such pride in his art. The creation was passed around for everybody to look at. It was the first civilized dish some had seen for 18 mths. The pilot ate it in addition to his yakimishi. No trouble. Tonight's dinner was the meal of the century.

During raid I was wondering what could be in Japs' minds as they watched these large-scale, unhampered raids. The Japs depend so much on belief they are invincible. Watching Big Ti out there with his binoculars somehow brought to my mind picture of a fading opera star in the stalls with opera glasses trained on the stage where new star was ascending. We felt blast of some of the bombs. They seemed to be on a closer target. The flights that passed overhead sent us to our foxholes but they also filled us airmen with joy. They were distinct and white against the flawless blue sky.

'Oh pretty to watch,' was one comment from a head jutting out of a hole as a flight moved across the sky in a formation out of the book. German bombs whistle, Japanese bombs swish swash but American bombs 'rush'. It sounds like a load of gravel being tipped out of a truck . . . a second and then the air flutters. Smoke out to the north but nothing else from the 90-bomber raid. Some other a/c were seen away to the south but they might have been a/c on way home after bombing.

We had no sooner finished our yakimishi when panic gong went again. Japs were in the trenches when we strolled out and another formation of B 29s was overhead flying NW to SE. They dropped bombs on a target about about 10 miles north of here. Then a single B 29 came out of the east . . . another B 29.

'It's either a photo recce -Joe- or the general,' said one Yank.

Just then there was a 'rush' of bombs and the thunder of bursts.

'Yes, he's dropped his camera,' said another.

We kept playing deck tennis during the raid. I am waiting for Big Ti to ask why we don't get into foxholes. My reply is ready: If our chaps are not aiming at us they won't hit us. If they do aim at us these foxholes won't be much use. Today is first time Japs have worn steel helmets for raid.

Initial bingo game won by RAF pilot who had eggs and steak for lunch. 1st prize two eggplant. His day. Second won by American flight engineer who is expecting that his wife will have a child today. 'My luck's in,' he cried. 'Now it's sure to be a boy.' I hope he finds out soon.

Off now to do some weight-lifting. Beans for dinner tonight. Certainly a full day. Rumour thru fence that Prome is ours. During the raid and after a few guards just looked and stared when we stood and bowed. Perhaps they perceived mockery within us.

23 March

Climax of yesterday's doings came at night. We soon had signs that the saki had been issued. A few tipsy guards had been seen about so I warned everybody to be on their best behaviour. There was a stir when a guard was seen patrolling on top of roof of Japs' billets. This is practice during air raids only. Japs were heard praying loudly when I went to 'bed'. I could see Japs from the balcony sitting around in their yard smoking. We had a forbidden sing-song earlier . . . whispering tunes.

Just before 10 pm Burmese time I was summoned. 'There's a Jap in compound,' said Gus. I looked out thru bars and could see down on the yard where a Jap was kicking awake the chaps sleeping out. I knew that some of the people there were out of the sick bay . . . very weak. Apparently, the Jap was taking objection to sleeping out. We had been seen doing it for a month but tempers were bad.

There was a second Jap who lined all the offenders alongside the water trough. Then beating started with both Japs swinging slaps and punches at the men who just stood at attention until they were knocked down or Jap passed on. One Jap was particularly bitter and at times when a man fell he kicked him heavily. There were about 15 men altogether. About ten others had escaped by hiding in foxholes. The Japs hit with all their strength but some of the boys used to taking beatings 'rolled' to take kick out of swipes. So from now on we know we are not allowed to sleep outside away from bugs.

Big Ti paid compound a surprise visit at 'tenko'. He has surly manner of walking length of line staring at people without saying a word or changing his expression.

I told him about King being seriously ill and asked that he be shifted to hospital. He said he would see him so I took him to bilky. It was a raw display . . . inert bodies covered with bags strewn all over bare room. I took him around, peeling off clothes to show him diseased bodies, nobbly and emaciated with rotting skins and others with large tracts of ulcers. Our mental case – a diseased mind – capped the display. I think it shook him more than a little. Being next to all this day by day we ourselves, perhaps, don't realize what a shock such a sight would be to a person living a clean life. He left me with feeling he would do something to help.

So that's the real Big Ti! I've been a little afraid of him until now. I thought he had dignity. But this is the first time I have a chance to stand up to him. I feel now it is only circumstances.

24 March

Shouting outside prison walls last night and dogs barked more than usual. I have not heard train whistle for couple of days. There are a few whistles from direction of the river during evening and a long spell of church bells ringing most evenings. Those are only sounds we hear that tell us there is an outside world. Rumour today that we have Singapore . . . but how?

One of English lads compiled a full set of logs and anti-logs while he was in the cells to pass time. It took him three months. During last few days somebody stole the lists of numbers. Not that he was interested in maths – just that he wanted the paper for rolling cigarettes. Bastard!

Sound of drums outside gaol last night and this morning. I.N.A.? or Japs trying to rouse Burmese.

Medical (Jap) Officer paid rare visit to us today and asked to see King. Did his inspection from distance and stamped off in a bad temper. It looks as though the Big Ti has been on to him about state of our sick and diseased.

From Pinky that Judson College, Jap A.H.Q., I.N.A. H.Q. and hospital near J. College among targets last raid.

Monty is among the weight-lifting pupils but he only uses one arm. His left one is only a stump. I just walked a hundred or so up and down the yard listening to Monty's story. As we turned I glimpsed now and again at his blue eyes – big, pretty blue eyes that still have pain behind them.

Monty is M/Sgt radio operator. Home town: Pittsburg, Penn. In October last year he bailed out over China after engine seized on way back from bombing Formosa. Took month to get back – walking, chaired, carted and poled and pulled up rivers.

Then Dec. 14 on raid. Target: Rangoon. Couple seconds after bombs gone heard explosion (never heard A/A before) . . . grey smoke in cabin. Monty, bending down, twisted to see whether bombs clear . . . right arm in air for balance when felt jab. Looked back to see hand hanging off from wrist by inch of flesh . . . spouting blood . . . recalled medical lecture . . . grabbed wrist, held. No pain. Own bombs? A/C in steep dive from 20,000 ft. On to knees . . . Lord's Prayer loudly. As he said it A/C straightened up. He had shrugged off flak vest, dragged off oxygen mask. Up to this resigned to crash. Dragged across to hatch. Watched two bale out. Others queueing up . . . so he dropped out . . . pulled ripcord then grabbed wrist again . . . surprised dangling hand not jerked off. Glasses swept away (eyes 20/40). Previous time sprained ankle in jump. Prayed all the way down . . . L's P, Hail Mary, others. This time chute let him down gently as baby into cot. Old Burmese scared, dragged chute behind . . . village 300 yards across paddy field . . . headman grabbed pistol, knocked him over . . . others murmur dissent. Mile or so to headman's house . . . arm twisted behind back. Weak, loss of blood . . . gulped water. Big hut . . . open-faced.

English-speaking Burmese fetched first-aid kit from chute. Burmese took his clothes . . . hot goat's milk until nauseated . . . shot of morphine. They said doctor coming – no Japs. 20 miles from Rangoon. Two crew members also. Another morphine shot . . . pain starts . . . dozed . . . sulpha powder. Then ancient Chinese bush doctor . . . he afraid to touch it. Bound arm against splint. Then Japs arrived . . . To barracks where Jap officers rough-handled others (4 of crew) but not Monty. No talk, no med. T. Others say they talk as much as allowed. To treatment room . . . Jap surprised at sight. To Pukk. dispensary . . . much concern, no skill . . . iodine, salt water. Cut off dangling hand . . . left jagged ends . . . tied arteries . . . one elusive. Hood of oil silk . . . doomed (?) . . . Jap faces commend.

Monty feeble. Tourniquets ordinary surgical cotton. To sleeping platform – others tormented – all this in early hours of morning. Told they all be shot at dawn.

At dawn Japs took them to Judson College. Stayed until Dec. 19. Water for Monty but not others at first. No food . . . two dressings. Welcomed at prison with face slappings. In cells constant pain for Monty. Wound became yellow green and smelt sweetly . . . more acrid daily. Complaint to Big Ti. Next day to pump building, centre of prison. Amber serum, enough for horse, into top of shoulder. Jap M.O. says 'cut.' Ti pulls chair up close. Monty in pain, side and lungs, shot miscued. Jap doctor angry – sent Monty back to cells. Monty resigned to rotting. Arm bad. Dec. 29 surprise! Out of cell block to pump room again . . . Wearie Willie apologetic . . . no speak.

British Army colonel doctor, famous surgeon . . . 30 years . . . says, 'Sorry, no anaesthetic but you can bear it . . . seen many take it battle fields in France.' Ordeal.

'Beautiful job. He wrapped skin neat as baseball,' says Monty. Doc said he had to cut off six inches of arm more than necessary because afraid to leave open bone. Circumstances demanded off at elbow. Infrequent dressings by Japs but now miraculously healing.

Monty refuses to be favoured. Is room chief over U.S. N.C.O.'s and their messing representative. Incredible man.

25 March

Short alert yesterday afternoon and again just before midnight. No a/c first time but two low-flying a/c at night. Japs had machine gun set up outside fence. Three new prisoners seen being taken in to cell block last evening . . . identified as British. Perhaps here is some real news. It can be obtained thru their cellmates interrogating them, then radioing it to compounds adjacent with sky writing. They would pass it on to us.

Incident in tree yesterday: A large lizard camouflaged blue-green spread itself around the hole to mango birds' nest – intentionally or otherwise. Anyway, one of the mango birds arrived home with mouthful of food to find the wolf at the door. It fluttered about the nearby branches in a proper panic making attempts to get into hole in branch and still avoid lizard which would have been to defy laws of gravity. The lizard remained inert although I suspected it observed every movement. We crowded window. Bird obviously concerned. Eggs or young ones? Then, after few half-hearted attacks by bird, anti-climax. The lizard scurried down tree. The nest had been relieved of invader. Pleasant morning but oh so dull! Church service in camera. Hymns softly for first time. Open testimonies. White silk of parachute on makeshift altar . . . sunlight . . . bible . . . B 29 crew all saved.

No medical orderly for five days. Is this because of bombed Jap hospital? Wounds smelling. Most people breaking out in sores and pimples. Jap guards appeared in afternoon wearing two cartridge cases . . . trouble brewing?

26 March

At least things are becoming a bit more consistently warlike. Yesterday afternoon a bombing cloud formed away in S.E. indicating that coast was being bombed. Softening up for invasion? Wind from that direction spread smoke over sky. Bomb rumblings also heard. Sour sgt. unusually attentive at 'tenko'.

Chit from Indian compound . . . curious . . . 6lbs of tobacco leaf. Brig's note . . . distrusted but big parcel over wall in moonlight. Good deal. These people are looking after us royally.

Two air raid alerts last night . . . a/c heard during first one. Curious thing: Rocket type of thing shot into sky in west half an hour before first siren. Two searchlights at play except for alert periods . . . burned all night until 7 am . . . just poking up haphazardly, one light in north, one in west.

Early air raid alert this morning. Guards now carrying tin hats permanently. The whole compound is as low as could be. Everybody touchy as hell . . . flaring up at slightest provocation . . . humble apologies ten minutes later. Everybody free with advice but nobody willing to abide by even own advice. Conflicting news . . . nothing to put faith into. Oh where in hell are the British? 'We will be here for monsoon' is the cry. Blokes still have hope but sad about their lot.

News from prisoners just in say we have Mandalay and Meiktila. Is that all? I must make determined effort to rouse morale of this confounded compound. I get fitter every day. Must make them interested . . . organize Easter celebration to give them something to look forward to. Toxon feast . . . deck tennis tournament etc.

Alert after lunch. Boys heard a/c in distance and faint bombing rumblings from south-east or south.

Today was my day for a beating. The likeable little medical orderly private arrived with a worried look. He gave me a note in English. It concerned the two complaints I had made to the commandant and the orderly sergeant. The first, a request that Jack King, critically ill, be moved to No 6 compound hospital. The other at 'tenko' last night that we had had no medical attention for six days . . . wounds smelling etc. The note asked who were the critically ill men and said I was not in position to say if a man was seriously ill or not. Also added that not proper to write to commandant or complain to orderly sgt on such matters but to report to him (we had but nothing had happened).

'You are always resting (not working)' note concluded.

As I finished reading (feeling a little indignant at the misinterpretation and unfairness) I was nearly knocked off my feet by a bang on the face. Jap justice, the only disciplinary action they know. Then another slap and another. I just stood there. The poor little Jap dishing it out looked frightened. I thought: Violence is not in your nature little fellow. Then he busied himself doing dressings.

Then came the Medical Officer – a fat 2/Lt. He hates us. Small eyes. He strode in, his sword banging his leg. 'Hill, Hill,' he said. I knew he meant me and went up to him. The medical orderly explained that I was C.O. He looked once at me with malice in his beady eyes. I looked back. The gathering held its breath as one man. Then, whop, he hit me with closed fist, swinging from low down and smashing my left ear. He wiped his knuckles with a handkerchief (very hygienic). The boys watching had fear that he was reaching for his sword. (Sword slapping is no fun).

Then came his left . . . wang. I reeled but came back to attention surprised at fact it didn't hurt much and that I was still looking back defiantly. That mean Jap looked me in the eye again, wheeled about and hurried out. Not a word. I went back to the medical orderly and stood about with my face sides red. The Chinaman with him was funny. He painted my knee with red Mercurochrome (it didn't need treatment) furtively and said 'Sorry' with his eyes. No damage to me but glad that we know we have two avenues for getting action even if it has such accompaniment. W/Cdr Hill was given some Vit.B powders for his beri beri and also an injection. Look after the rank,

Mr Jap, and rank will look after you. My assessment is that the note brought Ti here and he was not amused by state of sick bay. M.O. received a raspberry. I was beaten.

I have now set up a rule that all bits and pieces of cigars and tobacco leaf which comes over the fences from other compounds will be given in to pool and shared by whole compound.

**Public Records Office, Kew, England
28 April 1980**

Captain Tazumi Motozo, Commanding Officer Rangoon Gaol – seven years imprisonment

Lt. Onishi Akio, Medical Officer Rangoon Gaol – death by hanging

Superior Private Veno Koigetsu, guard at Rangoon Gaol – 15 years imprisonment

For the first time I know the names of these people and what happened to them. The War Office file in my impatient hands deals with the War Crime Trials held in Rangoon during May, 1946. I skip through the evidence but the cross-examination of the medical officer arrests my attention.

'What happened to Master Sergeant Montgomery after his arm was amputated?'

'I put him back into solitary.'

'Wouldn't you agree that was torture . . . to let a man lie on the floor of his cell in pain after his arm had been cut off?'

'No. We did change the bandage.'

'Could you not have giving him something to alleviate his suffering?'

'Yes, we could have but I was ordered to treat all the aviators as criminals.'

'Were there deaths in solitary?'

'Yes, several.'

'Is it true they did not get proper medical care?'

'Yes, I could have saved them.'

There is a hand on my shoulder. It's Audrey back from the Royal Botanic Gardens at Kew.

'Bill, you're just staring. Now, you must come and see the crab apple mound. It's the most beautiful sight . . . absolutely covered . . . pinks, reds. I want to share it with someone.'

I resist the invitation and go back to Lt Onishi's sworn evidence. He had had three month's medical training in Japan before joining the army at the age of 23. He had seen one operation and had been given lessons on treatment of malaria and battle wounds. He spoke no English. Rangoon was his first assignment and he went to the gaol once a week when wounded from the front slowed up. He said he had decided to amputate Montgomery's arm himself because such operations on arms were supposed to be easy.

'As it happened to be a dry season,' he went on, 'I splashed plenty of water on the floor of the temporary operating theatre in the centre of the gaol. I hung a few blankets to keep the dust away. In applying the anaesthetic, I decided on the 'Crain camph' method, which is to inject the drug into the upper nerve system, and it was considered to be the best way to alleviate pain . . . I had read over the text before the operation, but unfortunately I could not locate the shoulder nerve system, although I looked for it two or three times. I was embarrassed and lost all confidence in myself and had to abandon the operation. I then obtained permission to have the British medical officer, Colonel McKenzie, operate on him.'

The Butcher wound up his evidence with this complaint: 'I was brought to the Rangoon Central Gaol on Feb. 15, 1946 from Moulmein and I was not given supper that night. On the next morning I was interrogated by an American officer before breakfast. I was terribly tired and I was not quite myself to face an interrogation.'

(A year later Lt Onishi's death sentence was commuted to life imprisonment.)

Now the Big Ti, Captain Tazumi, whom I can picture clearly in my mind . . . a very short man, about 40 with grey hair and a small moustache. He always wore a white shirt.

Served in Manchuria as an artillery officer, he says, and then went to Singapore where he was first commandant of the Sime Road Camp, north of Raffles College and then was commandant of Changi Gaol, Singapore, from April, 1943 to January, 1944. My fellow Australian prisoners in Singapore may remember him.

He had special orders from the Kempei Tai, he said, to keep the airmen separate from the regular prisoners. They were not sent out to work and so they were not paid. The workers received heavier rations than the airmen.

Captain Tazumi said that a little less than 100 prisoners died in Rangoon Gaol during the year he was there.

I conjure up a picture of Superior Private Koigotsu Ueno. We used to call him 'Limpy' and 'Tarzan.' He is quite frank in his evidence: 'Yes, I beat the prisoners with my fists and with a wooden club taken from the limb of a tree because they failed to obey orders.'

I close the War Office file and go with Audrey to look at the crab apple.

March 27

Stripped to my boots and socks ready to do my 4-mile evening walk in 20 yard laps last night I was told 'Bearden is back.' Magic words. I found 2/Lt Al. Bearden, P 38 pilot, U.S.A.A.F., in an upstairs room flush with cigarettes and centre of attraction . . . striking real matches and telling an amazing story of the outside world to goggle-eyed men. Today I went around every room and told everybody in compound something. My fingers are too tired to put down everything. I must be very, very careful.

My knee is leaking again. Today I went around reviewing skin disease in compound. Horrible sights. Some blokes are thick with prickly heat standing out like butcher's blocks. They have scratched and then tracts of septic sores over rear and in crutch. Doodle disease is very prevalent. They are swollen and pussie and look as though amputation is only treatment. To me, anyhow. (I am still clean). The fellows suffering from ring worm are in agony at night. They sleep unclad at night below and to hell with the mosquito.

Air raid bulletin: Yesterday, alert in afternoon and bomb bursts heard in south. Two alerts during last night. A/c heard, not seen. Probably intruder Mosquitos. Two alerts so far today. Bomb rumblings heard in north and at moment column of blue-grey smoke rising not far away in N. Another alert this afternoon.

Peeved with all this fuss. Something is happening. And how! The Japs have just turned out in their full field equipment – everybody – Med. orderly, Q.M. included. Poor little men weighed down with water bottles, bed rolls, tin hats, cartridge cases, spears and rifles. Whence? For why? And blokes around me continue argument as to population of L.A. and don't even go out for raids. Japs scurry about. We browse.

28 March

Quiet after yesterday . . . 4 alerts in 24 hours. No sirens last night nor this morning. Heat and sweat, along with no baths for about five days, playing havoc with skin diseases, ringworm, festering rashes and prickly heat. Spirits low because of 'scoosh' (little) news. Doing best to keep chaps busy – making bamboo beds for themselves and sick bay, bamboo strip baskets and repairing our front walk with clay from the excavation of the air raid trenches. Easter deck tennis tournament gaining interest, bingo every second day popular. Arranging feast for Sunday (Easter) and sunrise church service in open if Japs will allow or secretly otherwise.

A dozen or so strange Japs seen about this morning. They looked rough and battle worn. Did some of our dressed-up guards leave for war yesterday? Could these be replacements? A/c overhead at the moment. Japs are out in their battlefield best again – full kit, washed grey uniform, riding breeches, puttees and tunics. Even pathetic little Weary Willie was dressed up to kill, polishing his spear. I cannot imagine what this is all about – unless it is a full-dress rehearsal for *der tag*.

This morning I watched a mynah bird tugging at a dry vine. It grabbed vine in beak and then backed and fluttered but the vine held – a Walt Disney incident.

Heard today that new prisoners in cells are not really new arrivals but people taken out of the compound a month ago . . . one of the other compounds. The report said they had been to Saigon for nothing. What does that mean?

King is having another relapse – fainting and becoming weaker. He is delirious at times.

Practically everybody who smokes has carved out a pipe for himself out of firewood or bamboo. They say tobacco leaf strong smoke.

29 March

There was blood in the full moon – red with rich yellow – when it first appeared above the wall last night. I was walking unclad. The boys were formed in groups about the yard discussing the quickening of events in the prison towards the real thing.

Before 'tenko' we spied a machine-gun sited on the verandah above the main gate building. It has a commanding position of the prison lanes leading to the gate. A blanket hangs on a rail as a screen but we can see the lean, black barrel from our side position. The gun is manned by the fresh troops. I consider there are about 30 but we had signal from Anthony in Chinese compound that there are 80. They are heavier type of Japs than our lot and their rough appearance gave impression that they are real troops.

Soon after moon up siren went and we heard single a/c. Then after few minutes we saw four star-like flashes falling in sky in north close by. There was series of explosions and we heard a/c turning away just before. Rockets! The Japs were out in force scattered all round the prison. There were seven Japs squatting outside our fence. The Big Ti sat alone and aloof on his chair – a little hunched and looking very small, his white shirt standing out in the moonlight. Everything pointed to fact Japs are worried about us making a break. All the guns are pointed at us. It's all internal. I wonder what are the preparations to stop our troops getting to outside wall?

Soon afterwards there was another alarm and the Japs poured out to mow us down if we attempted to escape. We slept on. In fact, most of us slept through the third and last alert for night – at midnight. Japs drooped out this time. I feel all this is not conducive to good-tempered Japs. I must warn chaps to be more poker-faced in case high spirits in front of Japs incurs their wrath.

I unveiled myself today to a pink-streaked morning. The full moon that sat on the wet, red corrugated iron roof was pale and anaemic looking. That was the roof of the Chinese compound.

Another calm Burma morning, still like Australian bush except for prison noises and it seemed incredible to me that war was close.

Yesterday's battle atmosphere was fading fast. But soon came first siren renting air with morning sprightliness and we were cheered.

That started it. From then on to lunchtime the alert sounded three or four times. Twice we heard a/c first, then sirens, and watched Japs scurrying about lugging their spears and rifles.

It was quiet for lunch and then a roar in the distance materialized into a B 29 raid. Lovely doll! From the edge of foxholes we watched happily as Libs passed close overhead spreading the pieces of flame that were incendiaries. The fire fell with a swoosh. There was a scream of bombs and a whumpff that was too loud and near to be comfortable, but we liked it. Target just north of prison and great clouds of grey smoke billowed up. We are becoming quite intimate with the war, thank goodness. About 40 bombers in all. Near end of raid there was strange sight . . . from high up in sky a smoking something spiralled slowly to earth. At first thought it was a/c but formation nowhere near. Perhaps it was some type of flare. Felt blast of bombs today but more the merrier. Never was bombing more welcome at the receiving end. I have to warn chaps to keep down their spirits in front of Japs.

Ack ack was sparse today and no sign of Jap fighters. (Yesterday corporal of guard made surprise visit to compound, looked around yard and building, then went off without a word – unprecedented.) After raid excitement we settled down to a game of bingo. Interrupted by air raid and sound of a/c but the game went on. We left spectator sport to Japs. This situation of ours is like a game of bingo. At the moment we have our cards full with only one number to go but that number is the elusive one and stays at bottom of bag. But we hang on straining our ears to hear that number called. As each wrong number comes out we tell ourselves it will be the next one.

(Brigadier . . . I don't even know his name . . . doffed his hat to me during 'tenko' last night.)

It has taken until now for me to fully realize the piquant position I find myself in. I had my back to the fence when I felt eyes behind me, I swung around and looked straight into the saddest, most vacant but 'I could kill you' eyes that any writer of thrillers ever imagined. He was a thick Jap with a snub nose, one of the new boys, and wore a camouflage net over his tin hat. He just looked through me and I had feeling of looking into an animal's eyes. Yet they were sad and inhumanly killing – not cruel. He was head and shoulders out of a foxhole. I did not have to look away but I did. Oh those vacant, but filled, eyes.

I looked about at the other Japs jutting out of their holes holding their toy, business-like rifles . . . so unlike the old-fashion models mishandled by our regular guards. I tried to imagine the course the miracle would take that would get me back to my suburb in Sydney.

These Japs, on the other hand, are resigned to dying in Burma. They are caught like rats in a trap. Their orders are to stay and fight. They know the British are coming soon with overwhelming majority and daily they see the might in the air growing. Their hope is draining fast. Death is only thing left for them but, perhaps, their Bushido is losing its charm. I don't really think so. That is the outlook of these men standing between me and yachting on Sydney Harbour.

At times there is a stillness about this place that is dreadful. Right now I could scream so as not to hear those bloody birds twittering so peacefully. I am sitting, sweating, writing and my arm is wet against my body and thigh. Yes, as the end of all this apparently draws near the formidable hurdle betwixt this and freedom looms larger . . . there is certainly an ordeal ahead. It may only be mental. The bombing targets are getting closer and we are not certain that the prison itself will not be pranged sooner or later. They are still stacking rice and wood here. The Japs could have plans for turning it into a fortress for a last-ditch stand. Then what price us? Then will come the actual storming of the prison. Somebody is sure to be hurt and, what's more, I'm reluctant to just lay doggo here and have chaps take risks to rescue me. I am able-bodied. Why should I not take an active part in my own rescue? The general feeling in the compound is that we should not stick our necks out. I agree if it is a useless sacrifice. But I think we could be effective if we await our chance. That is why I have made it known that there are 20 or 30 of us who are strong enough for action.

30 March

Three Japs have just marched into the open air solitary cells down across from our end window. One carried a piece of cord. They returned a few minutes later with a Burmese prisoner dressed in purple sarong, shady shirt and shiny brown Burmese topee. He hung his head as he walked. The scene looked a grim one. There was something tense about the little party and the way the rifles were formally shouldered. They disappeared into the main gate building leaving us with doubts that we will still be here when the British come. Will we be marched away? The most wicked thing to my mind is the doubt, the day to day doubt . . . suspense personified.

Last night was a nightmare. There were three alerts they tell me but as I attempt to conjure up in my mind what happened the sounds of sirens are mingled with drunken shouts and singing and then cries of a man being beaten, kicked and the revolting gurgle of him retching. Then more sirens screech, a swarm of flying cockroaches invade the sleeping area and in comes a fellow to tell me how he was just caught by a mean Jap for not bowing in the moonlight and how the guard had poked and hit him with the butt end of a spear and then 'braced' him (ordered him to stand rigid without moving even an eyelid). The Big Ti then appeared and said 'How are you doing?' He explained. B.T. sent him up to bed. A nightmare surely!

But this morning I awoke to the fact that it was all true. The drunk was our three-star medical orderly. Poor bastard. He was really happy. We heard him clapping his hands in the chapel and falling over furniture. His cries woke me and I looked down thru bars to see 3 or 4 Japs setting on him. He was obviously uncontrollable so they were beating, punching and kicking him to quieten him. It was all clear in moonlight through frame of mango tree leaves. They hog-tied him (arms and legs together up behind). Then they must have kicked him senseless because he was silent for a few minutes. Then we heard him being sick. He was lying with his face in it. One of his comrades went over, lifted him by the ropes and dropped him into the sick again. It was cruellest thing I've ever seen done to human . . . and Jap to Jap, too. I will always wonder.

It was about 9.30 pm. He was left there throughout air raids and someone saw him still there at 2 am . . . inert.

Anthony said Big Ti told him 'Free soon . . . 20 days.'

Upstairs area reserved for 3 hours this afternoon for Good Friday solitude worship. We have a bed of strong pink flowers in our yard. I will tell the chaps at 'tenko' they may be picked for Easter Sunday. Flowers don't altogether fit into this grim picture but they will suffice to make Sunday different if we are not allowed to have a service.

Deck tennis is claiming a little interest but the calisthenics class in the mornings has diminished. Nothing but freedom and food talk can hold interest for long in this compound.

I am not only becoming fit with the regular exercising but truly believe my body is stronger than it has been for year or so. I am clear of skin disease so far which is a miracle in itself and my stomach is in good shape. We are getting enough food but are hungry for a change from rice, soup, nuka and rice. We had a taste of fresh fish the other day and every few days are blessed with an infinitesimal piece of fresh pork – enough to make rice greasy.

I have no doubt that Big Ti and Japs at top are keen to keep us in fair condition for some reason or other. I take it as a hopeful sign but

AC2 Hudson, on boat heading for Southern Rhodesia for pilot training in 1940.

Wing Commander L V Hudson RAAF being interviewed outside Rangoon Gaol by war correspondents. (AWM No. SEA 240)

Above: Aerial photo of Rangoon Gaol, 1 May, 1945.

Above right: The diary spilling out of a Japanese Army despatch bag. It was vital to keep the diary hidden from the Japanese guards, so it was stowed piece by piece in an empty chutney bottle in the wall of an air-raid shelter.

Left: Rangoon Gaol gates 3 May, 1945 – Adjutant John Kerr with book in hand.

Former prisoners at Mingaladon airfield, Rangoon, about to leave for Calcutta. *Left to right:* Lt John Kerr; W/CDR Lionel Hudson; P/O Osboldstone, RNZAF; F/LT. Cliff Emeny, RNZAF.

Rangoon
29th April, 1945.

To the whole captured persons of Rangoon jail.

According to the Nippon military order, we hereby give you liberty and admit to leave this place at your own will.

Regarding food and other materials kept in this compound, we give you permission to consume them, so far as your necessity is concerned.

We hope that we shall have an opportunity to meet you again at battlefield of somewhere.

We shall continue our war effort eternally in order to get the emancipation of all Asiatic Race.

Harvo Ito,
the chief officer of Rangoon Branch Jail

Above and left: Th
photograph of Hud
son with the messag
in English left b
hind on the gate
Rangoon Gaol w
published in a Japa
ese newspaper.
brought results.

Above and right: Li
nel Hudson an
Harvo Ito at Ne
Otani Hotel, Toky
April 1985.

Rangoon Gaol Force, 3 May, 1945. With spear, Herb Ivens; on his left, John Kerr; on his left, Lionel Hudson. (Imperial War Museum.)

Prisoners who marched out of Rangoon Jail at Pegu.

Rangoon 1944. Centre table: Subhas Chandra Bose, INA leader and
Lt. Gen. Kawabe Shozo, C-in-C Japanese Forces at Imphal, replaced
by Kimura. Major Maeda on extreme right.

The ex-prisoners who stayed behind in Rangoon to hand over to the incoming Allied Forces, leave for Calcutta. (AWM No. SEA 244)

Major Maeda, who gave Hudson a beating during interrogation in Rangoon, is keen to be friends with Hudson when they meet in Tokyo, forty years later. He is now a retired banker.

you can't fathom these people. No medical attention for five days . . . no bath for a week.

Today saw first drunken Japs in daytime . . . new boys, dishevelled, staggering. A Chinese prisoner saluted and the Jap just managed to return it . . . shirt undone . . . very unJap. This follows last night's incident and shows uneasy Jap minds. Discipline going? It is noticeable that the mean guards remain mean but the good, almost human guards are more jovial.

Anthony signalled this afternoon that Burmese are evacuating Rangoon and Jap guards are all over town.

The few beards still left are disappearing one by one. Mine remains. I am determined to have something to show for my captivity.

Throughout today we have heard sirens in the town and there have been four or five alerts here. Often hear a/c but no big bombing. No Jap a/c have been sighted in ages. The Ti's chair is kept out permanently these days.

31 March

We could not leave flowers in garden until Easter Sunday because we wanted some for a wreath – King died early today. I told the orderly sergeant at dawn 'tenko' . . . 'itchi may shindow' . . . and they sent a rough-hewn coffin with the order to bring it back to gate with body in it. We did but lid would not sit down. I lined people up in yard as coffin was carried out with King's W/O cap and cross wreath on top and gave general salute. The coffin has been lying in the yard all morning and we have had to shift it twice so far out of the sun. Chinese will appear soon I expect and carry the coffin away with indifference.

There was a funeral yesterday from No. 1 O.R.'s compound. (In the morning light that looks more like No 6 compound.) We saw an RAF officer and some others carry the flag-draped coffin to the main gate preceded by the orderly sergeant (Jap). We are not so privileged. We are not to be trusted to bear one of our comrades to his grave. That would be too good for us. We are in course of being punished for something so we are not allowed to be decent. It makes me sick!

At least King was not killed by a Jap swan song injection – most of the chaps who have died here have been given an injection in the arm under skin (a large colorless, odourless serum) towards the end. Nobody has ever recovered from one. A 'waddy' shot, we call them.

This is one time I'm sorry to be right. I'm content we did everything possible here but the poor fellow would have had a far better chance if the Japs had agreed to my request to transfer him to the British Army compound where he would have had doctors to care for him.

King was a member of an RAF Liberator crew. His wreath was made up of a green vine intertwined with some purple and red flowers.

Yesterday at dusk a single-engine a/c -Jap – appeared at 2,000ft away to north, wheels down. Oscar or Army 97. This is first Jap a/c we have seen for about 10 days. There were three alerts last night but no untoward incidents. Strange that no searchlights or ack ack ever seen at night now.

The humorous types are going around asking, 'Is there an all clear on?' after this morning's consistent alerts . . . about six or eight so far. Hearing a/c frequently but only bombing in the north.

From balcony early last night saw flashes in sky to west which did not appear to be lightning . . . lasted for about an hour. Any little thing gives us a ray of hope. We keep scanning the skyline for a sign and straining our ears for a tell-tale sign. We have a strange outlook: Happy to be bombed and awaiting, desperately, an invading army with all the dangers that will accompany it.

A new prisoner came into gaol last night . . . an American officer with the beginnings of a beard. Only message from him so far is that war in Burma going well, we should be out by monsoon and incredible news that we have control of Canton.

Everybody awaiting Easter Sunday tomorrow with interest. No permission yet to have service. I just waylaid Weary Willie thru fence but he thought not.

Today I told all and sundry that they must go to air raid shelters when gong sounds for local raid. I explained stupid to stay in this flimsy building but, moreover, by ignoring alerts we indicate to Japs that this is a sanctuary from bombing. They could act on this idea and bring troops in here out of danger. Anyway, we don't really know that the prison will not be bombed. Another thing is that we don't want to show up Japs by not appearing to be afraid (that should read: by appearing to be unafraid).

TOP SECRET   IMMEDIATE

February 16, 1945.

From: SACSEA
To: Air Ministry

Following for Chiefs of Staff from Mountbatten

'*I much regret that Japanese, far from observing civilised standards in the location of POW camps, are deliberately using such camps to protect vital targets. In these circumstances I have decided on the following policy*
(*a*) *The presence of a POW camp is not repetition not to be permitted to divert air attack from a target, the damage or destruction of which is essential to the proper conduct of the war.*
(*b*) *The air forces are to observe the maximum practicable care in the tactical development of attacks in order to reduce the chance of hitting POW camps.*
(*c*) *Where an objective cannot be attacked without risking damage to a POW camp and its degree of vitalness is in doubt, the Allied C in C is to refer the matter to me for decision.*'

February 21, 1945
From: Air Ministry
To: SACSEA

'*Chiefs of Staff today took note with approval of SEACO's 316 17 . . . Although no call to formulate a policy in this respect in the European theatre, SAC thought it very necessary to form one in South-East Asia.*
    Where targets are of outstanding importance such as, for instance, Rangoon, no consideration should be allowed to interfere with our bombing policy.'
    Author's note: RAF Liberators bombed a POW camp at Hnong-pladuk, Thailand, on September 6 and 7, 1944 killing 32 British and 51 Dutch prisoners. There was what was considered to be an important strategic target nearby – a railway station and sidings.

I was unaware at the time but Rangoon Gaol was within 1,000 yards of the city's most important strategic target – the docks.

*   *   *

'Where are they now?' is question in everybody's mind.

I have just finished describing Toheroa soup to the recipes collector in our midst.

Rice and more rice! Wheelbarrows piled with bags of rice have been wheeled in like an endless procession for last three days. The Chinese compound ground floor is filled up and now they are filling next door Indian compound. Some of bags being stored are lumpy and not rice.

'This is a Bastille as far as food is concerned,' says Gus. 'Tomato juice, fruit cup, Virginia sugar-cured ham steak with two pineapple rings, baked potatoes, candied yams, raisin sauce, fried parsnips, cold milk, apple pie a la mode – NOT THIS BLOODY RICE AND SOUP.'

The Chinese came and took away the coffin while we were playing bingo.

This afternoon has been mainly quiet of alerts after a busy morning . . . another big parcel of leaf over fence from Indians last night so chaps are busy rolling cigs in leaf, paper and leaves.

It is amazing how we have slipped into this raw, down-to-earth existence. We are quite unconscious now, I feel, when we meander about yard in the nude, stopping now and again to bend our backsides to sun to kill any delicate germs. We feel quite dressed up in our loin cloths. Even today we saluted King's coffin dressed in such a way.

Responsible senior officers have no qualms about scraping the rice or 'nuka' barrels for every tiny fragment of food. All of our clothes are sweet-smelling with sun-dried sweat and our bodies caked with dirt. The med. orderly seems to have lost interest in us. Could he be embarrassed by fact that King died as we predicted? Not really. Already King's clothes have been divided among the needy.

1 April

This is Easter Sunday – and the RAF's birthday to boot. There is a good spirit in the air. 'Happiness' was this morning's greeting.

We picked the rest of the flowers, small and two shades of pink, and now these elongated cells are garlanded with bamboo tubes filled with flowers.

Breakfast was a gala meal – extra rice, nuka cooked in cow pea water, cow peas and compound chutney. How about that!!

The Japs have ignored my repeated request to hold Easter service so we had a secret service in my cell. A circle of bamboo cups on the floor denoted the altar. Lt. Erwin conducted the service. I felt God's presence. We sang three hymns so softly that fence guards could not hear us – Holy, Holy, Christ Lord, risen today and God our help in ages past. Coffin sang 'Christ Arise' and with Davis 'Hallelujah'. About 80 in congregation . . . cooks and cockatoos had to be on duty.

Read news first from Brig. (written in shorthand): 'We are using Meiktila dromes and reason for frequent alerts is wave of fighter sweeps down Pegu Road. European news, too.'

It was a strange and rough and haggard group who worshipped. They lined the cell in loin cloths, flying suits, jungle greens and battle dress . . . their Sunday best. Some who could not sit down because of sores and scabies stood up in the passage way outside. Thru wooden bars you could see some of them lifting their clothes off their sticky skins now and again. All the wounded men were happy with fresh dressings. The medical orderly corporal had been in an attentive mood. He gave a few beri beri injections. W/Cdr Hill and Sgt. Wells got injections. Quite a different attitude to four days ago.

There was another reason for the happy faces under the beards. I had paraded a row of the worst cases of skin disease. 'Toxon,' I said 'Sioka nay' (no water). Said Cpl: 'Air bombing . . . boom, boom. No sioka' . . . laughing. He thought it great joke.

Talk on Life of Jesus by Lt. Coffin punctuated by roll of cannon fire.

Unprecedented lunch – rice and soup and fish. All three! I notice that some of the old boys who appear quite fit and hungry cannot cope with an abnormal meal like this . . . so used are they to not getting enough for so long . . . and they have some of their lunch put aside for eating later. I must thank the cooks publicly for their effort today. I am told that dinner is to be a bumper. They have been working like niggers.

Lazy day . . . no exercise for me . . . I've been resting my knee that's gone bad again.

Who said Japs did not have sense of humour? Watched from above as Jap guards filed out of their mess. A large hog, all trussed up, lay there in a wheelbarrow. One by one they poked and prodded it with their rifles just to make it squeal and then looked around for applause from their fellow warriors when it did.

This reminded us of the Frisco Kid (he never tired of telling the Yanks of the good time he had in San Francisco when he visited on a ship before war). In the cell block he several times ordered prisoners to stand at attention close to the bars of the cell door while he pushed a rubber tube up their nostrils until it came into their mouths. When the end appeared he'd laugh his head off. Sickening for the blokes and made their noses bleed but great joke for Frisco Kid.

Other times he would make men stand braced with their eyes closed and mouths open, then pop in a dirty stone. Once he surprised the life out of one prisoner by putting in a piece of ice instead of a stone. That was his brilliant best.

One of the long-term prisoners told about one of the Jap guards when they were in the Law Courts cells. He was a husky type and the boys there called him 'Killer'. (Killed Capt. W. Wright) Once he punched and kicked a frail Chinese nearly senseless and then threw a big handful of salt into mouth, eyes and made him eat it. Somehow Chinese swallowed lot without being sick. This was punishment because Chinese was contemptuous of Jap and refused to eat the 'nuka' that was served to him.

Many of the prisoners there had black and blue fingernails from being hit with a club after being ordered to spread their fingers on a ledge. One Indian was driven out of his mind by the pain of having his fingernails pulled by a Jap sgt with a pair of pliers over a period of months. Guards sometimes made Indian stand up all night. Pottinger was told once to hit the Indian. Potty wound up twice and made mighty swipe. Guard pleased and went away. Potty had merely slapped his own chest and hardly touched the Indian.

Story told by old boys: In June, 1943, about 13 Rangoon merchants were rounded up by Japs suspected of having been using a radio transmitter to make contact with British. Jeweller, goldsmith, radio shop owner, hardware merchant, contractor. All rich and elite of Rangoon Indians. One was son of prominent Rangoon magistrate. At first they were kept in western lock-up cared for by bearers (their own servants) then to New Law Courts. They swore they were not transmitting but Japs persisted – torture.

Jeweller hanged by feet while being interrogated. His tormentor went to sleep and left the jeweller hanging there for 10 hours. He, the interrogator, had been drinking of course. Guards ignored the Indian's cries (four months before he could walk).

Another had score cigarette burns on body where Japs had pressed in burning cigarette when he could not answer their questions. Others beaten, starved. One of the wealthiest men in Rangoon. Finally, they decided to make up a confession to stop torture. They told of ficticious codes and said they threw radio into river. They were all released a month or so after that. One kept in gaol. Deal with Japs? Spy?

Working party from army compound report they read bulletins on wharf while out today telling Burmese not to panic if they hear gunfire . . . only Japs practising. Pegu airborne landing?

Three air raid alerts last night. One early this morning. No local alarm all day. Gloomy Sunday.

Outbreak of ulcers or boils noticeable even among new boys. Lack of water main cause?

2 April

Last night and for previous two evenings there has been unusual light flashing in west. It continues for an hour or two after dark and once when siren sounded stopped abruptly. Flash is intermittent and lights up big section lower w. sky. Not gun flashes. Most popular theory is that it is some type of furnace. Big fire pouring grey smoke away to N.W. at dusk yesterday. Two alerts last night but no bombing heard.

These new troops are said to be front-liners and have dug trenches outside the walls of the prison. It looks as though outside of prison is being patrolled now as well as inside. A successful break would be very difficult. It looks as though we have only one course left – sit and wait.

Some of the new Japs appear to be more friendly than usual and have waved to a few of us. They do not mix with regular guards. Some just stand and stare at us.

Easter parade festival last evening . . . forbidden, but what the hell! Half compound crowded into middle, upstairs cell, closed steel doors. McClosky and Davis sang solos. McClosky, sweet-voiced Irish tenor and Davis high-pitched tenor. Both emaciated bodies and it surprises that sounds from them could be so sweet. Green Eye of the Little Yellow God and Waterloo. Sat around in dark, cigar and cigarette ends glowing. It capped a happy Easter Day. (Byron's Before Waterloo . . . 'Arm, arm. It is the cannon's opening roar.')

On Easter Sunday we saw a Burmese type, dressed in long green slacks and a bush shirt, being led into the solitary cell block. Big Ti there. Chinese followed carrying bed roll. Prisoner appeared nonchalant. Since then Ti and interrogators back several times. Spy?

3 April

Quite a few stomachs still upset after Sunday's feast. White flashes in sky towards west again yesterday evening. Puzzling.

At 'tenko' offered Jap Q.M. more watches for sale. He asked for full list of what was on offer and prices wanted. Gave him list of 14 watches, 2 pens, 2 pencils, cigarette lighter and 2 gold rings which chaps want to sell considering they have little chance of ever getting them anyway. Personally, I think chance of getting back possessions in this prison is NOT so remote, but there is no doubt we need extra food. (I have nothing to sell . . . I was relieved of my watch by the Jap soldiers who captured me in the paddy fields.)

If we get money we might be able to get eggs and other wholesome foodstuffs to build up these frail bodies a bit. The cash amounted to Rs 6,400. Not such a fortune.

Our outsider estimates that our collection would bring in about Rs 20,000 if sold in Rangoon. With inflation so wild everybody is trying to turn their worthless cash into goods. B. actually witnessed a transaction of a second-hand bicycle selling for Rs 4,000.

It seems that a rupee is worth actually about five cents. But there is nothing for sale. We have figured that Rs 5,000 Jap is equivalent of Rs 300 Indian if both are converted to eggs. Mostly it is about ratio 6 to 1. Last week pork Rs 45 (3¼lbs), beef Rs 50, box matches Rs 5½ cheapest, onions Rs 50, cigs best Kooa Rs 75 asking price when find someone who has them. Pork was Rs 25 two months ago and beef Rs 28. Eggs were Rs 1, now Rs 2½ (chicken) and all this accounts for Q.M.'s keenness. He asked me for full list of things for sale this morning at 'tenko' and wanted to know whether figures mentioned were 'last price – rock bottom.' I said 'Of course.' He was in very good mood.

Said Gus: 'If you had told me a year or even six months ago that a Jap would stand up at tenko and bargain I would have said you were mad.'

Recce a/c overhead.

Rations in today to last for one week (usually five or six days).

Standard has improved if anything on when we first came into compound. The food is sufficient to exist on but is not good enough for sick and is lacking certain vitamins. We have all these sores and ulcers as a result.

Night quiet and this morning is as workaday and tranquil as any during last three months. Deck tennis tournament in full swing – calisthenics craze has fallen off even more. Myself out with only three others this morning.

Consensus of talk in here is that chaps generally want to go back to college, varsity and continue studies when they get home. I wonder? McCloskey – second tenor. Sang in Glee Club while at Bellevue High School, Penn. Choir, too. Voice cracked, sang with local band for hell of it. Learned Irish ditties from uncle . . . Irish from way back. Voice improved in range since been in Army. Sang in cadet orchestra, Maxwell Field. To Sicily as pilot of B 25 in August, 1943. Salerno was first raid . . . delousing, softening dromes, bridgeheads. DFC at Velletri . . . shot up before target but led squadron in. 'Earthquakers' name of group – 12th Bomber. To Foggia and then Salerno Bay . . . 48 missions. Cassino raid two men in crew wounded. Two weeks before due to go home . . . two more missions. Froze.

To India, operated Bengal . . . knocked down 5th mission in this theatre. Low level bombing railway Indaw. Ground fire . . . crew baled out. Extra 100 mph climbed as high as could and told them 'start walking.' Five out of six captured by Japs . . . 2nd pilot killed. Nav. died Rangoon Prison. Mc sprained ankles and was given up to Japs by Burmese. This May 20, 1944.

With another U.S. officer attempted break from Rangoon gaol

annex. Six took part. Mc's job was to attack guard on duty who was asleep. Broke lock on cell door with pipe, crept up to guard, hit him . . . blood spouted out of crack top of head. Jap fought. Two nailed him. Jap cpl also caught but Burmese flunky escaped and raised alarm. Both dashed to street door which unlocked. Mc had carbine, Bish, pistol. Street filled with Japs. Back into courtyard for another means of escape but cornered. Bish in dark covered with pistol/sword. Returned to cell where others and seven sick, who could not even attempt to escape, were beaten badly, untanned leather whips, belts, kicked in face and starved for five days. Sick also beaten and starved somewhat. 21 days later to prison. Cell 13. Scabies badly, raw from hips to knees . . . bad sores. Now clear. Half rations in prison for month. Overdid even that . . . weakened and lost 2/3 stone . . . 165 lbs previously. Songs: 'I'll take you home again, Kathleen', 'Adeste Fideles', 'Same old Shillelagh', 'Moosh, Moosh, Moosh', 'McNamara's Band', 'Begin the Beguine' and 'If I had a paper doll.'

Breath control, tone better now.

(*The diary for the next nine days is missing.*)

**Pittsburg, Pennsylvania,
24 January, 1976**

It is the top McClosky J. in the Pittsburg telephone directory. A male voice comes on the line.

'*My name's Hudson. I'm looking for a McClosky who was in the air force . . .' There is a chuckle the other end.*

'*That's not that bloody Orstralian. Don't tell me . . .*'

The rich timbre is still there in his voice, the voice that had brought tears to men's eyes in the prison.

I tell him I am on a five-month wildlife film/lecture tour of the western United States for the National Audubon Society and ask him along to the Sunday afternoon session of 'Kangaroos Can't Be Cornered' at the university auditorium. Audrey, too, is eager to meet this man. She has heard his story many times from me. I have no idea what the emaciated wreck of a man in my memory will look like now. McClosky's jungle sores were the deepest in the compound. The time comes for me to go up to the podium and McClosky has not turned up. Audrey keeps a seat vacant alongside her and we leave instructions at the door. When the lights come up and the questions start to flow I see this big hunk of a man sitting with Audrey. Surely not. It is McClosky.

'What a charming man,' Audrey said afterwards. 'He's so like Burt Lancaster . . . but better looking.'

McClosky's late model Cadillac is parked outside. He takes us home to meet his wife and daughter. While he mixes drinks I mention his singing in the gaol and how important it was in buttressing sagging spirits. They are wide-eyed.

'Daddy has never talked about life inside the prison,' says his daughter.

We have dinner at his country club. He flew for a while after the war, he says, sold a few light aircraft, but then got into making safety ladders for industry. He still sings in a choir.

On the way back to where we are staying he starts to sing softly and goes through his prison repertoire: 'I'll take you home again, Kathleen,' 'Same old Shillelagh' and so on. He leaves 'Paper Doll' until last. They had been poignant words for young prisoners wondering what was happening to their girlfriends back home:

> *'If I had a paper doll that I could call my own,*
> *A doll that other fellows could not steal . . .*
> *And when I got home at night she would be waiting,*
> *She'd be the sweetest girl in all this world.*
> *Oh, I'd rather have a paper doll to call my own*
> *Than have a fickle-minded real, live girl.'*

12 April

Afternoon . . . two silver fighters low in south. Afraid they are Oscars.

Out of 101 in compound 15 men have ringworm, 40 or 50 jungle ulcers or festering patches of pimples. About 20 with active beri beri . . . more than half compound have had beri beri at some time . . . always a score or so with diarrhoea . . . one arm amputated, one arm bullet wound.

Our physiological exceptional feats: No urinating – 72 hours. No defecation – 30 days. Most movements one day – 48.

Whisper thru fence that Pinky and three officers from No. 3 were beaten up badly last night for stealing soap. Pinky off duty today. Hope contact soon back. We need him.

Chess tournament under way. Also working on deck tennis

tournament and quiz+concert. Scoosh (?) behaves like full-grown but smaller than week-old kitten . . .

Far-off dates in sweepstakes strongly favoured.

There is a jack fruit tree outside southern fence. Fruit hangs oddly from thin branch low down.

My middle still wrapped in vest (?). I hate having to wear even one garment now. Most of us spend day naked. Hot sun, hot bodies, sweat, clothes filthy and stiff with baked perspiration. I wonder all this filth does not spread plague or something.

Birds still building nests. It must be their Spring.

Church steeple looks cool and serene over there against pale blue sky.

Boys talking about a crow dinner . . . and they mean it. I notice some eyes are following crow flights through the air.

13 April

Oh these exasperating people. Even we birds in a cage realize that everything is not quite all right with Rangoon . . . yet these confounded Japs gathered outside our fence at dusk yesterday and practised – wait for it – bowing. Yes, they bowed meticulously to each other for nearly an hour.

Then one of them came into our gate and punched and kicked diminutive Red Davis, thin and weak to begin with, for not bowing smartly enough as he passed. At least, we think that was the reason. One of the boys from another compound was braced and beaten last night, yet another this morning.

At 'tenko' today an Indian was thrashed outside our gate. This is quite a session of bloody-mindedness. We have not seen No 3 and No 6 boys treated like this before.

M.O. called me to fence this morning and handed me a note that said: 'With the onset of the monsoon rains it is likely that epidemics will spread if proper precautions are not taken. Consequently, people not convalescing or not engaged in W.P. or L.W.P. are to be employed in catching rats and killing flies. The bag for each day is to be shown at the M.I. room.'

This step is full of merit. I have had fly-catching details for months now but the flies have become fewer with the hot weather. Japs gave me two rat traps which have been set in cookhouse.

Just heard three bursts of fire away to north – straffing a/c – sounded like Mosquitos – on Prome Road. Good. How can these Japs be still making plans for being here for monsoon???

Along with half a dozen of chaps from my cell have been working in cookhouse today giving cooks a holiday. Cooking rice and slicing pumpkin squash and egg plant . . . fun. Six big bags of egg plant in yesterday. Lots of vegetable oil which is good. Yes, these Japs want us to live. For what?

Only four of us left with beards now. For the last few days there have been traces of blood and mucus in my stool but I feel fairly well.

The compound appears happier if anything. Odd people are seeking definite jobs to keep their hands busy and minds off speculation. I want to read lot of Kipling when I get out.

14 April

Fear in my heart last night. It started with a session with an angry guard just before 'tenko'. I was with another chap shielding me in front while I furtively signalled C.O. of No 6. Jap surprised me but, apparently, did not actually catch me signalling. He was just suspicious and that is par for the course for a Jap. He jabbered at me in Jap for a minute, growing more peeved all the time. I edged back from fence to be out of reach of a poke from his rifle. Then two scraggy white prisoners appeared and left their bows a little late. The attack swung to them. He hit them on head with butt of rifles, prodded them viciously. Really mean. They went and he swung back to me. He called W. Willy over. He was still uncertain in his muddled mind as to what I had been doing but I was surprised he did not whack me anyhow. It is not like a Jap to hesitate. W. Willy said something and then hurried off. Then bell saved me . . . 'tenko'. I thought this would only delay it but after 'tenko' I went back to fence and he waved me away. Apparently, he gave me benefit of doubt – unprecedented. Or was it something W. Willie said?

I walked the yard uneasy in mind as the Brigadier was standing out near his front fence looking over. He was evidently worried. Japs appeared more peeved than ever. There seemed ill in the wind. A cold front had caused a great building up of cloud – blue-grey mass at the base with crunchy white tops, billowing in firmness, growing as one watched. The sun setting caught the white with a russet redness.

There was another lovely and powerful formation in the west. There was an awe in the air, a tenseness . . . like a lovely woman who is also evil. It all dissipated as darkness fell . . . lightning chased around the cloud mountains . . . a brilliant display of nature mad and mighty. The two masses merged and the whole western sky was filled with menacing wall of cloud. I felt excited. My own small personal fear of an hour ago was replaced by a greater foreboding force. The storm moved on towards us with lightning flashing to light the way. There was something splendid about the approach of this monster. Dark now with the flashes all-revealing. Now and then we stopped pacing to watch the show.

Then light in block of solitary cells opposite took our attention. Japs were taking two prisoners to the dreaded cells. We listened and, sure enough, came the sounds of the poor beggars being punched and slapped. Here was 15th century brutality.

As we listened the roar was heard. It was in the distance . . . nearer, nearer. Then it was on us. Everything went purple. The great wind hit this prison with an accompaniment of rattling roofs and clanging of sheets of galvanized iron against the bars. There was no banging of open doors and shutters. This is a prison. The air was stinging with grit . . . and everything was still purple . . . frightening.

The bashing of the prisoners was over for the time being because we saw the lantern light moving away. We fled indoors.

The wind was raising hell. It seemed to be driving from every direction and the din was terrific. Trees waved at the mercy of this devil run amok.

The same thought leapt into everybody's mind – a grand night for escape. But caution said that would be foolhardy.

The tempo of the storm did not waver for a moment although a few stars were showing now and again. We went inside and laid on our rice bags in the shelter of the walls. Laying there I suddenly realized that not a drop of rain had fallen.

I slept immediately. It was all a horrible dream this morning.

I have not mentioned yet how the Indian babu in next door compound, who organized the tobacco parcels for us, tossed over a bag of gram (cow peas) to us the night before last along with some cigs and offered more food. I replied in a note that they must be sure not to deprive themselves too much but we could accept any extra food from them. He said that most of the Indians were very loyal to us and are willing to die for us. I believe him, too. These Indians are taking risks nightly to give us small tobacco gifts. The babu, in particular, is a great help and we need him. More cigs last night. I sent over our hot Rs 60.

Talk with W. Willy for Bearden yesterday. Then out with all belongings. He said to No 5 block-cells. Still stool-pigeoning?

More beatings all round us for the slightest thing. Japs very touchy. Then, ironically enough, M.O. tells us today that Big Ti is presenting prize to compound which gets biggest bag in rats and fly hunt . . . the schoolboy competition spirit. Amazing. We'll be having a picnic and sports day on the banks of the Irrawaddy next! We caught one rat while M.O. was here and one mice last night. M.O. pleased. Returned with a present of 20 cigs. Also with bottle for our dead flies. I respect Japs for this move anyhow and will do all I can. There seems to be no doubt in their minds that we'll be sweating out the monsoon here.

The rat prize of cigs was followed thru gate by the cpl of guard . . . compound inspection. He was in good humour and found nothing amiss downstairs but in officer's cells found maps and cartoons on the walls in charcoal. He was amused by map of China and Japan, England and USA and drawings over table which had cafe atmosphere. Then he became peeved. He asked for artist. A few fellows admitted to it and were thrashed with a piece of bamboo. All over in five or ten minutes. Twice he made as if to load his rifle and levelled it at fellows who did not flinch. He really had fun. He remonstrated with me for allowing walls to be marked but did not touch me. I wondered why not. Told him it would be cleaned and he went off happy. Nobody hurt, thank God. Vicissitudes of a day in this compound are amazing. Nothing dull. Every day, every hour is different. But God help the poor bastard who tries to reason why the Japs do things . . . how they will react. He'll go round the bend.

Lunch hour alert after a single-engine a/c flashed in sky to S.W. and fired at something on river (it appeared). Nothing else warlike today.

The next month threatens to be worst as far as skin diseases are concerned. Hot and filthy month with no washing may be disastrous. It seems popular opinion that everybody will have period when his

131

skin will go rotten on his bottom, crutch etc no matter what
condition or fitness. A lot of the newer inmates already broken out.
Horrible disease. I'm waiting my turn, dreading the thought.
Wrong-way-about sun worshippers.

Greeting here 'How is my rot looking?'

Pinky back – surprising! He says rumpus current started with Japs
being put on mat for stealing soap from the store. They were peeved
so searched No 6, found odd cakes so tried to put all the blame there.
Men beaten in solitary last night were from No 3. They were taken
back to No 3 again today. No reason yet.

Informed Brigadier of Bearden's movement.

Japs say in their newspaper that they are awaiting opportunity to
retake Philippines. Jap cpl today told us that Roosevelt was 'shindo'.
Bad news travels fast. Also M.O. said so today.

15 April

These noble Indians. They have won hearts of entire compound with
gift last night of nearly a full meal of beans and heap of salt and jagari
. . . over the wall in darkness. Sunny morning church service.
Peaceful . . . birds, green trees, bars. No air activity.

Lt. Walker punched by guard who did not see him bow.

'The daredevils are coming.' That is text of pamphlets dropped by
our a/c, according to news thru fence.

A month today to monsoon. Surely there will be a desperate army
effort to get here before the rains? Everything will be slowed down
horribly otherwise. Men here have lapsed back into resigned moods.
No excitement about an early release.

Glare of a fire in the north-west early this morning. Working on a
scheme to use bamboo pipes for catching water from roof to our
trough when it rains.

16 April

Walked under two-day-old moon last night and went up to sleep at
'shoto' with my body sticky with sweat. My clothes were soon
clinging to my skin and I could not sleep for some time. The east was
lighted with lightning flashes in quick succession and I had an instant
objection in my mind to the way the sky was paralleled off by bars. I
hate bars. My house after this will always have open windows.

I was awakened by the roar of the storm . . . heavy rain on the roof. Are these the 'mango showers' they talk about? Awakened again by excited whispers . . . 'Japs in compound'. Storm had passed . . . it was not long until dawn. I crept to balcony and watched Jap lanterns. Quite a few moving about. They were all over prison. The light in our yard moved towards the stairs so I raced to my bag and feigned sleep. Two Japs . . . by light of lanterns they counted the inert, but trembling, bodies. They were amazingly considerate, walked softly, whispered. 'Don't wake the baby.' They went and the talk soon died down. Either they suspected that the storm had given cover for an escape or there had been an alarm. Someone says he heard the Japs on the telephone during search.

Sky still had traces of night's storm at dawn . . . torn clouds strewn all over . . . Steely grey. Morning cool . . . a blessing.

Surprise when a Jap threw five tins of salmon or something like into the compound from the store . . . à la Pinky! Another rat, another prize. Medical orderly attentive . . . coming every second day now.

We were bent over our lunch rice when booming started. There was an alert on at the time so it could hardly be Japs at practice. The booms, sounding like field artillery or coastal guns, came out of the S.W. for about five minutes. We heard a/c overhead for a long period. Another alert this afternoon.

Three men in our compound punched, then braced in hot sun by a burly, scraggy Jap this afternoon because they did not bow to him. These Japs really mean to keep us suppressed no matter what.

17 April

Today's features have been in the air. During morning a/c heard on recce for several periods. Double vapour trail left by a/c which sped over N.W. to S.E. Early afternoon saw storm clouds in embryo . . . menacing castles of crunchy white and grey. Now storm has broken and it is cool while it rains.

This change in the weather has broken monotonous spell of fine, glary days but it augurs badly for a quick capture of Rangoon!

The 'daredevils are coming' pamphlet is amplified as being a reference to straffing a/c. The Japs are told in it to keep the Burmese away from battle zone as Japs are going to be straffed until they cry for mercy. Japs still show no trace of concern apart from being more vigilant about keeping the various compound populations segregated and ensuring there is no communication . . . still they fail.

Gus is wishing at the moment that he had a few of the lumps of fat off steaks that he has pushed to side of his plate in the past.

One of the old stagers just said that he'll need a real sign very soon that the army is coming or he'll settle down for monsoon season. That's general feeling. I am exception. I'm optimistic.

More beans from Indians over wall last night . . . and promise of jagari and 25 lbs of tobacco. I hate to think what state we would be in if it was not for outside compounds secretly supplementing our food and giving the smokers cigars and tobacco. Thank goodness I don't smoke. I can be impartial about tobacco road decisions.

Our news contacts are terrific morale lifters. All this forbidden but goes on merrily . . . and I'm not sure that chaps are at all grateful. They seem to take these sacrifices and risks by our fellow prisoners on the other side of the walls as a matter of course.

Chess tournament now in full swing. Quiz tomorrow.

18 April

Rifle shots heard last night – ten or so outside walls. One report close by. More rain and electrics last evening. Cooler afterwards. There is a very live feeling of expectation among few of us fresher prisoners. Day by day we wait for the climax. The veteran inmates have been through this before. They will believe it when they see it. These intangible premonitions don't count with them. But I, personally, can't rid myself of the conviction that it is inevitable that the army will strike at Rangoon soon. The Japs give no sign. Morose ones still morose, humane ones (for Japs) still humane (for Japs). If anything, Japs look a little more thoughtful. They still enforce their sense of superiority while we stand to attention as soon as we can recover from their blows, bow, and then say 'master' as we bow again. Of course, you salute if you can keep a cap on. The most insignificant of the Japs is still invincible in here. He has a rifle or a club and a key.

On my back naked in the sun today heard a/c high up . . . spotted it going S.W. at about 15/20,000 ft. No alert. No ack ack. But a/c too big for Oscar. I think it was Allied.

Quiz session and songs this week's show. Interest middling. Chaps prefer not to have to think. Some were even bad-mannered enough to leave during performances.

Ration of vegetables good if it is true, as Japs say, that they are for two days only. Our food is better now than we have ever had in here.

Beautiful, blue-torsoed lizard on our mango tree. They say this is the 'cuckoo, cuckoo' caller we hear each night. The sky is still storm-worried. About 5 pm air raid sirens. Hank Wilson commentating: 'The Ti's chair is out. Only his tin hat sits there yet. The M.O. has just dashed out brandishing his spear. There go the local alarm bells, an unidentified guard trots out, his rifle vertical in front of him (thunderclap sound effects). This is a great day, folks. I wish you were here. The daredevils have not appeared yet but here comes Weary Willie carrying his two satchels. Everything is tense. The spectators are nervously nibbling their rice. That's all. We'll now have some music.' Gus and Murph did not even lift their heads from over the chess board.

19 April

Last night cleared early of storm. Then things began to happen. Sirens announced a short air raid alert, then silence.

At 9.30 pm there was uncommon commotion and lights in Jap end of No 1 compound. After 20 mins 40 to 50 Japs marched out of the prison fully-kitted for field. We heard one phrase – a question – amid the babble: 'Messu toxon?' (plenty of water?). Shortly after they left we heard a burst of machine gun fire and some rifle shots. Rangoon dogs barked more . . .

After that I slept but I hear this morning that there was more commotion in Jap's quarters at 2 am and about the same time a white glare in the sky – not a searchlight – away to N.W. Someone else heard explosions and another dreamt of paratroops five times last night. All this builds up to . . . to what?

Perfect morning with ribs of colour touching up the clear sky. The working parties of prisoners went out into that other world as though nothing was happening there. I notice there are a few stranger Japs about this morning. Last night's arrivals?

Morning scene . . . nine men breaking up tobacco leaf in cell where five bar-marked sun splashes reach across from east side to wooden bars. Eight pounds leaf from Indians last night. Big parcel. Rs 60 worth of jagari, too. Note to me from B.Atar Singh written on back page of Bo Peep book for children saying only half tobacco demanded was received.

Breakfast late now since Japs have stopped us lighting fires for cooking before 6 am. Balcony gazing has been stopped, too, so now we watch movements in and out main gate and in store house from shadows inside building.

These 'stranger Japs' look travel weary.

I am making a strong point that everybody has to be ultra careful of this contraband tobacco. It must be concealed at all times in case of Jap search. If it was discovered that we were getting it from Indians we would cop the lot. Still, odd men are careless. Scores of pipes now being made from firewood.

20 April

Four months yesterday that I came down into captivity. Except for my cursed kneecap sliced in crash and still unhealed plus acute diarrhoea I am reasonably unaffected. Perhaps I am more bad-tempered but that is general.

Before-breakfast chess and then for the rest of the day is popular. There was a fillip of exercising this morning with an unusual number doing physical jerks in the yard. Needy cases, too.

Water buffalo slaughtered day before yesterday and two more today. Strong meat. Rations otherwise toxon. Biggest lump of meat ever today, most pumpkins for two-day period ever, bucketful of jagari today, too. Pinky says he threw in 8 lbs extra. Big bean-meat stew last night. Over-loaded stomachs too much for quite a number.

My six movements so far today record for me. Trace of blood again. Faced with decision whether or not to starve myself better . . . will decide tomorrow. M.O. maintains high degree of service . . . plenty of patient treatments today and then Yamamoto handed out cigs. Best regular medical treatment ever now. Japs showing common sense?

News today that Americans 60 miles up coast of Kurisha Is. (Japan) and that our army has broken thru 90 miles north of here. Anthony tells us that 30 new Japs moved in the other night.

No thunderstorms for two days now. Clear weather for anything – even a thrust south – and moon is growing nicely, thank you. Two alerts today – second time heard squadrons of a/c overhead. Boys saw three a/c unidentified.

I feel lousy . . . weak as a chicken . . . and I don't even feel like eating. Bad! More chili peppers today. Plenty lately. Practice is to boil them and make sauce. I give mine away. Here's the rice. My poor bloody stomach!

21 April

Cocoa and crumpets . . . lovely thought. It is early afternoon and thunderstorms just provided us with a bracing shower. High spirits . . . men cool and clean for first time for weeks . . . standing around drying off, skin tingling, smoking pipes and cigs, lively conversation. This is a change from blazing sun, sweating bodies, dirty skin. Last night it was too hot to sleep before midnight. The storm has passed on and the green scene thru the bars is yellowed again by sun. Trees look washed and I notice that bunches of red flowers on the acacia branches are bigger and redder. Aircraft above high up but no signs of ack ack.

Man from Leeds, England, squatting on floor in group on my right just said that he has lived there all his life and not once been to Bradford, seven miles distant. An Australian pilot is only man here who has seen Dickens' Curiosity Shop. Talk now about beer at Cheshire Cheese Inn where Shakespeare used to drink. None of the Englishmen present have seen the Tower of London . . . but they have seen Niagara Falls. One just said he will please his mother by telling her he's seen everything . . . whatever that means.

Bearden back in compound with depressing news of Burma campaign and the estimate that we won't be free for three months. How much can you trust a fellow who gets holidays away from the gaol courtesy the enemy?

Bearden thinks Roosevelt dead. He brought back with him this time three books . . . one by Agatha Christie called *Murder in the Mews* and another crime paper back. Third is J. A. Spender's *Short History of Our Times* which was intended for use as cigarette paper but I have had it reprieved. Surprising interest in the history book – crime novels overshadowed. 'Tear up crime novels for cigs' is cry. Anyway, I have organized communal reading of history book and week for week system of holding it. I read first chapter today and loved every word of it. History is going to be my forte when I get out . . . and that will not be in three months either. I consider Bearden to be our worst source of news in the circumstances.

Another bean meal tonight. Rations good again . . . vegetables galore. They are feeding us up for the kill . . . or something.

Bearden tells about a crazy inmate of the cell block. He sings all day and appears sublimely happy. Joe Wilson, our mental case, is unworried too.

One of the boys just said he supposes he will get married when he gets home if his girl still says 'yes' but he is not particular. It seems fairly general in here that the engaged men are not so keen to get married for a while. Yank just came into cell with his hair parted.

'First time for year,' he said.

My stomach is more settled today. Yesterday I had ten movements. I hope I can clear it up without the old starvation treatment. The Japs, annoyingly enough, are taking great pains to prepare for the monsoon season – building roofs, mending leaks and taking hygiene precautions. These incredible people. They go about so calmly . . . they don't show any signs that the near future will be different . . . they won't be 'master' any more. They're really digging in to stay. (Talk alongside me now on jobs after the war.)

22 April

Torrential rain thundering down. For an hour now there has been a full-dress rehearsal for the monsoon. This is more than the so-called 'mango showers'. Terrific thunderclaps . . . the yard below was at once a brown swirling lake . . . torrential rain driving thru the bars first from east and now from west. The wooden floor where we sleep is wet. Many took showers in the rain and are now exercising to get dry. In every mind is the thought that this bloody weather will hold up the rescuing army. This waiting, exasperating. Waiting day by day, week by week, waiting for just a sign from those poker-faced gaolers. The fear has crept into most hearts now that perhaps we won't get out until after the monsoon. There is a spasm of joking and high spirits but it is false and a little hysterical.

'As long as I'm out for Christmas nuts,' says one pilot.

Monsoon in here is not going to be fun. They say skin diseases are more rampant because of the humidity. Yet everybody seems strangely happy. It must be that it's an outlet to their nervousness at thoughts of future.

I was standing at the bars watching the downpour when the smell of lamb stew came to me . . . delicious . . . but it was from the Jap cookhouse. Anyway, food smells all I'm getting today, no food at all, starvation diet, and there was special chutney with the rice for breakfast. I feel feeble and have been horizontal all day. Last night was ordeal. I had 20 movements in 48 hours. Strings of red, green and yellow.

23 April

Odd alert, but nothing apparent. A dozen or so new Japs around prison today. Obviously raw recruits, a particularly sorry lot. All wore glasses and moved clumsily. Their rank tabs and stars looked new. It looks as though they have been recruited from Jap civilians in Rangoon. They stood in an amazed group and gaped as though we were pandas.

Some of the old guards got a new issue of shirts and breeches today. I have seen so much of their multiple-patched shirts of so many shades I was growing fond of them. At least their distinctive shirts were a means of identifying from behind the mean guards from the not-so-mean.

I still feel off colour but am eating again.

Strange cloud formation in S.E. this afternoon. Blue-black cloud tower with snow-white cloud as background. I could have sworn it was artificially formed but it could not have been bombardment smoke because, from that direction, it would have been meant invasion. Jap guard said thru fence 'Roosevelt dead . . . April 12 . . . no goodka.' He seemed sorry. My backside is itching to blazes.

24 April

My spirits won't stay down. At 9.30 pm last night a low flying a/c roared over W to E just south of the prison. It must have been within 600 yards of us. That's the closest I've been to a free man on our side for more than four months. Half minute later there was a cannon burst . . . looked as though he took a shot at something on the river. I could not sleep for my itching backside as I lay in my sweat-wet clothes, so I started thinking how that 'daredevil' could easily be from my own squadron. I might even know him. I might even have flown that a/c. It might be B for beer. And an hour, or less, from now that pilot will be drinking hot cocoa, at least, and eating bully beef sandwiches.

This morning's prison scene: Guards lackadaisical. There is the usual workaday morning atmosphere . . . breakfast is cooking, sujies are dicing up vegetables for tonight's soup . . . yard sweepers are swishing their bamboo brooms. There's somebody up our tree picking leaves for either binjo or to dry and blend with tobacco leaf. A special squad is digging two new holes for latrine. Dull morning.

Just after sunrise there was a purple mass of cloud slashed with pink in the east but now the sun is merely a brightness in the cloud. Half an hour ago there were three booms close by . . . explosions of some sort. A little later a volley of pistol shots rent the air. I thought I heard rat-tat-tat of machine-gun fire but it might have been someone chopping up vegetables.

Another pistol shot and a dozen Japs dressed in their battle best scurried out of their barracks in Chinese compound and thru main gate in twos and fours. They were from the new lot. That was all. The routine life carried on.

The pre-breakfast chess players remain crouched and concerned. Breakfast is ready. Here comes the rice and nuka.

The alarm for last night's intruder was given after the pilot had pressed the 'fire' button. Spears gleamed in the moonlight for a while then all clear. Another alert about 11 pm . . . more cannon fire. Indians next door gave us incredible news over the wall last night: Army only 30 to 40 miles away; Burmese National Army have revolted. They believe it, too.

What looks like a big oil fire is pouring up a great column of blue-grey smoke few miles north of here. Saboteurs? These bloody pistol shots have kept cracking away intermittently. Surely it's somebody keeping their eye in.

Two explosions shook building while we were having our dinner beans. One of the cooks said today: The army just has to be here tomorrow because tonight's bean soup was perfection and cannot be further improved. I dared not eat more than a few spoonfuls.

Smoke is rising from a fire in the east. Something untoward is happening down there with the Japs.

For the last half-hour Japs have been running out of the main entrance where they have their office carrying baskets filled with records or documents. There's a fire burning in the Jap's yard. (Ye Gods . . . stifle that imagination. It can't be about to happen.) But odd Japs are leaving their barracks heavy with kit and tottering out thru main gate.

An unprecedented pile of vegetables came in today . . . five baskets of celery (Burmese style). Also, four gross water buffaloes about to be slaughtered.

It is now tranquil late afternoon. Sky looks calm, strewn with white cloud. As I sit I can see the nearly full pale moon thru the bars waiting for nightfall. Last night's sunset had a piece of sky decorated with grey, curly Persian lamb's wool.

It's difficult to imagine that we are on edge of a big city full of people. It must have died.

Over the wall from Indians came copy of 'Greater Asia' dated April 14 (The 20th year of Showa 2605). The paper announces the sudden death of President Roosevelt on April 12 with the sub-heading 'Cause of Death a Mystery'. The Domei agency message is followed by a virulent attack on the President describing him as the greatest provoker of the war and the man most responsible for the great suffering of the world. The report says that rumours are rife that he was killed by some anti-war elements in U.S.A. It adds that prospects for conference of anti-axis countries in San Francisco on April 25 were gloomy.

Another article is headed: U.S. Political Crisis Bound to Worsen. Editorial: Wavell's conspiracy with Churchill. Inside report that Nainggandaw Adipadi had assumed post C-in-C Burmese Army. Refers to mutinous conduct of certain units of Burmese Defence Army (on Jap side) and threatens that anyone found helping them will be bombed or machine-gunned. 'All B.D.A. forces in districts being recalled' – in view of uncertainty and confusion.

Mention of profaneness to Pagoda shown by Prince of Wales in the Shwedagon Pagoda. And Thingyan water festival was 'gay and pleasant'.

And, oh yes, the editorial also made the statement that the occupation by the British army of some territories in Upper Burma had gained 'practically nothing'. Now that's comforting.

Yamamoto, M.O., did not show up today. First time for two weeks that he has missed alternate day.

It appears to me that the potential wealth of the thousand left in this prison is mind-boggling. Some have three years of accumulated pay awaiting them if we get freed. This is probably the richest concentration of people in Burma.

25 April

Even in the cool light of day last night's happenings are surely all that we have been so desperately awaiting. It has come! We do not know quite what it is but, at last, the poker-faced Japs have dropped the mask. Their faces and actions reveal that our days of Rangoon P.O.W. routine are numbered. A big event for us . . . the biggest in our lives, no less. This is the development we had to face. The last scene of the last act – or is it the last scene?

And still these amazing Japs keep up the suspense. We watched from balcony Japs scurrying about main building carting piles of papers towards the fire in their compound with suppressed emotions. We fought down our desire to shout but it just has to be the best sign yet. Then 'tenko'. A mild surprise . . . Funny Face, a corporal, took the parade. He was the one who was bitter sweet about the charcoal drawings on the wall of one of our cells. All I can say is that Napoleon must have had his manner as a corporal . . . glowering with importance. He was all dressed up in new clothes. As we strolled together around the water trough I felt a trifle self-conscious in my rags.

A whispered voice from the other side of the wall had told us the story so far: The Japs were burning records, medical and otherwise, and showed other definite indications that they were about to move. Either the Japs were evacuating Rangoon and/or Burma. The Emperor's soldiers had put their new clothing stocks on their backs and were throwing away old clothes. And . . . 200 men were to be taken away from here by Japs (nine officers). Yes, this is it for good or for bad. The ordeal is ahead for us.

A Burmese (Anthony), inmate of the Chinese compound, signalled with the aid of his fly swatter (sky writing) that we would be free in two days. The Indians thought we would be free by May 1. Excited discussion. The pregnant position was examined from every angle. Somebody recalled that no working parties had left the gaol today and we noted that work on the roof of the cookhouse had ceased. Yes, it was evident that the Japs were 'taking a powder', but, for the life of us, we could not see how we fitted into the picture.

Events of the night did nothing but fuel the fires of our imagination and curiosity. First, there was the celery, the prized celery. It was obvious that the entire garden had been stripped and there was no call for showering us with so much celery.

Soon a great cloud of smoke rose in the east . . . the crack of pistol shots continued. Smoke from another fire in the north pointed to fact that Japs were demolishing. Early in the evening an arch-shaped salmon-red glare filled half the sky, followed, in four or five seconds, by the roar of an explosion. That was south-east of us. There was the odd rifle shot in the distance.

The soldiers of Nippon kept busy scampering about the prison with their heads bent in concentration. Moonlight lit up the comings and goings of handcarts. Japs stood around with the general air of people all dressed up and packed waiting for the taxi to take them to the station. Many were flinging their unwanted equipment into a heap. It was all too much. Anybody will tell you that Japanese soldiers don't quit. They stay and fight to the death. What the hell??? My boys just dropped to the floor and pretended to sleep. There was nothing else to do.

Hours later – I carry on after a sickening interval. Those who got to sleep were soon awakened by explosions not far away and a cat giving a fearful scream. Then followed an hour of awe. There was a mighty rush of sound from the east and flashes against the clouds. The noise was like that which a thousand concrete mixers working at full tilt would make . . . a regular and tremendous cracking roar. It may have been caused by masses of steam escaping or something. We stood on the balcony, taking care to stay out of the moonlight, shaken and mystified. Soon we became accustomed to the roar and returned to our rice sacks still in a quandary. Heavy traffic was heard in the early hours of the morning.

We woke with questioning minds. What is happening? Only one thing was crystal clear: By now, Mountbatten and Slim and their beautiful boys, who were on their way to rescue us, just had to know that the enemy was scorching Rangoon and on the eve of leaving.

After all, we did have absolute air superiority and our intelligence people must have spies in Rangoon, surely. So, they could make their plans to rescue us.

'Tenko' was quite normal, however, and we bowed humbly when one of our masters appeared.

A score or so slobbering water buffaloes were driven into the prison and then a large number of pigs. Next, a herd of cows, some with calves at their heels. All was ready for the siege. Was the order from Tokyo that Rangoon Prison was to be held at all costs?

Pinky (our best source for 'good gen.') confirmed that 250, not 200, were going with Japs. Pinky appeared in good spirits. The funny thing is that although Pinky and I have been in close contact over the last few months I don't really know what he looks like. Our conversations are always furtive whispers from either side of a brick wall, never face to face. I have seen him in the distance from our balcony. I ache to really meet him. We all owe so much to him. He has smuggled to me most of the scraps of paper on which this diary is written. I asked him to put down something about himself on paper the other day. Over the wall came an amazing letter which started off: 'Dear Sir, I feel that it is not correct to call you Bill owing to circumstances which I will now relate. Who am I? A sergeant of the British Army who has twice escaped from the Nips. I was in the battle of France and came out via Dunkirk. . . .' It's a long letter . . . no space for it here. It ends: 'Have got a son now, 4-years-old but I have not see him since he was 5 months old and have not heard from home since I left there in '41. So you can bet I am looking forward to release with great impatience. Yours TAM.' The letter is written on blank spaces of three pages torn out of the front of a small book on Catholicism. I don't know the title but the preface was written at The Old Palace, Oxford, July, 1927. I don't know Pinky's name either. Just those initials TAM. I'll keep letter with diary.* Back to the drama . . . the Japs are still too busy to look up. They're packing all sorts of food and medical supplies on to carts. Somebodies are definitely going on a journey. But who?

'Wing Commander Hudson . . . Wing Commander Hudson.' That was the cry. I was wanted at the gate. Everybody stopped in

* See Appendix p. 219

their tracks and turned to watch as I made my way there, heart in mouth. Standing at the gate was Human Ape and he had in his hand the dreaded list. I was not surprised when he conveyed to me in gestures the question: Which men cannot walk?

26 April

Witness the date. I have not yet set down my troubled emotions of historic yesterday. At the time I felt so pent up with doubt, sadness and questions that I wanted to write my heart out but there was no opportunity.

Today, so far, I have been talking and laughing, living freely to a degree that I have not known for months, wandering joyously outside the walls of our compound and brushing past Japanese guards dressed as Nippon soldiers with not so much as a 'How do you do?', let alone a bow as has been my usual gracious custom. Overnight the situation has turned from a tense drama to a farce. All we need now to complete the scene is Gilbert and Sullivan's Koko to wander in singing 'Tit willow, tit willow, tit willow.'

But yesterday.

Heads were lifted in the groups dotted about the yard to hear me call for the cell chiefs. the officer i/c sick bay and my deputy commander.

The Ape was impatient and grunted disapproval while I took time off to explain to them the position. I was sick in the stomach and I felt myself shaking as I held up the list. My voice sounded strange and tremulous.

I turned and asked the Ape whether it was to be a long walk but he only grunted impatiently. I knew here was a ticklish decision to be made for every man. I went through the list with the various representatives – a red tick meant that a man was able to walk without discomfort. Those doubtful were left unticked.

Half of our 101 airmen were categorized as fit to walk. Then I sent the adj around the compound telling them that if they thought they had a reason for not being able to walk to come forward.

By this time the Ape was examining the unwalkables. They were called up, displayed their sores, wounds or explained other reasons. The Ape waved each one away with his head and noted something in Jap alongside the various names.

Half a dozen men we had classed as fit apparently impressed him they were not fit to walk. Several shammed sick to get on to the unfit list but I turned my head. After all they were chosing their own fate. Frying pan or fire . . . who knows?

Personally, I felt it was tempting fate to lie about it. I was among the walkers. I made that decision without hesitation. My diarrohea was on the mend and my damaged kneecap unpainful even though still unhealed. I could certainly walk better than most despite my slight limp. But anyway I wanted to go. I have never been able to risk the chance of excitement . . . for good or bad. Sucker! I did not really consider the consequences because it was quite firm in my mind: I wanted out. Also, things always turn out better when you give it a go. So I did. In the back of my mind was the idea that out on the road there would be escape chances. So started the turmoil, the questions and the preparations. Feelings were horribly mixed. To go or not to go . . . that was the question. The borderline cases could not decide. Speculation ran riot.

The most popular theory was that Rangoon was going to be defended and so, according to international law, prisoners o.w. would be moved to a sanctuary. This worried the sick. They had to stay for the battle and it looked as though the prison was being stocked as a strong point. As for the Japanese suddenly obeying international law as far as P.O.W's are concerned, to me, personally, that was a laugh.

Neither the Japs nor the fellows in the other compounds made even a trifling move without nervous observers giving a ball to ball description. News of any developments swept around like wildfire.

'Boys from No 3 are being given Jap clothing from the pile.' 'They're loading rice on to the carts.' 'There are strange Japs about.' 'Bloke from No 3 just gave thumbs up.' 'Pinky says the Big Ti has moved from his house into prison building.' 'Weary Willie is dressed up like a soldier . . . and with boots on.' 'Pinky says they're killing off the prison pigs.' 'All the old guards have rolled finger of rope hanging from their belts.' 'The Brigadier only has sandals on. He can't be going.' 'Carcases are coming out of the slaughter yard like a meat packer's dream.' 'All the meat is going into No 3.' 'There's a pile of Jap clothing outside No 3.'

The Ape had indicated he would return later. As usual we were at the end of the line. After all we are 'criminal prisoners'.

We waited . . . my stomach was frozen into a ball. I noticed a score or more fellows apart from those clustered around talking. They were just sitting or standing alone and gazing about vacantly. What was happening to those rosy dreams of going home?

Then there was a diversion, thank God, when a squadron of P 47 Thunderbolts came over high, attracted some intermittent ack ack from a battery near the gaol and then bombed something near the city docks. Their pilots went home happy judging from the great clouds of smoke that billowed up after bombs gone.

For the bombing I was in a trench near the fence. Some Japs went underground a few yards away. They popped up to ask what sort of a/c. I told them they were very friendly . . . made a noise like a machine gun and they laughed. This was something. These were not mean soldiers anymore. Surely that angured well for the trekking party?

Then the Ape called me to the fence. Who was next senior man to me? I told him Capt Hunt, the American pilot. 'Fetch him.' I did and stood there with him. I was ignored. Hunt was told to get his shirt on and go outside. He disappeared towards the main gate with the Ape. What in the hell was going on?

In the meantime, a pile of Jap rubber-soled canvas boots, old shirts, new underpants, old knee breeches and some coils of rope appeared outside our fence. It was soon brought in and those who were going on trek had their pick. The scenes that followed were hilarious. Cockney Sid Hill dressed as a soldier of Nippon caused a riot with his mimic of one of the guards. He shook a stick at the Indians who were watching from their windows. One by one the men appeared in their second-hand Nip clothes and each one prompted screams of laughter. It was like an artists' fancy dress ball, or dressing up on a rainy day as kids. There were even some thin, woollen blankets. The Jap creepers were unsuitable for walking so some of the sick boys staying put gave up their boots.

Four buckets of jagari came through the gate. These Japs were becoming overwhelming with their good treatment. Perhaps things were not so grim. A few of the chaps hung on optimistically to the hope that perhaps the Japs intended to march them to the British. I did not disillusion them! In fact, I was very worried. I hope it didn't show. I could not work out why I had been pushed aside. Did this mean that I was to be left behind? Hell! These Japs certainly have a faculty for intriguing one. Suspense to the last.

The pistol shots on the other side of the wall continued in occasional bursts startling our birds and it seemed appropriate when it rained.

Johnny Hunt came back . . . all the fit men, he said, were marching off at 4 pm. They were to carry their own kit and mess tins. The party would cook and take with it one meal in buckets.

Big Ti had done the briefing. The Brigadier and a Colonel from No 6 were there too. The trek was to be in three groups led by the Brigadier, the Colonel and Hunt. Our group would number about 70 which would include those now in the cell block.

Big Ti had been big enough to admit that 'we are moving because of the war' but went no further than that. The Ti going and the Brig going. Those going put a lot of faith into that.

But what about me? Hunt shrugged his shoulders? 'No mention,' he said.

The Ape came to the fence again and I passed the word around that anybody having second thoughts about going should grab this chance if they wanted to impress the Ape that they will not be able to cope. One man complained of rheumatism and his name was crossed off the list. M/Sgt Montgomery was still among the walkers but he reminded the Ape about his amputated arm, the stump of which is still unhealed, and off came his name. Others tried but our friend just turned his back and walked off.

In a flash he was back . . . impatiently asked for a typist. In came a typewriter and then followed a host of instructions. He wanted two lists – those going, those staying. I grabbed the original list, ran down it searching for my name. There it was . . . with a mark like an 'o' alongside it.

I turned to the Ape and said 'Am I not going?' He shook his head, eyed me queerly and pointed to my bandaged knee. Good God! It was my turn to shake my head.

'Okay,' I said. 'Very good.' I flexed my bad knee and then hopped around on that foot. 'Okay,' I insisted.

'You trouble-maker,' he hissed and stormed off.

I was stunned. Obviously, he had special orders concerning me. Ye Gods! Singled out again. Was it for some special torture? These Japs are grand masters at the art of keeping you guessing. I promise myself to read a Japanese mystery story after the war. It should keep one on edge.

I am disgusted at being dropped. I badly wanted to get out of here, whatever. Now I'm just one of the mob on the wharf holding a streamer in one hand and a return suburban train ticket in the other . . . hate farewelling travellers.

We had a quick lunch, then the cooks turned to preparing the meal for the road. Rain is falling heavily.

The departing men wrote telegrams for the others to despatch 'just in case' they don't make Calcutta first. Nobody has mentioned the word 'hostages' which is clearly what they are.

Fifty-two men are going, forty-nine staying. The atmosphere is morbid.

Then the cry went up 'Here come the guys from the cells.' Into the air force compound came the pale and rough-bearded men from solitary and there was excited talk for half an hour while we pumped news out of them. These men, recently captured, had news of the outside world.

I discovered from a Beaufighter pilot, S/Ldr Fenton, that it was known that I was a P.O.W. A captured Jap had told the British. I did not know whether to be glad or sorry at this news. My people would be worrying like hell. It was well known that being a prisoner of the Japs was no picnic.

Soon there was a scene in our yard like a continental railway station with Japs fussing about and eventually getting things straight. In front of the line were four tall buckets of steaming soup, two of sweet rice and one of jagari. The sixteen fresh from the cells had joined our lot.

They stood there in the teeming rain for 15 minutes. As I moved among them saying goodbye I told them that if we made first contact with our forces we would get the message to the air force that the walkers would identify themselves to Allied a/c by taking off hats and raising their arms horizontally. There was a remote chance that this would serve a purpose but what the hell! You had to say something. After all, many of our fellows were in Jap clothing and it would be hard for a pilot on a straffing run to pick them as Caucasians.

We had sad hearts when they marched out, surprisingly cheery, and facing the unknown like that takes guts. They are gallant men. There had been a final prayer meeting upstairs unknown to the Japs.

I watched the parade out of the prison from the balcony. First, an advance party of Japs, then the large British Army group led by a colonel. It was all very casual. The procession was punctuated here and there by a Jap guard or two, rifles shouldered with bayonets fixed. Each group was followed by heaped-high hand carts pulled and pushed by six to eight men . . . Retreat from Rangoon . . . a handful of Japs with 400 British and American hostages on foot . . . what chance did they have of avoiding the war machine that was the 14th Army?

The towering Brigadier was a glad sight. He marched erect and brisk ahead of his company. He and most of his men had been in captivity for more than three years.

Somehow the Japs had the look of serious little boy scouts except that the N.C.O Japs stood around haphazardly nursing sub-machine guns. There were no spears.

Our component of the column were a motley crew garbed in a mixture of Japanese army, American and British air force clothing. When they came into view they were marching exuberantly – nearly a goose step. I wanted to shout and wave but just stood there with my fingers crossed. By this time I think most of us realized the marchers had a tough time ahead of them. Some of our chaps had part bags of rice to carry. Others pushed barrows. There'd be no future for stragglers . . . those who could not keep up. They passed out of sight into the main archway and we turned to the comparative emptiness of our cells. At least the others were on the outside. We'd be trapped here in this cage while the opposing forces fought over Rangoon.

Supper of rice and celery was hard to serve because most of the buckets had gone with the column. It stuck in the throat a bit, too. Most of our jagari, salt and cigars went with them, too, but nobody begrudged this an atom. I started my meal in the sick bay but I could not stand the small talk, half light and gloom.

I fled upstairs, unhungry for food but craving a talk with a woman. I sat alone and thought things out. It was almost serene. Then I heard an a/c, ran to the balcony to see a Beaufighter come from west to east over the river. At this instant the rockets flashed off and the crumff followed. I hoped and prayed it was not the P.O.W. column. It will be lucky if it gets away without a strafe from our ground attack a/c.

That night was a restless one. Men went to the sack early to try and stop thinking. I noticed the men around me lay awake and were up and down like yoyos to scan the skyline for more fires. There was one in the east early and every time I woke (and it was quite frequent) I heard either an explosion or a rifle shot. It was clear that the Japs were demolishing and the rifle shots a sign that looters needed to be kept in check. Rangoon certainly looked like becoming a hot spot with us in the thick of it.

Sick of the uncertainty of it all, I tried to channel my mind into more peaceful thoughts. I tried to picture picnics I'd been on . . . with Mary in Kashmir . . . with that girl at Victoria Falls, Southern Rhodesia . . . but it didn't work. Every time I found myself back in Rangoon, Burma . . . wondering!

The cattle inside the prison were lowing because they were thirsty. Poor devils . . . they'd been forgotten in all the panic.

27 April

I awoke peaceful. What was the point of worrying anyhow about the why and the wherefore of the marching column? I even felt quietly confident . . . perhaps the freshness of the morning, clean after the rain, the buoyancy of the birds and that church steeple cross, brave against the misty sky, had something to do with it.

It turned out to be comedy all day and we made the most of it. (The war was a thousand miles away). Our old guards had been real soldiers. These new guardians were obviously raw recruits and, it seemed, with malice towards none. They were polite, but clumsy. Their uniforms were new and they wore flashy shoes. Our guess was that they had been civilians in Rangoon who'd been given guns. They were holding the baby while the regulars saved their own necks. They slumped around with a don't-care attitude and they didn't care if you bowed to them or not. We laughed as they shuffled in a daze through a change of the guard. This life has taught us to be opportunists above all.

So we set to work. Like a flash we were upstairs on the hitherto forbidden section of the balcony, unwinding the wire that held the gate shut. Previously, we had not been allowed to use the front upstairs cell or balcony because it was easy to signal Nos 3 and 6 compounds from there. An emergency sweeping party soon had this part of the building shipshape and the men were wandering up and down as though it was ever so.

Obviously the prison staff had marched off without giving the fresh troops a clue on how to manage we war criminals. Our gate was opened to allow us to carry water – unprecedented – and then it was left open. This was too much. We streamed out to the well in the centre of the prison and wandered into the other compounds at will. There were knots of fellows all over discussing the situation. The guards stood there self-consciously as though they were intruding. We carried a week's supply of wood from No 3 compound which was now empty.

There were 117 men left in No 6 compound of whom 50 were not really sick. We talked to these fellows who had been our silent neighbours for so many months . . . and we had lots to talk about.

They, too, had no idea where the walking column was heading but feared the way would be both dangerous and arduous. Most certainly eastwards, we all agreed. Big Ti had told the Indians that the Japanese would guard them well until British came. They supported our theory that these Japs with us now had been, until very recently, civilians.

It was strange talking to these long-term prisoners who knew so little about what had been going on outside for two and three years.

I was disappointed to hear that F/Sgt Harvey Besley, a fellow Australian pilot who was with me on No 11 RAF Blenheim Squadron on my first tour of operations, had walked off. It would have been great to have a chat with Harvey. Last time I saw him before catching a glimpse of him in the prison five months ago had been when he was dangling from a parachute over Meiktila in Central Burma.

The army prisoners had been left in the charge of a captain who had been shot in the mouth three-plus years ago. He was one of the first prisoners to be captured by the Japs in Burma.

One exciting event: Four of our men taking the rubbish and bingo tins out to be emptied were taken outside the . . . wait for it . . . thru the main gate, skirted the wall for a mile or so and eventually dumped it. They went with some fellows from No 6 and a couple of guards tagged along. On return they told a thrilling tale about the outside world. First thing they saw was a car loaded with six Japs and heaps of equipment careering along the road. A Burmese was walking along the road carrying a spear . . . another pedalled past them on a bicycle with a whispered aside: 'Two days'.

The guards did not pay much attention to the dumping party apart from slipping bullets up the spouts as a warning that they should not try anything silly.

Pistol and rifle shots continue to ring out all day and we still don't know the targets. Every now and again there's an explosion in the distance and smoke from fresh fires in the north.

We laugh at the absurdity of the situation . . . an Indian prisoner brandishing a shiny, silver revolver and shouting 'Toxon Nippon'.

At morning 'tenko' I handed the sgt a note asking that an Indian doctor be allowed to give our sick chaps medical treatment. Later I was told that this had been arranged . . . but he did not come. Then I heard that there was still in No 6 a doctor major.

An Indian interpreter (Madrasi prisoner) was almost running the place. He asked for our rations requirements. I wrote down everything . . . cigars, soap, sugar . . . luxury items.

Highlight of the day was collecting the rations ourselves from the storehouse. We sauntered about and talked to the other ration parties. I had a chance to thank Babu Atar Singh, a modest elderly Indian from Meerut, who hung his head shyly as I told him that a lot of the airmen would not have made it this far without the the smuggled food and inspiration from the Indian compound.

We were handed out ample supplies of pumpkin, potatoes, squash, marrow, fish, sugar, oil, salt . . . and when we told them it would not last a week the sharp, little, grocery boy-type Jap said to let him know if we ran out of anything.

When the Indians went to collect their wood they raided the jack fruit trees and the guards did not seem to mind. These fellows must have read the Geneva Convention.

Most of the morning there were a/c recces overhead high up. Those pilots up there could really see what was going on.

For a change of scene we had lunch upstairs in the newly-taken-over cell . . . bamboo tables we had put together loaded with goodies and a view. How about that? It was a jolly meal but supper was a feast. We had grilled steak, soup thick with meat and rice. Obviously

Sgt Edwards, B 29 gunner from New York State, was a good appointment as new boss cook. He has a few officers and NCOs under him. Eddie and his father back in the States are clam bake, chicken fry, fish fry specialists and now he is putting all his skill and experience into pleasing our palates. He's really enthusiastic.

It's already obvious that we can take over from his vulnerable bunch of Japs when the time is right. They are taking great pains not to ruffle us. They are out to please. It might be handy to take over the prison before the arrival of our troops as long as we have an indication as to the situation outside. How many Japs are left in Rangoon? Are they fortifying it? Surely they'll defend the place? One thing . . . we have nothing to fear from our hosts.

All this points to fact that I should endeavour to combine the blokes in the two European compounds so as we'll have all the fit men concentrated in case something happens. There could easily be mean Japs abroad against whom we might have to protect ourselves. Survival is the thing.

In the afternoon, Major McCloud, a British Army medical officer, who has been hampered in his doctoring over the last two years by failing eyesight, called on me from No 6. He proposed that we try to move to No 6 where there was a hospital established to make it easier for him to supervise treatment and nursing. He also thought that by pooling our rations we can eat better. I agreed with hesitation and wrote a note to the O.C. Rangoon P.O.W. camp putting the case to him.

The Major looked at our patients and gave F/Lt Emeny some advice on how to treat certain cases. I should record here that Cliff Emeny. New Zealand pilot who used to be a farmer, was fit enough to walk out of this place with the others but he volunteered to stay behind to look after our sick. He deserves a medal for the devotion he's put into this thankless task.

Some cigars came over as a present from No 6. We have salvaged a rice grinder for making rice flour from No 3 compound. It is proving invaluable.

Today has been just a series of memorable sensations for me. I've had soap in my eyes, sugar in my tea, real tooth powder on my teeth and have used paper and not leaves at the toilet. I had not experienced any of these wonderful things for nearly five months.

A beautiful fire just north of the prison last night lit a large space of the sky with red. I stood on the front balcony and watched the mass of flame shooting upwards spangled by sparks and glinting the golden pagoda which reaches upwards away to the NNW. This must be the famous Shwedagon Pagoda. We had not been able to see the top of the pagoda before we opened up the front section yesterday. Fancy that . . . I've been in the city of Rangoon for almost five months without setting my eyes on the historic landmark.

The fire burned merrily for some time and gladdened our hearts. How can one be so happy about a city being destroyed all around you? Well, we were. There were more explosions and rifle shots during the night but by morning it was peaceful again.

At present there are three big fires burning in the south. The Japs are certainly scorching Rangoon before handing it over to the Allies. An hour ago ash from a big blaze was falling in the prison yard like snow. The occasional rifle fire still startles us but we don't remark about the explosions any more.

This has been a gala day as far as food is concerned. We had minced chitlings with our rice and nuka this morning and fresh carrots with rich soup and rice for lunch. The sujis have been grinding rice for flour all day so dinner promises to be special. This is grand living. It won't be such fun to get out now . . . but all this high living brings to our minds those poor blokes on trek. I pray they're all right.

Things have settled down and it's obvious now that we are not to be given the key to the prison to enable us to come and go as we wish. The Japs have orders to tighten on our roamings and are now keeping our gate locked. A number of the guards speak English and are trying to be helpful.

A thick set Jap Lt. has become commandant of the prison. He called to see me without a by-your-leave and pointed out that it was against the rules to allow this compound to combine with No 6 but that he would arrange for an Indian doctor to treat our sick daily. He asked whether the food was sufficient. I had to admit that it was. Also, he wanted to know where I was captured. I said near Mandalay. He asked, 'Did you come down through the atmosphere?' I said no. I had crashed. I impressed upon him that we were a very sick lot in here. As we spoke two of our worst cases passed carrying water. He told them to put down the buckets and rest and indicated he would get the Indians and Chinese to do the heavy work for us.

The doctor did not arrive so I complained to the O. Sgt at 'tenko'.

Exciting raid today . . . a/c coming out of the N.E. in waves of three and at about 2/3,000ft RAF Libs bombed somewhere about a mile N. of the centre of the city, turned steeply before reaching the prison and swung away to the S E. Thick, but wildly fired, ack ack marked the sky as these heavies lumbered out of range. Libs so low is surprising and also, too, is the fact that there are so many ack ack guns left in Rangoon.

A truck loaded with rifles and ammo belts stood inside the prison all day and we did not like it a bit. Another truck arrived late in the afternoon, arsenal transhipped and away it went. Obviously, they realize that the prison is a safe place from the bombing.

There were signs of a big fire in the south during the afternoon and by nightfall it had grown to a huge blaze. Just after dark bangs from explosions in the fire were heard. They became more and more frequent . . . Guy Fawkes night . . . some shook the prison buildings. At midnight explosions were still popping. It must have been munitions of some sort. There was another orange glare in the north. Sporadic rifle fire continued during the night and there were occasional bursts of sub-machine-gun fire. We take all this firing as matter of course now. Wonder what's happened to the local population. Have they fled? Rangoon is dying.

28 April

It amazes me how we have slipped back into a humdrum routine already despite the momentous happenings of the last three days. This morning people are not agog anymore.

The commandant appeared at 'tenko'. He is a heavily-jowled Jap, quite unsoldierly. His trousers, new and purple braided, hang untidily. He understands and speaks English fairly well but when you speak to him his face is a blank and very disconcerting. I complained about no medical treatment again. He said he would consider. Ack ack for breakfast.

Our compound gate is locked again and the Chinese are carrying for us once more. We are not permitted outside as are the Chinese,

Indians and even the other compound with white prisoners. We are still the bad boys but, anyway, we had the acute pleasure of one day with an open gate.

The commandant has done nothing about regular medical treatment for this compound. It's a week now since our sores and wounds were dressed but F/Lt Emeny has kept a lot of the jungle sores and rabies in check with hydrogen sulphide and carbolic acid solution. From our secret stock we are now using sparingly odd bits of soap to wash down tracts of diseased skin. It's proving invaluable. There would be far more suffering here if it were not for our bush nursing.

Kandy, Ceylon April 28, 1945
Headquarters SACSEA

Meanwhile, with the fate of Rangoon (and ours with it) in the balance, the man we were depending on to rescue us, Admiral Lord Louis Mountbatten, is making an entry in his personal war diary on this most critical day:

28 April

Today I had symptoms which appeared to me to be either bacillic or amoebic dysentery. I reported to the doctors at once and they diagnosed it as amoebic dysentry.

As luck would have it, Brigadier Hamilton Fairley, one of the world's greatest authorities on tropical diseases, both in Bombay and London, and who is now in the Australian Army, came to have lunch with me on his way to Australia.

He immediately volunteered to stay and look after me which turned out to be a very lucky thing for him later on, as he himself had to retire to bed.

I accordingly called together all the senior members of my staff and informed them that I was retiring to bed to be treated for amoebic dysentery but that I would retain command and continue to hold the more important meetings in my bedroom and would be available on the scrambler telephone at any time.

That would have been disturbing news for us prisoners left behind in Rangoon Gaol and wondering what was coming next, but if we had been aware of two other communications dealt with that day at HQ SACSEA we would have been really alarmed.

One was a signal from the 14th Army front reporting that troops driving south towards Rangoon had encountered stiff opposition immediately south of the 62nd milestone. (62 miles away . . . ye gods.)

The other was a signal to London outlining a top secret appreciation of the situation prompted by the fact that the tempo of operations in the Pacific was faster than had been expected. It examined means of expediting the capture of Singapore.

The whole plan was based on the assumption that Rangoon would be captured by the end of May . . . END OF MAY!

Our hearts would have sunk to our filthy toes at that prediction by the top brass. In fact Lieutenant-General Kimura, Mountbatten's opposite number had fled from Rangoon five days before, on 23 April!

I keep worrying about some of the walking column. Some of those boys, although fit on the surface, are not strong.

The Indians shouted across today that the walking column had not yet left Rangoon. It is possible that they are awaiting boats or that their getaway has been cut off. They may be back . . . I hope, I hope.

Rangoon is being razed all around us. Every hour we see the tell-tale smoke of a new fire. In towards the centre of the city this morning blue-grey smoke belched in clouds from a blaze to the accompaniment of booms from explosions. There have been bursts of machine-gun fire but rifle fire has eased off. Apart from yesterday's daring Liberator raid the sky has been clear of a/c. I cannot understand why unless this grey weather is scaring them off. Perhaps the pilots have reported in their debriefings that Rangoon is being demolished by the Japs and the policy is not to lend a hand.

Naturally, I want to know just what the Japs intend to do about Rangoon. Will they defend it? Knowing that would make my decisions here so simple to make.

Yesterday's toxon ack ack does not tell me anything because the heavy guns would be hard to shift in the circumstances. I feel the Japs have already evacuated as much as possible but nobody can be sure that many of the Japs now at the front won't fall back here because they may be cut off and have no other place to go.

I had a brief talk today with the captain in charge of No 6. The left side of his mouth has been shot away and he has difficulty just talking. He seems a pleasant type. I told him about my desire to get our force concentrated and he agreed.

The rations today were good again. We have enough rice now to last us for a fortnight. We received the head and entire middle portion of a water buffalo (that's how the son of a Northampton butcher here with us described it). We will have to eat meat three times a day for the next two days.

The excitement of the approaching day of moment has simmered down and now all hands are engaged somehow or other on preparing our three feasts a day. There is an incredibly happy atmosphere. Food works wonders. Also, the boys from No 6 sent over 70 cheroots and the Indians cigarettes. Smoke is still rising over a large area down town. The Japs just stand there unmoved and showing no signs of emotion. They won't even look up at the smoke. This is a ridiculous situation. If I only knew for sure that our forces were within 100 miles of here.

Three rifle shots just rang out . . . another and another. Just what is going on? Last night at about 9pm there was another of those mysterious roars. It came from the south and sounded like several hundred invasion craft coming up the river. Then it stopped suddenly. Take a grip, Hudson.

29 April

I have just been told the story of how General Chi died. General Chi was the pleasant and polite, very cultured little Chinese general who was murdered on the compound stairs of No 1 block. He was stabbed and died days later.

The General was captured about three years ago while floating down the Chindwin River with a small staff trying to locate his division headquarters from which he had been cut off during the withdrawal from Burma.

He was a prize prisoner because he was married or related to one of the Pao sisters, one of whom was Madame Chiang Kai-shek.

From the beginning the Japs tried their hardest to persuade the General to join the Nanking National Government but the little general was staunch.

The Japs disliked him for it and on one occasion the Jap commandant of the gaol at the time asked him for his reasons. The polite, little celestial wrote a thesis on the subject with unbridled conviction and sent it to the Ti. After that the Japs did not attempt to conceal their hatred. The cultured General, who had been educated in an American military academy, was put on fatigues and working parties like a coolie but, it seems, he took all this pleasantly enough.

When the Captain became Commandant a year or more ago he ordered that the General be taken off working parties and allowed to remain in his compound cell block, but the Japs generally despised him.

In the Chinese compound was a small group consisting of several officers and some other ranks who had surrendered to the Japs with their arms which is an offence punishable by death in China. Naturally, there was a schism in the compound with this party antagonistic towards the General and his supporters. Also, they must have been somewhat apprehensive about their future.

On more than one occasion differences arose and the General flung their disloyalty at them, threatening courts martial when they returned to China.

The bad feeling intensified. Twelve days before the murder a kitchen knife disappeared from the cook house. During this period the murderer-to-be sharpened this knife to perfection. On the night of the stabbing he furtively slipped to the NCO of the guard a note which, I am reliably told, disclosed to the Japs his plan to kill the General that night. The Japs did nothing.

Early in the evening the General was walking down the stone steps to the yard. It was a dark, moonless night. There was a figure on the stairs. As the General made to brush past a knife was plunged into his thigh, whipped out and then sunk into his abdomen. The General tried to grab his assailant but sank on to the steps. His attacker ran to the gate screaming, 'I have killed him, I have killed him . . . now do what you like.'

The Japs put the knife man into the solitary cells block but there was no indication that he was in disgrace. It would seem he was put there for his own protection.

The Indian doctors were called. They feared that the abdomen wall had been opened but could do nothing by lantern light except to give him morphia.

Next morning when they were allowed to see him it did not take them long to discover that only an immediate operation would save his life.

They told the Japs and asked that Colonel Mackenzie, the British Army surgeon, be consulted.

That fat and sodden Japanese lieutenant who called himself a doctor went to Col. Mackenzie and asked him through the fence whether he would operate. The Colonel asked whether he could see the patient first or consult with the Indian doctors. The Jap said 'No'. Colonel then asked whether he could have chloroform for anaesthetic. Jap said 'No' and then walked off impatiently. He's reported to have said that the English Colonel had refused to operate.

The Jap doctor inserted a drainage tube but peritonitis had set in. The Indian doctors asked for saline but it was refused.

'Do not worry about him,' he told them. 'It does not matter if he dies. He is my responsibility.'

Before this Colonel Mackenzie was allowed to see the General. He did what was possible but could not operate abdominally without anaesthetic. Of course, the General died.

The Japs saw that the murderer was cared for properly and were very wild when he made an unreasonable complaint to them about not getting enough rice. They moved him to the solitary cells near the chapel.

When the Japs walked off the other day they took with them the killer of the General, dressed him in a Jap uniform and gave him everything but a rifle. Buddies. He was the only Chinese to go.

The bad feeling remains in the Chinese compound. Those who supported the dead General live in fear of their lives. They are a menace to the future of those who are facing courts martial. The patriots lock the door of their cells at night and take turns to sit up two at a time throughout the night on guard. There are about ten in each faction. The other 30 are indifferent. Chinese had a poll to decide C.O. of compound. One of the rebel party elected.

So much for the play within the play . . . what's happening in the war outside the walls?

30 April
Dawn is breaking on a 'No Man's Rangoon'.

The Japs have left (I think), the British have not arrived (as far as we know) and the Burmese must have taken to their heels (surely). That deduction leaves me Emperor of Rangoon.

I am free, too, but I don't feel a thing – except impatience at daylight being so long in coming.

The birds are beginning to squawk a little and soon I will not need the light of these five flickering candles that are spreading grease over the prison commandant's table forming an ice flow. A Japanese doll is raising dainty hands in the centre of the table. Half a bottle of saki is on one side of her, a cactus in a pot on the other. The boys have just brought in a bucket of tea.

This day is a frightening one. Anything may be in store for us. All is still now after several hours of frightening explosions that came from a fire to the east of the gaol.

Calm men sit about talking normally. One army Lt. just asked another browsing thru an encyclopaedia to look up a bishop's salary. Never has there been a stranger situation.

Birds are noisier so daylight is not far off.

I have locked the prison gate from the inside but before I did I pulled it ajar and stood and looked out on freedom. It thrilled me, too. The moon was there high in the sky and all was quiet.

The incredible Japs kept up their pretence to the last. Tenko was as ever – the same old routine – except that the sgt was a stranger and looked more like a soldier than our other custodians. He had several hand grenades stuck in his belt.

I complained that the food and bingo buckets had not arrived. The interpreter told the Japs and suggested he could fetch them now. The sgt said 'Tomorrow'.

We had a church service near the water trough and I went up to sleep quite early. I remember hearing a commotion down near the main gate but did not bother to investigate.

'Shoto' was accentuated by the Japs now that I come to think about it. And this was the first time for days that they had worried to tell us to sleep and keep quiet.

I lay on my bag talking for half an hour when I saw a reflection of a fire. I walked to the balcony to see a smallish fire just outside the gaol near the main gate. The Jap section of the gaol was suspiciously quiet. I had remembered the truck moving off. Some intuition, or

162

was it the extraordinary stillness, told me that something strange was in the air.

I went to the front balcony and could not find a guard. I waited for ten minutes but no guard. This was extraordinary.

I wandered about a bit, then started whistling and talking to the Chinese and Indians who were also aware that something was amiss.

I could contain my impatience no longer. I leapt up on to the wall and fell into the laneway. No bullets!

I tried to talk to the Chinese who started to dribble out. I talked with No 6 boys. Note. Booby traps? Indian doctor, Capt Thomas. Candles. Foreboding main gate. Dark and sinister.

The advice from the cautious was to return to our beds and sleep. Leave it until morning.

Oh no! Was I free or not?

Capt Thomas . . . adventure . . . here goes. Led party up the lane. Inner gate locked. Thomas scaled up into building and let me in. Chang Kun Chung – General's killer.

Two notes, or letters, neatly written in English, were left behind by our former hosts.
One read:

Rangoon
29 April, 1945

Gentlemen,

Bravely you have come here opening prison gate. We have gone keeping your prisoner safely with Nipponese knightship. Afterwards we may meet again at the front somewhere. Then let us fight bravely each other. (We had kept the gate's keys in the gate room.).'

Nipponese Army

The other I found at the main gate of the gaol:

Rangoon
29 April, 1945

To the whole captured persons of Rangoon Jail. According to the Nippon military order, we herby give you liberty and admit to leave this place at your own will. Regarding food and other materials kept in the compound, we give you permission to consume them, as far as your necessity is concerned.

We hope that we shall have an opportunity to meet you again at battlefield of somewhere.

We shall continute our war effort eternally in order to get the emancipation of all Asiatic Races.

Haruo Ito
Chief Officer of Rangoon Branch Jail.

Tokyo
22 April, 1985

'Mr Ito?'

'Mr Hudson?'

We meet again after forty years, not on a battlefield but in the backslapping foyer of the opulent New Otani Hotel here in Tokyo. The handshake is warm and we both laugh at the absurdity of the situation. I feel instant camaraderie.

Mr Ito's striped blue suit stamps him as a man of substance. He shuffles out three cards which announce that Haruo Ito is Counsellor for the Kikko Foods Corporation, Auditor of Mann's Wine Co. Ltd., Counsellor, Japan Amateur Association, Chairman, Hitotsubashi University's Veteran Rowing Association and President of the Japan Oarsmen Club.

The media is with us. I had sent ahead to the Mainichi Daily News *a copy of the letter he left behind for the prisoners in Rangoon Gaol saying my wife and I would like to get together with this Japanese Army officer.*

We walk in the hotel garden and, predictably, are photographed together on a traditional curving bridge.

Mr Ito chuckles.

'I feel like a film star,' he says.

He comes with me to our room in the tower to meet my wife, Audrey. We have a beer.

'That night,' he says. 'When did you know we had left? When did you know you were free? We crept away just before midnight. I remember it was the Emperor's birthday.'

He tells us how he was recruited with all the other Japanese civilians under 45 in Rangoon during March and April and put into uniform.

He knew about the evacuation of the city on April 26.

'*We were the very last troops to get out of Rangoon,*' *he says.* '*There were sixty of us but only 17 survived the march through the jungle to Moulmein.*'

I ask about Captain Tazumi Motozo, commandant of the gaol before he took over.

Mr Ito lights up another Chesterfield and his lips tighten around the cork tip.

'*Did he survive?*' *I persist.*

'*I don't know,*' *says Mr Ito.* '*I never met him.*'

I wonder.

III

The Evacuation and After

The 'mango showers' sweep out of the vast Bay of Bengal at the same time each year as April turns to May and the fruit on the massive mango trees ripen. Then, in the second week of May, invariably on cue, cyclonic storms generate in the intense heat and the remorseless south-west monsoon swiftly blankets Bengal and Burma. The rains have come and they last through October. Life becomes sluggish in the towns and villages of Burma. Travelling, playing, plantings, weddings – no plans are made at all that do not take into full account the flooding monsoon deluge and the inevitable mud.

So, early in April, 1945 as the battle lines for Rangoon were being drawn no factor was more in the minds of the commanders on both sides than the menace of the monsoon.

Pushing on after punishing victories in Central Burma, General Slim's Fourteenth Army was still 300 miles short of Rangoon with thirty days to go before the scheduled arrival of the monsoon. The Japanese forces were clearly in disarray but with the suicide resistance they had shown at Meiktila and Pyawbe they could still deny Rangoon to the Allies for months as long as they held out until the rains came.

Slim freely admits he was haunted by the prospect of being stranded in the mud short of Rangoon with no supplies. His forward troops were already on half rations. Once the weather closed in air drops would become extremely difficult. Anyway, the Americans were adamant they would be withdrawing their Dakota transport squadrons by June 1, at the latest, for operations in China.

At Slim's headquarters they had dubbed the two-pronged south-ward thrust Operation SOB – Sea or bust. Without the port of Rangoon by the monsoon they would have to retreat. Disaster.

In London, Prime Minister Churchill was demanding the early capture of Rangoon at all costs because General Marshall had indicated that a good deal of American aid would be withdrawn once the monsoon began.

Also, Mr Churchill described as 'chilling' the fact that any hold-up in the capture of Rangoon 'would delay operations against Malaya on which both the United States and ourselves are relying to relieve the rubber shortage.'

Mountbatten's Army Commander-in-Chief, Lt.-General Sir Oliver Leese, was to write later: 'I could not contemplate with anything but dismay a repetition of the Meiktila battle around Rangoon at the end of a precarious supply line in the midst of rain.'

On 17 April, as a desperate measure, Mountbatten went firm on Operation Dracula, an amphibious and airborne assault on Rangoon from the south. This plan had been shelved earlier as, among other things, too hazardous. The weather was the main enemy at this time of the year, not the Japanese. Tidal conditions were most difficult and it was not possible for the fleet to come in close enough to shore to provide naval gunfire support. Also, known Japanese gun positions on both sides of the river threatened the landings.

With Slim's overland thrust held up south of Meiktila, Mountbatten had no alternative but to gamble on a scaled-down version of the original Dracula. He immediately flew to Meiktila himself to stress how vital was the need to capture the airfield at Toungoo within a week to ensure close air support for the amphibious landings. He told 4 Corps commander, Lt-General Sir Frank Messervy, he would personally take responsibility for his getting up to 3,000 men killed in an attempt to speed up the advance.

The capture of Rangoon before the rains had over-riding priority.

Both Mountbatten and Slim were facing up to a typically Japanese last-ditch stand in Rangoon with an estimated 40,000 fanatical defenders and Field-Marshal Terauchi, who commanded from remote Saigon all Japanese troops in South-East Asia, was grimly willing to accommodate them. His 'hold to the death' type message sent to Rangoon had the authority of Imperial General Headquarters in Tokyo and was expected to be carried out in the same glorious spirit of sacrifice which, at that very moment, was inspiring the kamikaze pilots to make their death dives on the United States warships around Okinawa.

However, Lt-General Kimura Hyotaro, Commander-in-Chief of the Burma Area Army, who had been Vice Minister of War under General Tojo at the outbreak of war, had other ideas. On 22 April he ordered that Rangoon be abandoned and flew off himself next day to Moulmein, near the border with Siam, leaving what was left of his 100,000 strong army to get away from the oncoming British as best they could. It was so contrary to the accepted Japanese 'divine wind', fight to the death, tradition that Mountbatten, Slim and the men around them were all fooled. Their conviction that Rangoon was to be a last-ditch stand was hardened when the forward units of the Fourteenth Army ran into stiff opposition on the outskirts of Pegu, 50 miles north of Rangoon on April 29. The tenacious enemy was going to resist doggedly all the way. Then the rains came. They had lost the race to Rangoon.

Of course, they did not know that the force blocking their way in Pegu was the Rangoon defence force, a mixed brigade of odds and sods, many of them civilians who had been living in Rangoon. They were also on the run.

The surprising thing to me is that the Allied command, with all the resources at its disposal, knew less about the situation than did we prisoners behind gaol walls. At least we were aware the Japanese had fled the city.

*　　*　　*

The following is an objective account of what actually happened inside Rangoon during the next four days. It is not based on faded memories but on a detailed official report I wrote on the spot to the Supreme Commander. I have my own copy but I found copy no 19 in a file with Lord Mountbatten's personal war diary in the Public Records Office, Kew, England.

F (for Free) Day
30 April, 1945

Dawn, reluctant as ever, finally reached Rangoon and we, metaphorically, held our breaths. What now? Where was the victorious 14th Army or the dreamed of invasion?

It was incredible to us all but, clearly, the Japanese had abandoned the crucial port and communications centre of Rangoon in inglorious fashion without a fight. Would they return? Would the advancing British forces cut off their retreat and force them back into the capital? The Japanese had been in occupation here for two years and ten months and must have stores and fortifications here. They must have had a plan for defending the city. There even could be a suicide force in the city somewhere, lying doggo.

Everybody in the gaol was freed but I made sure that the padlock on the main gate into the street remained secure, locked from the inside. For the moment we felt safer with the gaol walls between us and the unknown on the outside.

A quiet muster in the darkness established that we had 668 officers and men of different nationalities inside the gaol – 474 Indians and Gurkhas, 123 British, 54 Chinese, 39 Americans, three Anglo-Burmese, two New Zealanders, one East African, one Canadian and one Australian. I was the ranking officer so I took over command automatically.

We were a tense lot, apparently free but afraid to venture out. Rangoon in Burmese is 'Yan Kon' which means 'end of strife'. It was extremely difficult for even an optimist of my persuasion to imagine that we had seen the end of our strife. We were sure something sinister was around the corner.

With a few exceptions the Europeans left behind in the gaol after the 400 able-bodied prisoners had been marched away four days before were either sick and feeble or disabled.

However, our Indian and Gurkha soldiers generally were fairly fit. They were loyal, too, having resisted frequent attempts to persuade them to join the Indian National Army and fight on the Japanese side. They were our strength. The Chinese stayed in the background. Communication was difficult.

Obviously, the situation screamed for action. We could be in a fight for our lives within the hour.

I was no soldier. I needed an army staff right now.

'What was your name again, John?'

Lt. J. M. Kerr, 13th King's Regiment, who a few minutes ago had told me he had been captured by the Japanese after he had been wounded on General Wingate's first expedition behind the lines two years before, looked at me intensely across the candlelit table.

'Kerr as in car,' he said.

'I need someone like you to handle the army side. What job do you want?'

'How about adjutant?'

'Okay, you're it. Now we need some others.'

Within minutes Lt. R. C. Fullarton, Burma Frontier Force, had been appointed Intelligence Officer, Major N. I. McLeod, I.M.S., part of whose face had been shot away, became Medical Officer and Warrant Officer J. J. Finnery, Royal Inniskilling Fusiliers, Quartermaster. They were all complete strangers to me.

Our headquarters was established in the Japanese commandant's office and a guard of three officers and twelve men posted inside the main gate. Their job was not so much to stop anybody leaving but to check intruders. We were suffering from a dose of agoraphobia – fear of the outside.

There had been shooting in the streets north of the gaol in the middle of the night and at least one rifle shot hit the building at the main gate. Explosions and raging fires lit up the low clouds over the city.

By first light all was strangely quiet. It was tantalizing. From an upstairs window I watched as our Burmese neighbours dribbled out of their flimsy shacks. Even they knew more about the battle for Rangoon than we did.

At 6 am we hoisted the Union Jack that had been used by the army prisoners for their funerals. It hung limply in the morning calm. Then we called to several civilians in the street outside who were acting as though it was just another morning.

'Good morning, gentlemen,' one of them said with a friendly grin.

I shook his hand and told him to go and find some official, somebody in the government, a police officer, anybody, and bring them to the gaol at once. It was an emergency.

'Most certainly, sir,' he said and hurried off hitching up his longyi.

The cloud cover was low but I kept searching and listening for the Dakotas that surely would be over soon dropping medical supplies and paratroops now that it was obvious that the Japanese had evacuated Rangoon. We had some very sick boys inside the gaol and it would be a crying shame if even only one more died unnecessarily at this point.

One blessing was that the sick airmen had real doctors to care for them at last. Major McLeod was amazed at the sterling job New Zealander, Cliff Emeny, had done with his farmyard nursing without medical supplies.

The doctor was concerned about some of the prisoners who had been marched off as hostages.

'They simply weren't strong enough to take to the road,' he said 'but you couldn't talk them out of it. They were convinced their chances of surviving were better on the march than staying here and risk getting involved in the fight for the city.'

After my first full-length wash with soap in five months I felt good, but I must have looked pretty wretched in my torn flying clothes that I had slept in every night.

'You don't look much like a commanding officer,' said one of the old-timers. 'Here, take this.' He took off his RAF cap and put it on my head.

So I had a token stamp of authority when Major Hla Gyaw, of the Burma Defence Army, drove up to the main gate of the gaol at 10 am. It was all very formal. Two guards escorted him and his aide to my upstairs office where John Kerr and I were putting on a show of working something out on a map. The game of bluff was on.

The cold-eyed little major refused to sit down. He claimed he was in command of the civil and military administration of Rangoon. His 500 troops, all with rifles, 200 police, half of them armed, were deployed within the city boundaries. Obviously he was trying to intimidate us. For some reason, perhaps political, the Burmese wanted to be in control of Rangoon when the British arrived. He did not want a bunch of helpless former prisoners-of-war to inter-fere with this strong bargaining position. I decided to go in boots and all.

'You and your troops,' I asked. 'Were you part of the Burmese forces who joined up with the Japanese?'

He clenched his teeth.

'You know what I mean . . . the Traitor Army. Whose side are you on now?'

'We are now the Burma Defence Army,' he said pugnaciously.

'We did not revolt as the Japanese say, but dispersed from within and reformed as the BDA.'

'Are there any Japs left in Rangoon?'

'We haven't seen any since last night.'

The major said his transport consisted of one car, the city's fire engines and a few trucks. I stood up and faced the Major.

'It's important for all of us,' I said, 'that there is no fighting in Rangoon. If the Japs are cut off by the British forces they will almost certainly fall back into the city. We have to be ready to repel any such withdrawal. We are a thousand strong here in the gaol,' I lied, 'all good soldiers . . . Gurkhas, Indians, Chinese as well as the Europeans. We need more weapons.'

The Major appeared to be convinced. He promised arms and ammunition and to try to find a radio transmitter for us. He ordered two of his soldiers to stay with us permanently to act as runners.

My parting shot was that I would hold the prison force in reserve. He was to alert me if I was needed to maintain peace in Rangoon.

Within an hour or so the Burmese Defence Army had handed over to us 17 .303 rifles, 430 rounds of SAA and 12 hand grenades. We were no longer toothless.

At noon Captain Fathekhan, chief police officer of the Indian National Army in Rangoon, reported to the gaol. He told me that before the Japanese had left last night they had shot one INA officer but there had been little trouble in the city since, apart from casual looting.

After the British had evacuated Rangoon in 1942, he said, the Burmese had slaughtered scores of Indians and Anglo-Indians. The INA was staying put to make sure this did not happen again. They had 2,000 men in a dozen camps scattered about the city but had only 150 rifles all told. The INA had no plan to cope with any Japanese who might fall back on Rangoon but were prepared to protect the prisoners if this did happen.

'Thank you, but we can look after ourselves,' I said as casually as I could. 'We're turning this gaol into a fortress.'

My thinking was that these Indian traitors would not be very effective anyway against their former allies.

Captain Fathekhan said that on paper Rangoon was under the control of a government that was pro-Japanese but this government had virtually fallen when the Japanese evacuated. Most ministers had left town but the former Finance Minister, U Set, had taken over as acting Premier.

The INA estimated there were two regiments of Japanese troops, each numbering 5,000, between us and the advancing British Forces.

John Kerr and I were washing down a fine lunch of rice and water buffalo with a mug of strong tea when the next lot of VIPs turned up for an audience. The word had spread that there was a force to be reckoned with in the gaol.

The Chief of Staff of the INA, Lt-Col Arshad, had brought along the Secretary to the War Minister during the Japanese régime, Thein Han, and the acting Commander of the BDA, Kyaw Nyein. They brought information to the effect that there were 400 to 500 Japanese in the South River area and another 1,000 in the vicinity of Mingaladon Airfield.

Lt-Col Arshad reiterated that the INA would not fight the Japanese, but were quite willing to do police work in the city under my gaol force.

It was time for some name-dropping. I stood up to show who was the boss and tapped the wing-commander stripes on my shoulder for good measure.

'I speak for the Supreme Commander of the Allied Forces who are about to enter this city,' I said with all the authority I could muster in my voice. 'And this is my plan to preserve peace in Rangoon until the British arrive: The INA to police the town area. The BDA to mop up any Jap stragglers who turn up in the city and then to move north towards Mingaladon forming road blocks and patrolling the river to prevent infiltration of retreating Japs into Rangoon. The Allied force in the gaol will remain here in reserve.'

To my surprise they all nodded agreement to the plan and undertook to set it in motion immediately. The main objective was to try to get the Burmese forces out of the city.

Of course, it was John Kerr's plan, not mine. His appointment was the best snap decision I have ever made.

'They went off meekly enough,' I said to John. 'But it's Mountbatten who is our trump card not our army of a 1,000 warriors here in the gaol aching for action.'

'Yes, you're right. The only action our fellows want is to go home.'

In the evening we spotted armed, uniformed Burmese soldiers high in the branches of trees outside the east and north walls of the gaol. The Burmese had us under surveillance.

During the afternoon eight more rifles, three revolvers, five grenades, two swords, a bayonet and 126 rounds of ammunition were handed in through the main gate, mostly by INA deserters.

John Kerr's prison defence and alarm scheme was in operation by nightfall. Guards patrolled the walls inside the gaol and others were placed at vantage points to keep a lookout for anything likely to jeopardize the safety of the former prisoners so near but yet so far from safety.

We knew that many of the rifles they carried lacked parts and were next to useless, but they looked lethal.

Where the hell was our army? The cloud had been low all day and we had only heard the odd aircraft but they must know by now that Rangoon was waiting with outstretched arms.

Perhaps they would roar down the road from Prome under cover of darkness.

In the main gate building was a real bed with a mattress. The big Tai-i had slept in it. Here, I told myself, was one of the perks of rank. I flopped onto it, but, although I had not closed my eyes for 36 hours, sleep did not come. It was too soft. I had to evacuate and sleep on the bare floor.

Meanwhile, outside Rangoon that day 30 April

At Pegu, 50 miles to the north, a meagre Japanese 'odds and sods' force is still tenaciously holding back the armoured might of Slim's 14th Army. They had blown the three bridges over the river there which was swirling with a flash flood. Their commander, Major-General Matsui, has just received an order from his superior, Lt.-General Kimura, who is safely ensconced in Moulmein. It reads: 'Your brigade will return with all speed to Rangoon and defend it to the death.'

Matsui resists the temptation to become an immortal hero. Instead, with his band of 'amateurs' facing certain annihilation, he takes them off at night into the hills of the Pegu Yomas to lick their wounds and regroup to fight for Rangoon another day.

175

Away to the west of Rangoon in the Bay of Bengal the main convoy of the assault force for Operation Dracula has left Akyab and is catching up with the other five slower convoys off the Arakan Coast. They have a 500-mile voyage to the mouth of the Rangoon River in the Gulf of Martaban. Four escort carriers are there to provide fighter coverage in addition to the close tactical support from the land-based RAF, but not a single enemy aircraft is sighted.

In the remote chance that the Japanese Navy is still looking for a fight, a formidable force of two battleships, two escort carriers, four cruisers and six destroyers from Ceylon is covering the landings. The fleet makes its presence felt by bombarding airfields and shore batteries on Car Nicobar and the Andaman Islands. However, it cannot buy a fight. The ocean is theirs. If there is any enemy, it does not venture out today.

F Day+1

All was quiet in Rangoon at dawn on May 1. It was now 31 hours since the last of the Japanese had fled the city. For a minute or more I lay there listening intently for any tell-tale noises announcing that the 14th Army had turned up overnight, but there was no rumble of tanks and trucks drowning out the bird twitterings. Then it hit me that I no longer had to rely on 'noises off' for news of what was going on outside. The walls meant nothing. I could now look out of the window and see for myself. I could even walk the streets to find out what was going on.

I bounded down the wooden stairs and experienced the sheer joy of helping myself to a mug of hot tea from a bucket inside the main gate of the gaol.

'What's happening?' I asked a bunch of guards standing around haphazardly.

'Fuck all,' said a British Army corporal. 'The war must be over. They've all gone home.'

John Kerr and some of the other officers had got wind of the fact that tea was on so we had an instant staff meeting.

'It's bloody hard to believe, but they can't know that the bloody Japs have gone.'

'Yes, if Slim knew that, the place would be lousy with paratroops.'

'The cloud ceiling is pretty low.'

'It's not that bad. There are breaks now and then. They could drop us medical supplies. They must know we're here.'

'I wonder?'

'Well, we're just going to have to tell them . . . just in case.'

So we decided to paint messages on the roof of two of the gaol buildings. 'JAPS GONE' was to go up in the largest possible letters on one roof and 'BRITISH HERE' on another.

An hour or so later while the end letters were being painted an RAF Beaufighter swooped in at low level and shot up some target near the gaol. On his fourth strafing run the pilot flew over the gaol at 60 feet. Cheers went up. He must have seen our messages.

'I saw the pilot's face,' said one of the signwriters after he had climbed down. 'I waved to him with my brush.'

Captain Fathekhan, the INA's chief police officer, reported dutifully to me at 10 am. He said Allied aircraft had machine-gunned the banks of the Rangoon River early this morning. Their target could have been Japanese coming down the river in small country craft. He, too, had seen the Beaufighter strafing the town near the gaol. At least five ack-ack guns had been left behind by the Japanese and it was possible that the Burma Defence Force had taken possession. Japanese stores had been looted of rations, cigarettes, candles, medicine and clothing but his police did not interfere because there was an acute shortage of these goods among the civilians. Otherwise, everything was quite orderly in Rangoon.

Where was the British Army? The INA had received reports that severe fighting had been in progress around Pegu on April 29. One estimate was that there were 15,000 Japanese blocked between Pegu and Rangoon. This figure, however, was doubtful because only 2,000 had been reported on April 28. There was a chance, of course, that the force had built up with Japanese trying to get through to Thailand from the west.

All this was very disquieting, especially the fact that the captain agreed with me that, so far, the British were unaware of the Japanese evacuation of Rangoon. I restricted all this information to a handful of officers to ensure that the dubious news did not reach the ears of the men in hospital desperately trying to hold out.

Major McLeod had been depressed about the condition of a number of his charges this morning. The excitement of an early release had been too much for many of them. He needed drugs badly. Captain Fathekhan left the gaol with strict instructions to step up his efforts to hunt down a radio transmitter.

All was not rosy inside the gaol walls either. Captain Meyer, the American pilot who took over the air force compound, confided to me that two or three of his fellow Americans were threatening to 'deal' right now with Lt Bearden, the Texan P 38 pilot.

'They're saying they don't want the world to know that the United States Air Force had a stool pigeon in its ranks and want to bump him off,' whispered Captain Meyer. 'The cover story would be that he just disappeared.'

I could not agree with that sort of kangaroo court justice. So I told Captain Meyer that Bearden was his responsibility. He could lock him up in one of the cells with a guard for his own safety if he wished.

Then there was the case of Havildar Abdul Karim, head clerk of a pioneer battalion, who claimed that Captain Thomas, the Indian doctor, had yesterday struck him four or five times on the face and knocked him down. He said the Captain had accused him of going to the Japanese over his head with complaints about the medical treatment, assisting the Japanese in inducing Indians to join the INA and of being a 'dog of the British officers'.

Captain Thomas, the man who had jumped over the wall the night the Japanese left to let me into the main gate building, had refused to apologize so the havildar insisted we proceed with the complaint.

'This is army, John,' I said to my adjutant. 'Over to you.' He grimaced.

I preferred to dwell on the fate of Rangoon. However, I did find time to write a report on the murder of Major-General Chi ready to hand over to the British when they turned up. The Japanese had given his alleged killer a uniform and taken him with them. His name was Chang Kun Chung and I was able to put it down in Chinese characters in the report as well as phonetically in English. I wonder what happened to him.

Gifts, mostly from Indians, poured into the gaol during the day. There were bananas, soap, razor blades, candles, sugar, rice cakes, cigarettes, tins of milk, bananas and more bananas.

One letter offering help came from a Gulam Mohamed who said that under the British he had been a 'jailor of this very Rangoon Jail'.

His letter started with a flourish:

'Long live Emperor of India

Long live the English and Americans

Long live Mr Churchill (We are sorry to hear unexpected death of
  Mr Roosevelt . . . R.I.Peace)

Long live the Australians

Long live the Chinese nation and those who are co-operating

Long live the Indians' and so on . . .

'Long live the Rats of Rangoon – us,' muttered one of the boys
bitterly.

We heard aircraft over Rangoon for most of the night, but at least
they did not bomb us.

Meanwhile, outside Rangoon that day 1 May

Before first light 82 bombers pound 'enemy positions' on both sides
of the river south of Rangoon and then Pathfinder aircraft mark
out a paratroop dropping zone with fluorescent panels and smoke
pots.

The weather is foul but, between rain squalls, a battalion of
Gurkha paratroops on their first operation are dropped into the
sticky mud around Elephant Point. As they advance to attack the
gun positions defending the mouth of the river a United States Air
Force Liberator miscues with a stick of bombs. The Gurkhas suffer
more than 30 casualties.

The Gurkhas press on and, with flame-throwers, grenades and
mortars, attack the entrenchments. They find there 36 Japanese
dead and one seriously wounded. These hapless creatures turn out to
be the only defenders of Rangoon. It seems nobody had bothered to
tell them that their army had withdrawn.

North of Rangoon, an impatient Slim, who is well aware that
tomorrow is D-Day for Dracula, is in the air above Pegu looking
desperately for a break-through point. He can see Rangoon in the
distance. The tall columns of smoke rising from the city tantalize
him. It could be the results of bombing. Then again, it could mean
that the Japanese were evacuating. He tells his pilot to fly on south.
They do not get far. A burst of anti-aircraft fire hits the aircraft,
severely wounding one of the General's staff officers, an American.
Also, an unexploded shell buries itself in the radio equipment

179

immediately behind Slim himself. They turn back. Slim seems fated not to know that the birds have flown.

At dawn on May 2, 55 hours after the last of the Japanese had sneaked away from Rangoon, waves of Allied aircraft bombed something or other near the river across from the gaol and then lower down towards the Gulf of Martaban. Our guess was that the bombardment which lasted for two hours was somehow connected with an amphibious operation but what, we asked, was there to be softened up?

Captain Fathekhan turned up on the dot at 9 am. He had counted 26 bombers over Rangoon this morning. Also, he reported that the Acting Premier of the so-called Burmese Government, U Set, had hoisted two red flags over the city. The political offensive was also under way.

The police chief had found a reliable Indian who had volunteered to go through the Japanese lines with a message to the G.O.C. British Forces in Southern Burma that the last of the Japanese had abandoned Rangoon on April 29 and that the headquarters of Allied forces in the city was in the Rangoon Gaol. The Indian, who had been educated in Malaya, went off on a bicycle with one companion and the letter in his belt. His cover plan, if caught by the Japanese, was that he was trying to join his INA unit.

At 9.30 am an RAF Mosquito skip-bombed the gaol wall behind No 6 compound. We have several casualties but nobody was killed. Within minutes I was surrounded by a bunch of angry faces.

'The sonofabitch . . . what the hell does he think he's doing?'

'If the bastard comes back I'm going to start shooting . . .'

'I don't believe it . . . surely we are not going to buy it at this stage . . . not with our own bombs?'

I was sick in my stomach.

'Perhaps his idea was to breach the wall so as we could escape,' I ventured.

'Can't your RAF pilots read? For God's sake . . . we've been advertising for days that the Japs have gone.'

'Obviously they don't believe our messages on the roof. They must think it's a trick.'

'What can we do about it, sir? How can we get them to pull their finger out?'

'That's it,' I said. 'Paint a message on another roof. Just say: EXTRACT DIGIT. That should stop the bastards.'

'You beauty, they'll know that no Nip could have thought that one up.'

'EXTRACT DIGIT' was on the roof of No 7 block in no time, admonishing every pilot who flew over. It helped to calm down the frustration that was building up in the gaol.

If the Mosquito was the second visitor of the morning to the gaol then Major Khin Nyu was the third. He said he represented the Supreme Commander of the Burmese Defence Army who wanted to inform me that the Supreme Council would be forming a Peace Preservation Committee tomorrow. I said that was a good idea, adding that, of course, the meeting to form the committee would be held here in the gaol. The Major nodded. When I asked about the present military situation in Rangoon he said Lt. Colonel Kyaw Nyein had occupied the city with 500 troops. The runways at Mingaladon had been blasted by the Japanese to prevent aircraft landing and there were reports that the Japanese still had boats on the river.

Obviously, the Burmese had most of the cards. I pulled Admiral Mountbatten's name out of the hat again and ordered in his name that the Burmese troops were to throw away all Japanese caps, that their trousers be cut down to shorts and a white band must be worn diagonally across the chests of all B.D.A. soldiers. Otherwise, the Allied forces could not be responsible for their safety when they entered Rangoon. In fact I was quoting the astute John Kerr.

The Major smiled; I did not.

'They'll be here,' I said, 'sooner than you think.' I tried to sound confident. Also, I made the point that the B.D.A. should hand over more arms to my Allied force in the gaol in case the Japanese were forced to return to Rangoon.

Minutes after Major Khin Nyu had driven away Captain Fathekhan was back again. The Indian police chief was a worried man. He said the B.D.A. was assuming power in Rangoon without the consent of the provisional government. Personally he thought that this was a good idea as long as they acted under my orders.

'It's high time everybody around here realized that I'm running Rangoon,' I said angrily and could hardly believe my own ears. Then and there I called a conference for 1400 hours at the gaol to be attended by the top people in the Burmese Defence Army and the Indian National Army. I gave Captain Fathekhan written authority to act as liaison officer for the meeting.

Tension built up during the afternoon. At times there was a queue of Indians outside the main gate of the gaol handing in weapons. The receipt we gave them they saw as a badge of their loyalty to the incoming British.

There was a scatter when four RAF Thunderbolts and a Mosquito fighter-bomber came over at low level and 'beat up' the gaol a number of times. No bombs this time. Clearly, their mission was to check out the writing on the roofs. As they flew away they waggled their wings acknowledging that our message was understood. Note the time: 1535 hours on May 2.

Minutes later the top brass of the INA arrived looking splendid in their freshly-laundered uniforms. They brought with them a message from the commander of the Burmese Defence Army saying he refused to attend a conference in the gaol. We could see him at his headquarters if we wished. John Kerr agreed that we were not too proud and, with an armed escort of three of our officers, we set out by car for the B.D.A. Headquarters in Lewis Road. The ridiculous situation amused us. It was essential that we kept up our big bluff but, frankly, we were not in the least bothered by the Burmese bid for independence or that the Burmese quisling army might clash with the Indian traitor army. Our sole concern was to ensure that nothing at all happened to the Rats of Rangoon, our men back in the gaol. They had had a rough time and deserved a safe passage home.

From what we saw of Rangoon as we drove through it, we were much better off in the gaol. It was just a shell of a city with piles of garbage everywhere. It was still smoking but the high stench of decay won through. Lumbering water buffaloes wandered in the streets but few civilians showed themselves. Red flags fluttered here and there, apparently put up prematurely by the Burmese Socialist Republic leaders. B.D.A. troops in Japanese caps and uniforms were well in evidence.

The Burmese commanders were not at their headquarters but while we waited Colonel Arshad, Chief of Staff of the I.N.A., told us he had heard on a BBC news broadcast yesterday that 400 Allied prisoners of war whom the Japanese were attempting to evacuate had been retaken by the British forces.* Slim's foward troops were 36 miles north of Rangoon and Hitler had committed suicide.

The B.D.A. Commander of the Rangoon sector, Thein Han, turned up after 35 minutes with a supercilious grin on his face and opened the interview with the words 'And what can I do for you, gentlemen?' I said I had given orders that the B.D.A. was to mop up Japanese stragglers and to tail them as they retreated as well as setting up road blocks outside Rangoon and securing tactical positions in case the enemy is forced back. Instead, according to my reports, Burmese troops were being recalled to the city. The plan was for the I.N.A. to keep law and order in the city and the presence here of Burmese soldiers was causing trouble. Thein Han glared at me and I could not resist grinning back at him. It was a scene out of a film.

'I take my orders from General Aung San whose H.Q. is in touch with your Allied H.Q.,' he said defiantly.

I tried to sound angry.

'Well, I give orders in the name of the Supreme Commander, Admiral Mountbatten. If there is any trouble in Rangoon you will be held responsible.'

I reiterated that there was no need for the main body of the B.D.A. to concentrate in Rangoon town.

'Also, I notice that your soldiers are still wearing Japanese uniforms and caps. They're asking to be shot. When the British Army turns up they're going to be very trigger-happy. My orders were to cut their pants down to shorts and to wear something white.'

---

* Lord Mountbatten's war diary, 1 May:

'Signal from War Office to Allied Land Forces South-East Asia says: "Press here reports 400 B/A PW formerly held in Rangoon released by British forces whilst being evacuated by Jap. Report adds some hundreds sick PW still left in Rangoon. Grateful you signal soonest."'

It would seem that we POW's trapped in Rangoon were at least as up-to-date with the news as was the Supreme Commander's headquarters.

My parting shot was that if the I.N.A. gave up their arms for any reason they were to surrender them to my force at the gaol and not to the B.D.A.

'He wasn't very scared of us,' I said to John on our way back to the gaol.

Waiting there were two clean-shaven RAF officers fresh from civilization.

'We saw the Union Jack and your nasty remark on the roof so I put down at Mingaladon,' the pilot said casually. He was Wing-Commander A. E. Saunders, 110 Squadron, RAF, who, with his navigator, F/Lt Stephens, was on a reconnaissance flight in a Mosquito when he decided to take a gamble and land to check whether the enemy had really run away. The runway was full of holes and a tyre burst, so they could not take off. My duty officer had received a report from the I.N.A. that the Mosquito had landed. He told them to bring the airmen to the gaol. They had been driven from the airfield by an I.N.A. colonel.

'The Nips have really fooled us on this one,' the Wing-Commander said, slowly shaking his head. 'The brass up there are convinced the bastards will be making a last-ditch stand in Rangoon. We saw your messages but couldn't take them seriously.'

'You did.'

'Yes, but I'm an idiot.'

'Just the same they'll believe you if you report that the Japs have pissed off.'

In my absence the I.N.A. had delivered a radio transmitter to the gaol. We promptly sent off a message on the correct frequency which read: 'Mosquito K110 landed Mingaladon 1500Z. No enemy in Rangoon – Saunders.' Again and again the signal was repeated but there was no acknowledgement.

Taking me aside, Saunders confided that paratroops had landed near the mouth of the Rangoon River the day before and that an amphibious operation was on the way. He was a very worried man.

'If we don't get word to them they could be knocking shit out of this place even tonight,' he told me. 'You know how they're apt to go to town on these things. I'd better get a boat and go down river to tip them off.'

Our visitor who had just dropped in certainly had panache. The

I.N.A. hunted up a couple of sampans but strongly advised against going on the river, turbulent with the high winds and flood-waters.

'Spend a night in gaol,' I suggested. 'It'll be much healthier.'

'Somebody has to tell them. Even an hour could make a difference,' said the pilot, and he went off into the night with his navigator and the Indian colonel. We went back into the security of the gaol.

Our radio operators tried frantically all night to make contact with the Allied forces but nobody was at home. Perhaps our troops would come storming ashore in the morning.

Meanwhile, outside Rangoon that day

It is just as well the D-Day landings south of Rangoon are unopposed. The assault troops have enough to suffer without having to fight as well. A storm of cyclonic fury comes in out of the Bay of Bengal and heads for the invasion force as the troops are being lowered from the seagoing transports into the assault landing craft. In pouring rain and with lightning flashes coming closer the seasick soldiers have a five-hour, cramped journey through wind-whipped seas to their landing points. The convoys cannot come closer because the sea approaches are shallow for 30 miles off-shore. The battle fleet has to stand off so far that their guns cannot reach the enemy concrete pillboxes so 58 bombers fly in and unload to 'soften up' the enemy while the landing craft are on their way to their objectives.

The rain is falling in sheets. These are not the 'mango showers'. This is the monsoon. It has come ten days ahead of schedule.

The assault commanders are aware that the well-sited gun batteries at Elephant Point have been silenced but they are braced for stiff opposition as the force heads up the river to Rangoon.

One landing craft carrying key medical and engineering personnel and two 15-cwt trucks is blown up by what was more than likely one of our own air-dropped mines. There are few survivors.

Late at night, just when the worst was expected, a sampan approaches from upstream and hails one of the leading assault craft.

'Ahoy there, Dracula. I repeat . . . ahoy there Dracula.'

It is Wing-Commander Saunders and F/Lt Fletcher bringing the news that the Japanese had fled Rangoon on April 29.

North of Rangoon the 14th Army is bogged down by mud and mines just south of Pegu.

F Day+3

Those in the gaol who slept at all woke on May 3 to a morning heavy with heat and suspense. This was to be our fourth day of freedom from the Japanese but we were still prisoners of a sort in an embattled Rangoon.

Rain had fallen in torrents during the night, enough to bog down any army. Anyway, we still had no idea as to whether the British were aware that the enemy had cleared out of the city. At a staff conference by candlelight before dawn we had agreed we could not afford to sit back and rely on Wing-Commander Saunder's desperate bid to make contact with trigger-happy invasion forces.

At first light John Kerr went off to Colonel Arshad's bungalow and ordered him to have white flags, ten feet by ten feet, raised over all I.N.A. camps in case Admiral Mountbatten had ideas of 'softening up' Rangoon as part of his amphibious operation. Also, the Indians were told to close off sections of the Prome Road and St John's Road and to fill them with these messages: 'DON'T PRANG RANGOON', 'JAPS EVACUATED RANGOON', and 'BRITISH REPAIRING MINGALADON'.

I went off by car to the Mingaladon airfield with the two New Zealanders, F/Lt Cliff Emeny and P/O Eric Osboldstone and F/O Bellingen, RAF. Our mission was to do what we could to repair a runway ready for landings by ambulance Dakotas to take out our serious cases and to establish an air traffic control party.

Rangoon was beginning to breathe again. Women were carrying water and buying food from street sellers who had spread their meagre stocks on the pavements. Children were knocking mangoes off trees with long poles. Apart from Burmese soldiers the only man I saw was repairing a roof.

Our I.N.A. escort told us some Japanese stragglers had been seen on the other side of the river last night.

Mingaladon was a mess and it was a miracle that the Mosquito crew had been able to walk away from their landing. Their aircraft had been man-handled off to the edge of the field and was being guarded by an armed Indian. Locals told us that the Japanese had mined the airfield before they left and one man said he had an idea where the mines were laid. We immediately recruited some bystanders and set about repairing a section of the runway which had been established as clear of mines. Before long we had 800 yards of the east to west runway serviceable and marked with white strips of sheeting. We had reports that groups of Japanese soldiers up to 300 strong were moving at night north of the airfield trying to link up with their units to the east but Cliff Emeny and his men volunteered to stay put armed only with a couple of dubious rifles. They showed incredibly unselfish courage.

'Some of our fellows back in the gaol will not make it unless we get them proper treatment in the next day or so,' said Cliff.

I went back to the comparative safety of the gaol and asked for volunteers to reinforce the airfield party. There were only a few fit enough to make the journey but Sgt. Davis, British Army, and 2/Lt Richard Moore, a P 38 pilot from Des Moines, Iowa, promptly put up their hands. (When he was shot down in September '44 Moore had been put in a cell for four days with a 17-year-old Burmese girl. He told us the girl whimpered the whole of the time but the Japanese blamed him for her distress and kept making cracks about American morals.)

It was back to dull routine at the gaol headquarters. Indian merchants handed in food and clothing. Another radio transmitter was presented and also a Burmese revolutionary pamphlet.

John Kerr went off to reconnoitre the city. He raised a Union Jack on the Town Hall as a counter to the rash of red B.D.A. flags bursting out everywhere.

'It's strangely quiet in the city,' John reported. 'Seems like the whole of Rangoon is having a siesta.'

Then, out of the afternoon haze, a B 24 loomed up large on a bombing run heading straight for the gaol. The bomb-bay doors swung open with purpose and hearts stopped.

'Christ! He's going to bomb us.'

The arm of an American alongside me froze half-way as he raised it to wave. Nobody dived for cover. We just stood and gaped, feeling sick in the stomach. So this was to be the end to the last four incredible days. Our desperate efforts to identify ourselves as allies had failed. Two days ago the Mosquito had blown a hole in the wall. This heavy bomber load would be different. It was . . . 22 containers packed with 'K' rations and one with medical supplies gently lowered into the gaol and adjoining streets by parachute. At last. The time: 2.30 p.m. on May 3.

At 4 p.m. a British war correspondent and two official army photographers knocked on the main gate and were given a warm reception.

'We were with the invasion fleet,' one said. 'But our boat was hardly making headway against the strong current in the river. So we jumped off and walked cross-country. Don't tell me we're first here?'

Suddenly, people around me were laughing, a rare sound in this gaol. After half an hour the press men hurried off to tell the world that Rangoon was British again.

At 6 p.m. there was the sound of marching boots in the street outside the gaol. Looking down from my office above the main gate I was stirred by the sight of a Royal Navy party approaching. When they reached the entrance their officer with a colour sash across his chest pulled out his sword and crashed it several times into the wooden gate.

'The Navy's here, the Navy's here,' he yelled.

I put my head outside the window.

'The Navy can fuck off,' I called. 'The Press was here two hours ago.'

Some might say that I could have been a trifle more diplomatic but, somehow, I was not in the mood for mock heroics.

Naturally, we opened the gate for the Royal Navy and our guard made a show of presenting arms.

'You're a rotten lot,' a sailor said to one of the Rangoon Rats sporting a Japanese rifle.' At least you could have let us rescue you. We haven't been able to find one bleeding enemy to shoot at.'

John Kerr and I walked down to the river, boarded the headquarters landing craft tied up at a wharf and were ushered into the presence of the navy and army commanders of the seaborne assault. I noted that the reception was very formal and even on the cold side. News of my greeting to the sword-brandishing naval officer at the gaol must have reached them.

Major-General H. N. Chambers, commander of the 26th Indian Division which provided the assault troops, had a few patronizing words to say.

'Well, Hudson, you chaps can consider yourselves mighty lucky. I only called the show off at 3 a.m. Good job I heard you were here.'

'How did you know, sir?'

'Some pilot tipped us off. Came down the river in a sampan. Just as well. I was going to give Rangoon a hiding.'

The frustration showed in the eyes of this battle-hungry fighting man.

I tried, but could not resist my next remark.

'You know, sir,' I ventured. 'The Japs abandoned Rangoon four days ago.'

The General glared at me for what seemed ages.

'The 14th Army are not here yet, young man. They're stuck in the mud at Pegu and that's 30, 40 miles away. We've beaten them to it. My 26 Division has won the race to Rangoon.' He spat out the words and then turned away as if to dismiss me.

'Escuse me, sir,' I persisted. 'We have a lot of very sick boys back in the gaol.'

'They'll be all right. We've got a hospital ship out there.'

'Some of them are on their last legs, sir. We have a doctor in the gaol and he says they could die if we don't get them into hospital pretty quickly.'

'I told you. We'll get them down the river and out to the hospital ship.'

I then told the General that we had a party of ex-prisoners out at Mingaladon and that they had repaired a section of the runway, enough for a Dakota to land on. He was surprised. I then asked if I could dictate a signal to the effect that Mingaladon airfield was serviceable for Dakotas and that a party of air force officers, former prisoners-of-war, was there to handle air traffic. The General consented and listened with apparent interest while I briefed him on the situation in Rangoon with regard to the B.D.A. and the I.N.A.

It was getting dark but General Chambers and a brigadier went back to the gaol with us and were cheered by the prisoners. He spoke to the Indians in Urdu and spent some time with the sick in our hospital. It was a mighty morale boost for them all.

Later in the evening the Brigade Commander, Brigadier Lauder, turned up to deal with our administrative problems. There was the apparently unsavoury case of the American pilot, Lt. Bearden. He said he would arrange for him to be evacuated the next day and would send a signal ahead so the United States authorities in Calcutta could arrest Bearden on arrival, if it was considered necessary.

The Brigadier was told about the murder of General Chi and was given the name of the Chinese who did it.

We were still handing over Rangoon at midnight.

Meanwhile, in Kandy, Ceylon that day

According to War Office file number 203, class number 2733, piece number 173/6 in the Public Records Office in Kew, London, there was a meeting in Admiral Mountbatten's office at HQ SACSEA, Kandy, Ceylon on Thursday, May 3, 1945 at 0930 hours. This meeting, attended by all the commanders, discussed a Joint Planning Staff Paper on expediting the capture of Singapore. It is in the minutes that Admiral Sir Arthur J. Power submitted that, on the assumption that Rangoon would be captured by May 20, D-Day for Zipper (Singapore) should be 16/17 days earlier than had been assumed. May 20?

At least King George VI of England apppeared to be more up-to-date. His message to Mountbatten in Kandy was dated May 3 (obviously London time). It read: 'I send you and all in South-East Asia Command my hearty congratulations on the brilliant success achieved by all arms and services in the capture of Rangoon.'

In his report to the Combined Chiefs of Staff, Mountbatten said that although Slim's 14th Army had lost the race for Rangoon, it was their drive, helped by 221 Group (RAF), which had really won the battle; for if their rapid advance had not forced Lieut.-General Kimura to evacuate the port, Dracula, which beat the monsoon by only a few hours, would have met with severe opposition.

Mountbatten was still excited about the Dracula operation on 8 May when he wrote to his daughter, Patricia, later to inherit the title of Countess Mountbatten of Burma: 'I can't tell you how thrilling the race to Rangoon has been. Unless we could capture the port by the monsoon we should get the 14th Army bogged down and confined to a single tarmac road which could easily be held by the Japs, and further the storms would be so bad we couldn't do a landing. If we landed before the 14th Army was within 50 miles from the City, the defences could be so strong as to resist the assault. You can imagine what a thrill the race was. The first day it was OK to carry out the landing was also the day on which the monsoon broke, as it is a fortnight early this year. We watched the monsoon predictions advance with horror in a race with the 14th Army, and we won out after more than a year's constant advance by a few hours!!'*

No mention of the fact that the entire amphibious assault operation happened to be unnecessary.

F Day+4

Evacuation of the 659 ex-prisoners from the gaol began at 7 a.m. on May 4. The 60 stretcher cases carried by I.N.A. soldiers to the landing craft at Phoongyi Jetty included our two mentally unsound men, one British and one Indian, whom we had kept in solitary confinement since the departure of the Japanese.

The British and Americans sailed off first down the river to the hospital ship and were followed in the afternoon by the Indians and the Chinese. I stayed behind with my hard-working staff of four and handed over to the army our 25 rifles and 800 rounds of mixed calibre ammunition, our water buffaloes, rice and other food.

At 4.30 pm we hauled down our Union Jack, surely the only one to have been flown over a command headquarters in a prison during World War II. Ten minutes later the I.N.A. prisoners began marching into the gaol. Now I could stop acting. The big bluff was over. I had a facetious thought: Perhaps I should seek out some rich Burmese and take advantage of my unique position to sell to him the trading rights to India. I smiled inside. Here was a sign that my perverse sense of humour was coming back. After all, that RAF officer nearly got away with selling for a large amount of United States dollars the trading rights to Burma after the war. That, surely, must have been one of the more intriguing confidence tricks perpetrated during the war. It is another story that has never been told.

July, 1943 it must have been. I had been posted to Calcutta as Squadron Leader Air Plans and was involved in the planning of Operation Bullfrog, an amphibious assault on Akyab, off the Arakan coast. An Englishman who was on the staff of RAF Headquarters,

*A quote from Lady Mountbatten's papers by Mountbatten's official biographer, Philip Ziegler.

Calcutta, was about to be court-martialled and my name was on the list of officers of equivalent rank from which the panel would be drawn to decide his fate. I missed out and was disappointed but I went along to the court martial one day.

This was the story: The exclusive Saturday Club in Calcutta was the scene of a regular poker game and the stakes were high. One of the school was a general in the Nepalese Army and a member of Nepal's royal family. Our officer was also of the school. He could be persuaded now and again to give the odd tip as to what to buy on the London stock market. One night at the club the officer let slip a remark to the effect that the 'trading rights to Burma after the war were to be put up for sale by the Allies. What a bonanza they would be for the far-sighted devil who snapped them up. There was the rice, the teak, the oil, the rubies just for starters.'

The Nepalese General was immediately interested and said so. The officer was horrified when the General wanted to know more. The General must, please, forget what he had told him. It was all frightfully hush hush. He should not have even mentioned it.

However, when the General persisted the officer agreed reluctantly to think about passing on the fact that Nepal could be interested. Names like Churchill, Roosevelt and Mountbatten were dropped in strictest confidence. However, if word got out the deal would be off for sure.

So 'negotiations' got under way with the poker-faced officer as the go-between. Eventually, a fat deposit was agreed upon. It had to be paid in United States dollars. Some time later a big swag of 'greenbacks' was found by a passer-by in a street in Calcutta, who took the money to the police. They were in a bag that had been dragged from under a bed by a dog.

Our friend did not have many nights left in that bed. He was booked to fly off in the USAF's 'fireball' service to Miami, Florida, on his way to South America to sit out the war. He went to gaol instead.

No, I decided, I had no desire to do any deal in Rangoon. The idea of gaol did not appeal. Been there, done that.

F Day + 5

On the morning of May 5 Group Captain John Sandy flying a

Dakota made the first landing on the newly-repaired runway at Mingaladon and was greeted with a salute from a grinning, red-haired New Zealander in a loin cloth. It was F/Lt Cliff Emeny, for the moment Officer Commanding RAF Station, Mingaladon, now putting into the task of filling holes and clearing up the debris on the airfield the same sort of dedication he showed nursing the sick in the air force compound.

Some of the desperately ill and weaker former prisoners were flown off to hospital in Calcutta but Emeny and two of his men refused to go until the following day when airfield staff were airlifted in to relieve them.

Back in Rangoon I, too, had a last mission – to see close-up the great, golden Shwedagon pagoda, one of the wonders of the world. I had seen from the gaol the morning sun flashing off the top of the pagoda's colossal spire and had wondered whether I would ever get out to see inside it. Now I was walking towards the great pagoda, head back, quite moved by the sheer purity of its line against the leaden sky. The story was that the pagoda had been covered with pure gold leaf, plastered on strip by strip by thousands of Buddhist pilgrims, but the Japanese had looted this sacred treasure and replaced it with cheap gilt paint. Whether this was true or false I did not know but the faithful Buddhists were still climbing the long stairways in their hundreds to meditate in this dramatic pagoda which, according to legend, enshrines eight hairs from the Buddha's head brought from India more than 2,500 years ago.

The stamp of army boots brought me out of my reverie. A squad of Indian soldiers led by a brisk, fresh-faced English officer was marching past with a Burmese prisoner.

The officer must have recognized me. He called a halt, came back and saluted.

'This Burmese chap was shooting at our patrols from an upstairs window, sir. I thought you would be interested.'

'What are you going to do with him?'

'Execute him, sir. Right here and now. We need to do this now and again as an example.'

'He's only a boy.'

'Old enough, sir.'

He excused himself, barked a few orders and inside a minute the trembling Burmese youth was facing a firing squad.

His bare feet shifted nervously on the pebbly road. He was wearing khaki shorts and a red shirt. His hands were roped together behind his back but he was not blindfolded.

At first he watched the soldiers busy with their rifles and then jerked his head away and found my eyes.

Twenty years later I wrote a book about Australia's much maligned wild dog, the dingo, a magnificent, highly affectionate animal. It is called *Dingoes Don't Bark*. I describe in it how a dingo bounty hunter, my cameraman and I came upon a dingo in a trap in the desert heart of the country. It stood like a statue, straining the chain that held the trap to the post.

'Once in Burma during the Second World War,' I wrote, 'I was obliged to be an observer while a Burmese youth was executed. He was not blindfolded and, for some reason, he looked at me for the last thirty or forty seconds. Just before the bullets hit him he lifted his questioning face to the sky. This yellow dingo also held me with questioning eyes. He just looked at me steadily until the bullet went home.' Somehow these two horror moments in my life are inexplicably linked in my mind.

Bodies of Indian looters killed by booby traps and in fights over spoils were being taken out of the Bank of India as I walked back to brigade headquarters.

It was now a week since the last of the Japanese had fled the city but human life was still cheap there.

I wandered up to the gaol to see John Kerr, still busy with his adjutant duties, and was pulled aside by a military police officer who appeared to be in charge.

'We've got one of your Jap guards in there,' he whispered. 'He's yours. Do what you like with him. We won't see a thing.'

This was an offer I could refuse.

Forty years later I was in Tokyo talking about the war in Burma to Major Noguchi Seiki who spent 100 days in Rangoon Gaol after the surrender as a suspected war criminal. In fact, he was locked up in what had been in my day No 8 block, the air force compound.

'There was one British sergeant among the guards who was very bad,' the Major told me. 'He kicked and punched us and took our watches and valuables, even our mosquito nets. We used to call him The Fox.'

Two days after British Indian troops had occupied Rangoon, the Commander of the Japanese Burma Area Army, Lt.-General Kimura, who led the hasty retreat from the city, was promoted by Tokyo to full general.

It is difficult to imagine Kimura's Chief of Staff, Lt.-General Tanaka Shizuichi, joining him for a congratulatory saki at their new headquarters across the Gulf of Martaban in Moulmein. He had violently opposed the decision to retreat so ingloriously from the strategic port and had clashed with Kimura over the matter. In fact, it was only because Tanaka persisted in arguing the point that Kimura ordered Major-General Matsui on April 30 to return to Rangoon and defend it to the death. Matsui declined. Tanaka did not last long after that. He was sacked and packed off to Tokyo.

On May 7 Lt.-General Slim, whose dogged assault had forced Kimura to quite Rangoon, was also sacked.

The disappointed Slim was cooling his heels back at his headquarters in Meiktila when Lt.-General Sir Oliver Leese, Commander, Allied Land Forces South-East Asia, flew in and, acting under a half-hearted acquiescence from the Supremo in Kandy, he brusquely told Slim he was giving Lt.-General Sir Phillip Christison command of the 14th Army for the invasion of Singapore and Malaya. Slim was to take over the 12th Army and mop up in Burma.

The reason Leese gave was he did not consider Slim was capable of planning a large-scale amphibious operation and so it would not be fair to the 14th Army to leave him in command. Slim was stunned and said he would rather resign.

When Whitehall heard of Leese's presumptuous move there was a closing of ranks and in the end it was Leese who was sacked and Slim was promoted to his job.

He was to become Field-Marshal Viscount Slim. His protagonist in Burma, General Kimura, was hanged in Tokyo as a war criminal, dressed in U.S. Army fatigues and devoid of insignia of any kind. He had been Vice-Minister of War, under General Tojo, at the time of Pearl Harbor.

Away in a Calcutta hospital on May 7 I, too, was facing a crisis of sorts. Just talking with people was too much for me. After a few hours as a patient I was at screaming point.

Apparently, we were the first large group of prisoners of the Japanese to be released so we were getting special attention and in my hyped-up state I could not take it. I was poised ready to abuse the next woman from the Red Cross who told me I was a 'poor, dear boy'. (All this has nothing to do with Rangoon but I enjoy relating it).

Some women were approaching my bed, so I closed my eyes tightly.

'So it *is* you, Bill Hudson. This Wing Commander L.V. fooled me.'

I opened my eyes. It, was, incredibly, Pat Jarrett, my mate Pat, from Melbourne. She had been editor of the women's pages of the *Sun News-Pictorial*.

Standing there with Pat was Maie Casey, wife of the Governor of Bengal. Pat had become her press secretary.

'Okay, Bill,' asked Pat. 'Is there anything you need?'

'Yes,' I blurted out, 'get me out of this bloody place or I'll go crazy.'

Maie Casey took over.

'Come home with us,' she said. 'Is there anybody you want to bring with you?'

John Kerr was in the next bed.

'I can't go anywhere without my adjutant,' I said.

Within minutes John and I, dressed in pyjamas, were on our way by Rolls Royce to palatial Government House.

Calm and wise, the Governor's lady had our situation diagnosed by the time we reached there.

'You can have a wing to yourselves,' she said. 'Just stay there quietly until you sort yourselves out. Nobody will bother you. When you feel like it come and have meals with us.'

For the next few days John and I were in solitary in Government House, Calcutta. The four-poster beds were too soft for us. We slept on the floor. We did not talk much.

The Governor came up to check whether there was anything we needed but said he was under strict orders from his wife to stay for only 30 seconds and 'not to make a nuisance' of himself. Richard Gardiner Casey, D.S.O., M.C. (from World War 1) was a conservative politician in Australia who became his country's ambassador in

Washington. He was selected by Churchill for the difficult post in troubled Bengal after a stint in the Middle East for the British Government.

John and I slept a lot, walked in the garden and relished the specially-prepared food brought by the bearers to our rooms. After a few days I had calmed down to the point where I could sit at a dinner table and make small talk with the maharajahs, generals, statesmen and other celebrities who turned up as guests.

It was a far cry from Cell 35, Rangoon Gaol.

There was one awkward period. Apparently I had brought with me from Rangoon an itch mite or two. A female had tunneled under the layers of skin around my genitals and laid its eggs. Within a few days I had scabies which is intensely itchy but you are warned never to scratch it.

Of course, I was 'disinfected' but on several occasions at dinner the itch became almost unbearable and I started wringing my napkin and clenching my teeth. I am sure that Maie Casey and Pat Jarrett, who had me under close observation, were wondering whether my mind was about to snap, but I could not explain my problem. It was hardly table conversation.

John and I were part of the entourage when the Governor moved to Darjeeling, a hill station in the Himalayas, for ten days. We all travelled in splendour aboard the viceregal train. A fellow guest was Lt.-General Sir Richard O'Connor, a charming wisp of an Irishman, freshly-released as a prisoner-of-war in Europe.

'And how did you get into the bag, Hudson?' was his opening gambit at dinner that night.

'It's not one of my favourite stories, sir.'

The tenacious, little General, however, did not take my hint to drop the subject. In fact, it goaded him on.

'Why, what happened?'

So, I looked him in the eye and told him that because of a burst of exuberant flying, I had presented my navigator and myself to the enemy on a platter.

Now General O'Connor was really interested and cruelly pressed me for all the embarrassing details.

'I know how you feel,' he said at the end of my reluctant story. 'You should hear what happened to me.'

The whole table went silent while General O'Connor, who had been the British Commander of the Western Desert Force in North Africa, made his confession.

He told how he and another general were bumping along a desert track at night in a big blue sedan that was serving as a staff car. General Rommel's Afrika Corps had the Allied forces on the run. In fact, it was a helter skelter race across the Libyan Desert with the Germans in hot pursuit. The Australian troops had dubbed it the 'Benghazi Handicap'.

'You might say it was a confused withdrawal,' said the General. 'We were taking a short cut when two trucks ahead of us stopped short and so did our driver.

'We sat there patiently for a minute or two chatting away. Then a soldier came out of the darkness and we were staring into the barrel of a machine gun. It was a German. We were prisoners. It was only a day or so after I had been knighted. But what really hurt was an intelligence report I read recently after I was released. Apparently, this German who captured us and the trucks was one of a party of four who had raced ahead of the German army on motor cycles to direct the traffic.'

Life was good at what they ironically called the 'Governor's Camp', Darjeeling.

Then, on May 24, I wrote this letter to my fairy godmother, Mary Marlowe, who worked on *The Sun*, in Sydney. She had been an actress and played the juvenile leads in 'On Our Selection' and 'The Squatter's Daughter' when they were first produced on the stage in Australia. She had also written seven novels.

> **Government House,**
> **Darjeeling**
> **May 24**

My Mary

My mind has cleared up and I am sitting up and taking notice. I want to start doing things again so the first thing is to write to you. This last 10 days in the clouds has worked wonders. I'm afraid I wasn't worth a bumper at the end of all the fuss. I hadn't slept for weeks and this was the first time it had happened to me. O gosh. I think they call it living on your nerves or something. It turned me from a very thoughtful young prisoner into a tormented and bad-tempered, mind-in-a-mess wretch. Everybody was very kind and so here I am almost sane again. To-day is Thursday. On Sunday I leave the clouds along with His Ex and his lady, Pat (power behind the throne) Jarrett and the rest of the party to return to the plains and all that. Then will follow Bombay and a boat and Australia and a family party. God give me strength.

Your prayers were really good for me, Mary. I used to lie back on my bed board in the cell with my head on my boot and feel them. They made me strong to take it all. Sometimes I saw you going alone into a big cathedral or something. You knelt down and prayed for me and there were only a few other people there. I know I should not say all this now. It's hardly fair. But it was so clear. The strange thing was that I felt that you were the only person really praying for me. I could not feel that anybody else I knew was capable. After a while I got around to feeling I might pray for myself and I felt all right as I did. I prayed that I might retain my commonsense and I did. It was most important. Not until I reached Calcutta did I flop. . . .

John Kerr flew off to London, but, before he left, the military authorities in Calcutta made a point of taking away from him three copies of our report on how the prisoners took over Rangoon. Apparently, it was for official eyes only. (My own copy of the report was safely tucked away in my kitbag with my gaol diary and went back to Australia with me.)

On the first morning back in Calcutta a copy of *The Statesman* was on my breakfast tray at Government House with a note from His Excellency referring me to the editorial page. The newspaper's leading article was about the gaol exploits of a young Australian airman, Wing Commander L. V. Hudson, who had been a prisoner of the Japanese in Rangoon and 'became virtual ruler of the city with an assorted force of Americans, British, Chinese and Indian servicemen when the enemy left the city.' 'This must rank first in high adventure,' the newspaper said. 'Before the war, Hudson was a journalist. There is no direct evidence that his civilian professional training equipped him for his remarkable enterprise.

'Journalists are not in the normal course of their duties required to impose and direct martial law, disarm doubtful characters, repair airfields and organise returning forces. But it may be thought at least that the painting of the words "Japs Gone" was the outcome of Hudson's training on the *Sydney Sun* which had taught him the importance of big headlines on big occasions.' (*The Statesman* was too dignified a newspaper to mention the angry 'Extract Digit' roof headline that finally got the message across.)

Well, all that cost me a round of pink gins when I met up later that morning at Firpo's bar with fellow Australian, Hank Wilson, and a few of the 400 others who had been marched away by our Japanese gaolers on 25 April, ANZAC Day, the one day in the year in Australia when the nation remembers its war dead. This was the day in 1915 when the Australian and New Zealand Army Corps made its ill-fated landing on Gallipoli in the Dardanelles. It was the nation's first 'glorious defeat' and the irony of the occasion was not missed by the Australians among the marchers.

There, at Firpo's, I was told what happened on the forced march. None of the prisoners knew where they were headed, but the guess was north to Pegu and then eastward. There was no question about it. They knew they were just pawns, expendable hostages. The first night they covered fifteen miles up the Prome Road. They were a ragged lot, many barefooted, some looking ridiculous in discarded Japanese shirts and shorts.

Next day they kept under the cover of the roadside trees, out of sight of marauding Allied aircraft. The second night they had to march twenty-two miles. They ran out of drinking water. The weak were getting weaker.

At this point four long-term Australian prisoners decided that escape was less of a gamble than being at the mercy of their unpredictable hosts. Three of them were pilots, Peter Wilson, Ron Hadden and Harvey Besley, the man from X1 Squadron, RAF, whom I had seen bale out during a raid on Meiktila airfield two years before. The fourth was Douglas 'Lofty' Eastgate, who had been with the A.I.F. 8th Division when it surrendered to the Japanese in Singapore in 1942. He had escaped in a sampan only to be taken prisoner by the Japanese again two months later in Burma. They were a tough bunch. I knew about them but had not had a chance even to talk to them in the prison. The four waited until Mosquitos and Beaufighters were low overhead on strafing runs and slipped away one by one into the jungle. They eventually turned up in Calcutta.

On 28 April the feeble column of men holed up during the day and at night went through a smoking Pegu which had been pounded by our aircraft.

'That was the night S/Ldr Fenton bought it,' said Hank. 'He was our newest prisoner and couldn't have really recovered from his crash. He collapsed and the Nips made us leave him there at the side of the road. We heard later from the Army that the Nips must have finished him off with their bayonets.'

The Air Force was still being singled out for special treatment. Colonel Mackenzie, the surgeon who amputated Montgomery's arm, could not keep up, so some of his men put him in a wheelbarrow and took turns to push him.

An hour after dawn on 29 April Hank saw a party of Japanese cutting across the paddy fields heading south-west. Their guards had vanished. They were now on their own but with the 14th Army shelling targets all around them there was little they could do but wait and pray.

Later in the morning Brigadier Hobson passed the word that he had been left a note by the Japanese commander saying that the POWs were now free men. It was a frustrating situation. After three years in gaol for most of them they were free at last, but had nowhere to go. They were under fire in no-man's-land. The attack by the Hurricanes came in mid-afternoon. The men, spirits high, had moved into a deserted village to lie low but an army spotter plane noticed movement in the area and called for a strike. First, the Hurricanes bombed. Then they came back for two strafing attacks with their 20 mm cannons. One man only was killed. It was Brigadier Hobson.

'Oh no! Was he out in the open?' I asked. 'Was he asking for it?'

'No,' said Hank. 'It was sheer bloody bad luck.'

The towering Brigadier who for three years had held his head high, too high for some of the smaller Japanese to reach without jumping, to slap his face, had been cut down on the brink of freedom.

An Indian National Army officer who had surrendered to Slim's forces alerted them to the abandoned prisoners and patrols were sent out to pick them up.

It was 30 April. Back in Rangoon the prisoners left behind still had four tense days to go.

I met up with 'Lofty' Eastgate in Ceylon on my way home. One night at the Galle Face Hotel in Colombo he told me about the great hole they had to dig near Rangoon University for our Japanese 'masters.' It was early in 1945 and all fit prisoners were put to work digging with picks and shovels. The earth was carried out in baskets on poles.

Six men were needed to carry the 30-foot lengths of teak, 12″ by 12″, which were used as uprights and barely reached ground level. The excavation was roofed over with heavy timber. Obviously, this was intended as a bunker in case there had to be a last-ditch stand in Rangoon. No doubt there were other earthworks as well and an Indian prisoner told me that in April gun emplacements were being dug in the high ground around the Shwedagon Pagoda, the most sacred of Buddhist shrines. Nobody was surprised that the Japanese were preparing to fight to the death to hold Rangoon.

An Order of the Day found on the body of a Japanese officer in Burma had said: 'If your hands are broken, fight with your feet. If your hands and feet are broken, use your teeth. If there is no breath left in your body, fight with your ghost. We must have the determination to defend our positions to the death, and even after death . . . There must be no retreat in the Imperial Army without order . . . It is still easy to remedy the dangerous battle situation if the enemy command system can be annihilated by suicidal attacks. There must be no room for historians of the future to say that we have left undone something which we ought to have done.'

So why, for Pete's sake, did the Burma Area Army slink away from Rangoon without firing a shot?

Conceded they suffered some terrible defeats in Central Burma but what happened to the plan to fall back to Rangoon and hold the city to the death as ordered by the Southern Area Army commander in Saigon, Field-Marshal Terauchi?

Of course, if they had stayed put in Rangoon, I, more than likely, would not be here writing this today.

*   *   *

For forty years I wanted to know the inside story behind the Japanese retreat from Rangoon. In April, 1985, I went to Japan in search of it.

'If the Allies hadn't hanged Kimura, we should have . . . because of the way he abandoned Rangoon.'

I am riding the Tokyo underground listening to my interpreter, Commander Sadao Seno, a retired intelligence officer with the Japanese Marines.

He balances a boxed sponge cake precariously on his finger tips in the rocking train while he carries on emotionally about the defeat of the Japanese Burma Area Army.

The real fault, he says, lay with the Prime Minister, General Tojo. He was desperate for some success that would help him prolong the life of his cabinet, so he ruled in favour on the hopeless invasion of India from Burma which had ended in disaster at Imphal. Without this defeat the Japanese could have held Rangoon, at least until the monsoon of May, 1945. The cake, a traditional gift when you go visiting in Japan, is intended for our next target, another eye-witness of what actually went on behind the scenes before the fateful flight from Rangoon in April.

Previously, Colonel Noguchi Seiki, who had been on the staff of the 33rd Army, had told us how General Kimura had come to the front a few weeks before the battle for Meiktila to hand out bravery awards. At one point Lt.-General Honda had ordered all the staff out of the command post while he tried to persuade his commanding officer to allow an orderly retreat from Meiktila, so as they could fight a delaying action and make a stand further south at Toungoo. The plan was to play for time until the monsoon bogged down the enemy's tanks and cut off his air supplies.

Kimura would not hear of it. He insisted on a suicide defence of Meiktila. It was a decision that sealed the fate of the Burma Area Army.

Our next call had been on Major Maeda Hiroshi, the Intelligence Officer on Kimura's staff who had grilled me on my arrival in Rangoon on Christmas Day, 1944.

After we had presented our sponge cake we harked back to those days in Rangoon.

Kimura, he said, had been very nervous about pulling out of Rangoon. His honour depended on the defence of the city. He had been ordered to defend Burma and Rangoon was its capital. It was an important point for politics but not from the viewpoint of strategy.

Rangoon had lost value as a base. It had been destroyed by bombing and also the ships came no more.

Major Maeda poured the tea and lit up a Mild Seven cigarette. 'The

*General decided at the end of March to evacuate Rangoon,' he said
calmly.*

Commander Sadao juggles the cake to the fingertips of his left hand.

*'You've been hearing the army point of view over the last few days,' he
says. 'This next man is neutral.'*

*We take a taxi from the station through a maze of pocket handkerchief
wheatfields to the home of Mr Tamura Masataro, who had been Third
Secretary in the Japanese Embassy in Rangoon at the time of the
evacuation.*

*Mr Tamura, now 76, has a ready laugh and penetrating eyes. His
fingers are continually working on the recalcitrant fringe of his grey,
shaggy hair which is parted in the middle.*

*The room has a delicate air. An interior garden of fragile African
violets in pots claims attention. Pinks, purples, white and even green.
There are 21 plants in all.*

*Mrs Tamura, a gold chain around her slim waist, arrives with a basket
of hot hand towels so as we can freshen up after our journey. Then the
inevitable sponge cake followed by hot house strawberries.*

'General Kimura should have defended Rangoon.'

*The voice of the former diplomat is low and unemotional but his charges
blunt and brutal. The impact to me is incongruous in this charming room.*

*'The retreat from Rangoon is one of the most shameful chapters in the
history of the Imperial Japanese Army.'*

*I accept the offer of some more fragrant tea. The gracious Mrs Tamura
is still smiling. Obviously, she has heard all this before.*

*'I hated to have to witness this disorderly retreat.' From the street comes
the cry of a street vendor selling poles for clothes lines.*

*'General Kimura was ordered to defend Rangoon to the last. Instead he
ran away. It was the first time in the history of the Imperial Japanese
Army that a high ranking officer so blatantly disobeyed an order from his
commander. Three Japanese colonels who ran away during a skirmish
with Soviet forces on the Manchurian border in 1939 were ordered to
commit hara-kiri . . . and they did.'*

*Mr Tamura says Japan's official war history does not 'show the shame'
of General Kimura's flight from Rangoon. The account there is merely on
the surface. So, he thought it was high time someone put the record
straight. It was important for future study of the 'essence' of the Japanese
Imperial Army.*

I am presented with a copy of a book he has just written. On the cover is a photograph of the towering stupa of the Shwedagon pagoda. The title translates to: Record of Exodus from Burma The Day of Defeat of Burma Area Army Seen by a Diplomat.

He says I am free to use the material in the book.

Why, I ask, did he write the book?

'I do not begrudge the truth. I have recorded what I saw with my own eyes. I am sorry that it will invite bad feelings from some of my army friends.'

This is the gist of his story in my words:

By the end of March, 1945, the front in Central Burma was collapsing and the fate of Rangoon in doubt. We were following the situation closely at the Japanese Embassy in Rangoon and it became clear that with our forces retreating so rapidly they could not fight again in good order.

On April 21 we considered it urgent that the leaders of the Burmese Government and all Japanese civilians in Rangoon should be transferred to a safe area.

I discussed the situation with the Consul General, Shimazu Kyudai, and it was decided that I should make a call that night on a staff officer at the Burma Area Army headquarters, Lt.-Col Okamoto Iwao. He insisted that the Japanese forces would stop the advance of the British at Pyinmana and that we should not be in a hurry.

I disagreed strongly, pointing out that the last place that remained where we might stop the British tanks was the Sittang River, only 50 miles away.

He had no answer to this except to say, with a forlorn look on his face: 'At the last stage the kamikaze will blow.'

The kamikaze, the wind of the gods, is the name for the typhoon which saved Japan from an invasion by Kublai Khan and his Mongolian hordes late in the 13th century. It destroyed the great Khan's armada.

At this stage of the war we often heard the word 'kamikaze,' but it conveyed little hope, only deep despair.

The following day there was a call from Lt.-Col. Okamoto asking me to please arrange the retreat from Rangoon of the Ba Maw Government on the night of April 23 and the evacuation of all Japanese civilians the next night. Later there was a further call to say the situation at the front had worsened and that all civilians would need to leave after dark next day as well as the Burmese Government leaders.

There was much to do, but we also had the problem that the army was insisting that even at this last moment we must handle the recruitment of civilians for the fighting force. Officially, this was consulate work.

The only food we could round up was one bottle of saki and a bottle of sochu liquor made from potatoes. The two staff members we had sent to Bangkok for emergency food had not returned.

We all dressed in jungle green army clothing. I was wearing a straw hat held on by bootlaces and carrying a loaded Lee Enfield rifle provided by the army. I looked like a mercenary on the Amazon River. At least I provided some comic relief.

On that last day, April 23, I went to Burma Area Army headquarters with the Consul General to say goodbye. He went to the office of General Kimura. I called on Lt. Col. Kazuta Jiro, one of his staff officers.

His office was in a terrible mess, with documents scattered wildly, but the officer had a smile on his face. I had always assumed that the army would stay behind and defend Rangoon but now I was not so sure.

'I'm leaving here tonight by truck for Moulmein with the Japanese civilians,' I told him.

'Thank you for the formal farewell,' he replied. We shook hands and he presented me with a couple of packets of Java cigarettes. The Consul General followed me back to the Embassy. He had a disgusted look on his face.

'The Commander, Kimura, was trembling terribly and could hardly talk,' he told me.

Eventually, he asked me in a very low voice whether we were going by plane or by sea. I was so angry I could hardly speak myself. Just by truck, I said. Then I came back.

In the two years I had been in Rangoon with the Consul General it was the first time that I had seen him angry. We both knew then that the Japanese army was about to abandon Rangoon.

That evening, April 23, General Kimura made his surreptitious departure from Rangoon. With one of his staff officers he flew off across the Gulf of Martaban in a three-seater scout plane to Moulmein.

The small plane made return flights on the next four nights bringing out a further eight members of Kimura's staff. His Chief of Staff, Lt.-General Tanaka, who was angry at the decision to withdraw, flew out under protest on the second last flight.

I fail to understand why seats in the only aircraft available were not offered to the Prime Minister of Burma, Ba Maw, the leader of the rebel Indian national movement, Chandra Bose and the Japanese Ambassador, Mr Ishi-i and the Minister of the Embassy, Mr Hachya. They were obliged to get out as best they could by truck, running the gauntlet of strafing by enemy aircraft. They could move only at night and finished up doing a lot of walking.

Tinsa, daughter of Prime Minister Ba Maw, was expecting a baby any day. She and her father waited for a promised truck that did not turn up but eventually got a lift out of Rangoon. They were soon foot-slogging. The baby was born just over the Sittang River about 50 miles out of Rangoon.

Indeed, the scramble to get out was humiliating for all of us. We walked most of the way to Moulmein travelling at night along rain-sodden paths through rough country. On the way our party came across the bodies of several of our colleagues from the embassy.

After the war, Lt.-General Tanaka claimed that at the time his commander, General Kimura, flew out of Rangoon no concrete arrangements had been made for the evacuation from the city of Burmese Government leaders, the Japanese Ambassador to Rangoon, or his staff, the pro-Japanese Indian National Army or the Japanese civilians stranded there. The Army was looking after itself.

The fighting at the front was no fiercer than the battle that had raged at Burma Area Army Headquarters in Rangoon between Kimura and his Chief of Staff, Tanaka, as to whether or not the Japanese should pull out of the city at this point.

Tanaka had a reputation as a fanatical, never-retreat, general. He was commander of Army Operations in Tokyo when General Tojo agreed to the evacuation of Guadalcanal. Tanaka scolded Tojo saying it was a 'stupid' decision. He also had words with another high-ranking officer over the issue and slapped his face.

It was no surprise that Kimura firmed up on his decision to quit

Rangoon while Tanaka was away in Toungoo desperately trying to bolster the Emperor's forces there.

When he returned to Rangoon on 23 April Tanaka was furious and refused to sign the draft order for the move of the headquarters to Moulmein. He argued strongly that they should defend Rangoon to the last. A retreat was too premature. They should wait for the Kamikaze. God's wind was sure to blow.

He kept making the point that Rangoon was the Japanese army's brain centre. If they retreated they would lose control altogether.

It was a bitter clash and in the middle of it the air raid sirens screamed. The two generals carried on their wrangling in a shelter.

Kimura refused to countermand his order, stressing that the headquarters radios were already in Moulmein. Also, the Burmese Government had already been informed.

Kimura flew out that night. He was first to go.

Word of his departure spread rapidly to the front but it was not clear to his field commanders what was happening about the defence of Rangoon. The confusion that ensued did nothing for the morale of the retreating troops.

One of the last men to hear about the headquarters pulling out of the city was Major-General Matsui Hideji, who at the last minute had been given command of the Rangoon Defence Force, a mixed brigade mostly made up of Japanese civilians in uniform.

Three days after Kimura had flown away he was still busily recruiting. It was left to Matsui to deal with the prisoners-of-war in gaol. He ordered that any fit prisoners be marched to Moulmein. This amounted to 400. The other 700 were left in the gaol.

The first he knew that the headquarters staff had fled was when a security patrol he had sent there reported that looters were ransacking the offices searching for cigarettes.

'I was so angry,' he recalled after the war, 'because the headquarters staff had left for Moulmein without telling me . . . and I was supposed to be the Rangoon defence commander.'

Lt.-General Sakurai Shozo, commander of the hard-pressed 28th Army, asked Rangoon for orders but was told to wait until after Kimura's headquarters had established itself in Moulmein.

The flight from Rangoon of the Burma Area Army headquarters was so sudden that the bulk of the military stores, badly needed at the front, were left behind in the supply depots. Several units sent parties into Rangoon to help themselves to trench mortars, other arms and ammunition but the bulk of the supplies fell into the hands of the Burmese Defence Force which had switched sides and were now opposing the Japanese.

Among the last Japanese to leave Rangoon was a party of about 100 women and children.

Major Shirakawa Senji, one of Matsui's men, has told that when he asked Kimura's headquarters what to do with them they instructed him to send them away with the soldiers.

This, he thought, was unrealistic, so he went down to the river and found a wooden fishing boat that was about to sail. The women and children were crowded aboard, along with some 40,000 boxes containing the ashes of soldiers killed in recent months. The boat ran the gauntlet of the British air and sea patrols to reach Moulmein safely.

All this points to the fact that Commander Kimura and his senior staff officers were afraid of the rapid advance of the enemy tanks and panic set in. Is it not shameful behaviour that they did not follow the principles laid down for the Emperor's army to attack and defend to the death in any emergency?

The main cause of the Rangoon disaster was Commander Kimura's fear of being captured.

Of the 303,000 Japanese who fought in Burma 61% were killed. People always talk about the Battle for Imphal, when we were defeated on the verge of invading India, as being the great tragedy of the Burma campaign. This is not so. The damage to the Japanese army caused by the panic retreat from Rangoon was three times more than we suffered at Imphal.

*   *   *

It surprises me that nobody, not even Mr Tamura, makes the point in their writing about the war in Burma that the gods did blow for the Emperor's army in the defence of Rangoon. The kamikaze came at exactly the right moment.

Like Napoleon at Moscow, Slim was stretched to the limit at the end of a hazardous line of communications. The forward troops of the British 14th Army were on half-rations. Trucks bringing supplies from the rear were in poor shape and the roads chopped up by tank traffic.

The British troops were dependent to a large degree on food and ammunition flown in by transport aircraft that were about to be taken away by the Americans for their operations in China. In fact Washington was not at all keen to be seen helping the British re-establish themselves in S.E. Asia.

Close air support to Slim's advancing columns was coming from squadrons which had flown into forward airfields which were turned into quagmires by the first showers of rain.

The early 'mango' showers had bogged down the British tanks and the low cloud ceiling had hampered attacks by the RAF. It is true that a formidable invasion force had sailed from Akyab at the end of April but even Mountbatten himself looked on the planned landings at the mouth of the Rangoon River as a dangerous gamble.

As I have stressed earlier, his battle fleet could not get close enough to the coast to bombard Japanese defences and, because of the shallow waters, the convoys had to stand off 30 miles out to sea. The attack troops had an extremely vulnerable journey to the landing beaches. The situation definitely favoured the defenders.

Then, bang on schedule, at just the right psychological moment when the first of the landing craft were heading for the beaches the gods blew with a vengeance, the kamikaze came in the form of the monsoon, the annual deluge so feared by the architects of Dracula. By a quirk of fate the monsoon broke two weeks ahead of schedule.

The trouble was, of course, there were no Japanese left in the Rangoon delta to take advantage of their blessed kamikaze.

They had not had the faith to wait for it.

Canberra, Australian Capital Territory, 1953.
The public bar in the Hotel Canberra is hardly the place I expect to run into Martin Gilliatt, but here he is and we have a beer together.

'You must come up and have a drink with the old man,' says Martin. 'He'll want to have a talk with you.'

Sure enough there is a message next day from Yarralumla saying the Governor General, Field-Marshal Sir William Slim, wanted to see me the following evening.

Lt.-Col. Gilliatt is Slim's private secretary. I had got to know him in Singapore several years before when he was private secretary to the Commissioner-General for South-East Asia, Mr Malcolm Macdonald.

*He had been based then across the Causeway in Johore. I was covering
the region for AAP-Reuter. On the way to the Governor-General's study
Martin puts his hand on my shoulder.*

'Of course, Bill, you understand this will be off the record?'

'Of course.'

*I had never seen the old soldier before in the flesh. He looks even
tougher than his image and even sets his chin to ask me whether I want ice
in my whisky. Martin leaves us.*

There is no small talk.

'How long were you in the bag?'

'Five months, sir.'

'You must have been mighty glad to see my chaps.'

'I didn't have the pleasure, sir. I was back in Calcutta before your
troops reached Rangoon.'

'Nonsense. The 17th rescued your lot near Pegu. Where were you?'

'Back in Rangoon Gaol, sir. The Japs wouldn't take me on the march
out.'

'Why not?'

'They said I was a trouble-maker.'

*The Field-Marshal looks at me steadily through narrowed eyes and
nods as if he fully agrees with the Japanese assessment.*

I try to take the initiative.

'Kimura. General Kimura, sir, the Jap commander . . . what did you
think of him as an opponent?'

'I didn't know much about him. That was one of my big problems in
Burma. Our intelligence had nothing on him or his field commanders. It's
mighty important to know something about the character of the commander of the other side.

'Anyway, I made sure he handed over his sword to me. General
MacArthur had sent out an order that we were not to insist on them giving
us their swords until after the big surrender ceremony in Tokyo Bay. I
didn't wait.'

'Rangoon itself, sir. You know how we prisoners took over there for
four days before its recapture. Well . . .'

Field-Marshal Slim's fist hits the table.

'Rangoon was not recaptured. It fell. They ran away.'

*His mouth shuts tight and I am sure his teeth are clenched. His look
silences me.*

'*And you know when Rangoon really fell? Early in March, two months before, when the 14th Army knocked the stuffing out of the Jap in Meiktila.*'

He pushes aside my empty glass to make space for his rigid forefinger, hovering over the desk.

'*Meiktila,*' *he growls. The finger circles a piece of desk top.* '*We killed so many Japs there we got tired of counting them. There must have been 2,000 dead in the town area alone. Then came Toungoo. That's where we beat Kimura . . . in Central Burma . . . And if our rapid advance hadn't forced him to get out of your Rangoon in a hurry that amphibious operation would have been very tough going.*'

I have no argument here. This is my thinking, too. However, I do not get a chance to say so. Field-Marshal Slim is on his feet looking meaningfully at his watch.

I am not offered the other half of that whisky.

Postscript

The date is March 6, 1987. The proofs of this book are due any day now from London so that I can check them before publication. One nagging worry persists: It is the Lt Bearden enigma that has haunted me for 42 years. What was the whole truth about this Texan pilot who had been branded a Japanese collaborator by so many of his fellow prisoners? A slither of doubt about this accusation still lurks in my mind.

It was just before dawn, a time when, for me, thinking is sharpest. I lay there reproaching myself for not trying harder to get Bearden's side of the story. Now it was too late. He was dead. *Rangoon Ramblings*, the newsletter of the American POW's who survived the Japanese prison in Rangoon, Burma, listed A. L. Bearden as having died in the years after liberation. There was a report that he had died in 1985 and was interred in the Fort Sam Houston National Cemetery in Houston, Texas. A few years ago I had tried, in Washington D.C., to track down Lt Bearden and got nowhere. More recently, I had contacted the United States Military Personnel Records Centre in St Louis, Missouri. The fact that the Texan had finished up in a national cemetery was proof that he had been honourably discharged and I wanted confirmation of this. However, you needed to be a next-of-kin to get any information from the records centre.

Without the full story, the least I could do was to make the point in this book that there was no slur against Lt Bearden's name when he died. I owed him that, but first I had to be sure he had been buried at the National Cemetery.

I was not conscious of having made the decision to do it but, in the dim, dawn light I found myself sleepily dialling international directory assistance. There was an A. L. Bearden listed in Houston. Again I hesitated.

'How can you be so insensitive to call a widow like this out of the blue?'

My wife's words were ringing in my ear while my fingers were dialling. A woman's voice answered.

'My name's Hudson. I'm calling from Sydney, Australia. Would there by any chance be someone at this number who is related to Lt Bearden, a pilot, who was in prison in Rangoon, Burma, during the war?'

'Al's here himself. Would you like to talk with him?'

Now I was fully awake.

'This is Al Bearden.'

'You couldn't be the Lt Bearden who was in Rangoon Gaol during the war?'

'I sure am.'

'But you're supposed to be dead. All the blokes in the gaol with us, they said you died two years ago and were buried in the Fort Sam Houston Cemetery.'

'Well, I'm not feeling too good, but I'm not dead yet.'

'That's good news. I'm glad the report of your death was exaggerated.'

There was a chuckle over the phone.

'So am I.'

'How come? How could this have happened?'

'The 80th Fighter Group in Assam got it wrong. They listed me as killed in action. That started it off . . .'

I knew by heart his entry in my gaol records: '0-748524 Lt Bearden, Aaron L., Houston. Texas 459 Sdn. P 38. On 3.9.44 D. bomb Myting, bridge. Rammed other P 38. Baled out, captured by Burmese, handed to Japs in Mandalay. Slight ill-treatment at interrogation, 4 days. Then talked bull. 14.9.44 City Jail. Leg wounded, no med. treat. 'til C. J. Rangoon Prison 22.9.44. Cell 29.' I had to be 100 per cent sure this was my man.

'How old would you be?'

'Sixty-nine.'

'What were you flying?'

'P 38.'

214

'Where were you shot down?' This was my trick question.

'I wasn't shot down. I rammed into another P 38 over the target.'

Yes, this was our Bearden. We chatted on. To my surprise he had never heard of the newsletter, *Rangoon Ramblings*.

'I haven't kept in touch with any of the guys,' he told me. 'Too busy getting on with my life.'

Neither had he heard about the Rangoon POW reunion in St Louis, Missouri in two months time. Anyway, he would not be able to make it.

'I'm not much on reunions. In any case, I'm not well enough.'

I said I was sorry about that, told him to look after himself and hung up.

I stood there for minutes agonizing over my dilemma and hating myself for not having had the guts to go further. Did he, or did he not, collaborate with the Japanese?

I dialled Texas again.

'Al, do you mind talking a bit about the gaol?'

'Shoot.'

'Well, you know most of us thought you were collaborating with the Japs?'

'Yes, I knew you were talking about me. Nothing I could do about it. You didn't know what I was going through.'

'Were you in trouble when you got out, back in Calcutta?'

'Oh, there was a lot of investigation stuff. First of all there was an air force investigation. They cleared me. Then the FBI.'

'The FBI?'

'Yes, I cleared myself with the people who count. They couldn't have been too worried about me. I was recommended for a Silver Star after my release. General George Stratemeyer gave me a commendation. I brought a Jap rifle back with me. They gave me a letter to carry it home. I've still got that rifle.'

'But, Al, the Japs kept taking you out of the gaol. It looked to us you were collaborating.'

'I never did. Hell, no. I was feeding them false information, and they were buying it.'

I reminded him how he was put into a cell for a few days with Herb Ivens, a Canadian, and myself.

'No, it was a Canadian and an English pilot.'

'That was me. I'm Australian. I was just flying with an RAF squadron, and I say in a book I've just written that you did not ask us any leading questions.'

'That's right. I didn't want to know anything factual. In that way I could not let anything slip. At one time they had a half-colonel, an American pilot, and they were beating the hell out of him until I persuaded them to let me have a go. We made up a lot of bull between us and after that they laid off him.'

The incredible thing, I told Al, was that he didn't say anything about all this to the other Americans when he was put back into the gaol.

'All the time I was lying to the Japs. I had to be real careful. If they had found out they would have slit my throat.'

'But feelings were running pretty high. A lot of us were convinced you were a stool pigeon.'

'That didn't bother me. I had no option. I was in a tough spot. If they told you to do something you did it, or else. You know that.'

'Yes, no doubt about that, if you wanted to survive. But, later, after the Japs had left, I had to tell Captain Meyer to put you into a cell for your own protection. Why didn't you speak up then?'

'Things were happening fast. Nobody wanted to listen to me. Carl, my buddy, knew the truth.' ('T-1643 Beardslee Carl M. Elmira, N.Y. 459 F. Sqdn. P 38. On 11.3.44 straffed Heho, attacked by Oscars. On fire. Baled out. Hit tail. Unconscious five days. No memory opening chute. 17.3.44 City Jail. R. Prison 17.7.44. Cell 18.')

'What happened when they took you out of the gaol? We all had the idea you were living off the fat of the land.'

'Yea? I went in at 170lbs and came out weighing 110. No, they treated me like a dog. Believe me, I'd rather have stayed in gaol. They used to take me to a house near the gaol. The main interrotagor came from Saigon. Their intelligence H.Q. was there. I had to keep my wits about me to survive. There were always two guards on me. We all slept in a double bed with me in the middle. If I moved a muscle they were on to me. I tell you, it was hairy. I'd say it was worse being knocked around outside the gaol than inside.'

'What about this story that you were helping the Japs to reassemble a wrecked P 38 near Rangoon?'

'Ah, you heard about that. That was a wild idea the Japs had. They had all sorts of parts from P 38s and had the crazy idea they could reconstruct one. I led them on for as long as I dared, knowing they'd never get it into the air. They were like little kids getting parts from a dump yard to build a motor car. Let me tell you a story. It was around the end of December, 1944. This Jap captain from Saigon asked me how long I thought the war would last. I said about two years. He insisted it would be all over next August. I said again the American people would fight on for another two years. But, he confided, not the Japanese people. They could last only until August. Japan would lose, he said, and then I will shake your hand and be your friend. But right now you are my prisoner. Then, slap, slap. He gave me a hell of a beating. Let me qualify that. It was just slapping, but those Jap hands are hard. As you know, we dropped the atom bomb on Hiroshima on August 6.'

'Wish I'd heard all this before. Can I write about it?'

'I don't care. Write what you like. Look, I'm pretty tired. I'd better get back to bed.'

'What's wrong with you, Al?'

'Cancer. Cancer of the lung and the hip. They say it's terminal.'

'Oh, I'm sorry to hear that. Do you mind if I tell the other fellows who were in the gaol with us?'

'I wouldn't bother. Who would be interested? Do what you like. I'd better get back to bed.'

So, at last, I'd heard Lt Bearden's side of the story. At one point he had said, 'I don't want to talk about it. That's all over and done with.' Yet the feeling came through as we talked that he had been wanting for a long time to put the record straight.

Karnig Thomasian, a gunner turned advertising man, and his wife, Diana, co-editors of *Rangoon Ramblings*, were stunned and happy at the news that Lt Bearden was still alive. Their information about his demise had come from the Veterans' Administration. They put me on to Roy Wentz, a navigator in the gaol, now an attorney in Wilmington, Delaware. He had mentioned the Bearden case in his diary of events in Rangoon Gaol written up after the war.

'Yes,' Roy told me, 'I wrote after the war that the whole compound was widely split over the situation. Many believed he was helping the Japs. However, through my daily walks with another P 38 pilot, Carl

Beardslee, Al's best friend and probably the only one in his confidence, I learned that Bearden was finding it tough fooling the Japs and he was fearful of his ability to stall them for much longer. Carl was convinced the Texan was really performing a veritable service to the United States.'

Yes, that was an important 'phone call.

Appendix

Letter from British Army sergeant, T.A.M., known as Pinky.

Dear Sir, I feel that it is not correct to call you Bill owing to the circumstances which I will relate. Who am I? A sergeant in the British Army who has twice escaped from the Nips!

I was in the battle of France and came out via Dunkirk. After a short stay in England I came overseas to Singapore. I was in the Battle of Malaya and Singapore. On the fall of Singapore I was captured but escaped later (18/2/42) . . . four others and myself got a small boat and arrived in Sumatra, after much hardship, on the 10/3/42, where I was once more captured on the 16/3/42. I stayed there as a P.O.W. for two months when they shipped me to Burma. I arrived at Mergui with 500 other British troops and worked there on the drome for a couple of months and was then sent to Tavoy, once more to work on a drome there.

During the whole of this period I was making plans for escape. We stayed there for a couple of months also. I had almost got my plans completed when we got word of a move to Moulmein. We went there and then on to Thanbuzyat, 40 miles north of Moulmein. I saw that this was the last possible move towards the north and decided that I had better leave my hosts in the very near future. All told I stayed there for 17 days then did a flit on 13/9/42. I made my way north by following the railway tracks moving at night and sleeping during daylight.

So as to avoid going through Moulmein and Martaban I crossed over on to Bilujon Island which lies in the mouth of the Salween, then landed on the mainland two miles west of Martaban, got on to the railway tracks again and proceeded west toward Sittang and Pegu. At

Jaikto which is one mile east of the Sittang I was stopped by an Indian and informed that he had orders to escort me to an English captain in the jungle who had had me followed from the time of my escape. So I took the chance and went with him to meet the Skipper on 30/9/42.

Well, we got together and decided that he be the big Chief and also in command of the northern sector of an area 250 miles long by 30 miles wide approx and that I be in charge of the southern sector to administrate it, attack all small enemy forces that I thought we could beat. Well, this worked very well for 8 months when the skipper sent for me and told me we were running too short of ammo' and as we were not in contact with the Allies somebody had to go and inform them of the situation in whole area absolutely free of Burmese-Nips and also a possible landing strip and a few other titbits.

I told him I would go so he sent myself and four Karens in five different routes myself taking the most dangerous but quickest i.e. Toungoo-Prome-Arakan Yoma-Akyab getting up close to the Nip line then going round by boat to our own lines. Well I had got the most dangerous part of my journey finished right across the plains and the Pegu Yoma.

I arrived on the banks of the Irrawaddy between Paungde and Prome when I got into the water the current was too strong for me and I had difficulty in getting to the shore again. I finally got ashore exhausted about five miles lower down where I was set upon by Burmese fishermen and have a few lovely scars on my back to remind me of this episode.

Anyway, they nearly killed me, then took me to the Nips at Prome who stitched me up but left me with four broken ribs which have not yet got better. I stayed in the hospital there for 28 days and was then sent to Rangoon still very ill on the 9/5/43. Was lodged in the Town jail for six weeks then sent here to spend a further 4½ months in solitary.

During my stay in Prome I was questioned – managed to bluff my way through as Lt . . . American Air Corps and have stuck to my story ever since but had some very hard times with American-educated Nips. I got a few bits of information about the B 25 so was the pilot. I know nothing at all about aircraft but have a mechanical mind as I am a member of the Recce Corps and can drive tanks, Bren gun carriers in fact anything which has four wheels or tracks.

Appendix

I am a regular soldier with 13 years service . . . have got a son now four years old but have not seen him since he was five months old and have not heard from home since I left there in '41. So you can bet I am looking forward to release with great impatience. Yours TAM (or TAIM).

Postscript

The date is November 18, 1987. At last, nearly 43 years later, I know the identity of 'Pinky' or, as he signed himself in the above letter, 'TAM'.

He is Roy Pagani, formerly of 18 Reconnaissance Battalion, part of the ill-fated British 18th Division captured in Singapore in February, 1942. He now lives in Clacton-on Sea, Essex.

I had many whispered conversations with him through the gaol wall. As the aircrew compound's main contact with the other Allied prisoners, he was invaluable to our morale. We caught glimpses of him now and again from a distance and dubbed him 'Pinky' because of his colouring. Names were not bandied about. It was too dangerous. He now tells me he signed the letter to me 'TAM'—his baby son's initials—in case it fell into Japanese hands.

Now I have had a letter from him. He has four children, eight grandchildren and three great grandchildren. Also, this incredible man has had a book written about him, *The Flame of Freedom,* to be published by Leo Cooper.

It transpired that 'Pinky', among other things, was the only man to make a successful escape from the Japanese on the Burma-Siam railway. After the war he was awarded a well-earned Military Medal for his work behind the lines.

The Australian pilot, Harvey Besley, (pages 42 and 200) was also awarded the Military Medal for his work as a medical assistant in the gaol hospital and for his part in the escape from the hostage column marched out of Rangoon by the Japanese.

Bestselling War Fiction and Non-Fiction

☐ Passage to Mutiny	Alexander Kent	£2.95
☐ Colours Aloft	Alexander Kent	£2.95
☐ Winged Escort	Douglas Reeman	£2.95
☐ Army of Shadows	John Harris	£2.50
☐ Decoy	Dudley Pope	£2.95
☐ Gestapo	Rupert Butler	£4.50
☐ Johnny Gurkha	E.D. Smith	£2.95
☐ Typhoon Pilot	Desmond Scott	£2.95
☐ The Rommel Papers	B.H. Liddel Hart	£5.95
☐ Hour of the Lily	John Kruse	£3.50
☐ Duel in the Dark	Peter Townsend	£3.95
☐ The Spoils of War	Douglas Scott	£2.99
☐ The Wild Blue	Walter J. Boyne & Steven L. Thompson	£3.95
☐ The Bombers	Norman Longmate	£4.99

Prices and other details are liable to change

ARROW BOOKS, BOOKSERVICE BY POST, PO BOX 29, DOUGLAS, ISLE OF MAN, BRITISH ISLES

NAME. . . . .

ADDRESS. . . . .

. . . .

. . . .

Please enclose a cheque or postal order made out to Arrow Books Ltd. for the amount due and allow the following for postage and packing.

U.K. CUSTOMERS: Please allow 22p per book to a maximum of £3.00.

B.F.P.O. & EIRE: Please allow 22p per book to a maximum of £3.00

OVERSEAS CUSTOMERS: Please allow 22p per book.

Whilst every effort is made to keep prices low it is sometimes necessary to increase cover prices at short notice. Arrow Books reserve the right to show new retail prices on covers which may differ from those previously advertised in the text or elsewhere.

A Selection of Arrow Bestsellers

☐ The Lilac Bus	Maeve Binchy	£2.50
☐ 500 Mile Walkies	Mark Wallington	£2.50
☐ Staying Off the Beaten Track	Elizabeth Gundrey	£5.95
☐ A Better World Than This	Marie Joseph	£2.95
☐ No Enemy But Time	Evelyn Anthony	£2.95
☐ Rates of Exchange	Malcolm Bradbury	£3.50
☐ Colours Aloft	Alexander Kent	£2.95
☐ Speaker for the Dead	Orson Scott Card	£2.95
☐ Eon	Greg Bear	£4.95
☐ Talking to Strange Men	Ruth Rendell	£5.95
☐ Heartstones	Ruth Rendell	£2.50
☐ Rosemary Conley's Hip and Thigh Diet	Rosemary Conley	£2.50
☐ Communion	Whitley Strieber	£3.50
☐ The Ladies of Missalonghi	Colleen McCullough	£2.50
☐ Erin's Child	Sheelagh Kelly	£3.99
☐ Sarum	Edward Rutherfurd	£4.50

Prices and other details are liable to change

ARROW BOOKS, BOOKSERVICE BY POST, PO BOX 29, DOUGLAS, ISLE OF MAN, BRITISH ISLES

NAME. . . . .

ADDRESS . . . .

. . . .

. . . .

Please enclose a cheque or postal order made out to Arrow Books Ltd. for the amount due and allow the following for postage and packing.

U.K. CUSTOMERS: Please allow 22p per book to a maximum of £3.00.

B.F.P.O. & EIRE: Please allow 22p per book to a maximum of £3.00

OVERSEAS CUSTOMERS: Please allow 22p per book.

Whilst every effort is made to keep prices low it is sometimes necessary to increase cover prices at short notice. Arrow Books reserve the right to show new retail prices on covers which may differ from those previously advertised in the text or elsewhere.

Bestselling Fiction

☐ Hiroshmia Joe	Martin Booth	£2.95
☐ The Pianoplayers	Anthony Burgess	£2.50
☐ Queen's Play	Dorothy Dunnett	£3.95
☐ Colours Aloft	Alexander Kent	£2.95
☐ Contact	Carl Sagan	£3.50
☐ Talking to Strange Men	Ruth Rendell	£5.95
☐ Heartstones	Ruth Rendell	£2.50
☐ The Ladies of Missalonghi	Colleen McCullough	£2.50
☐ No Enemy But Time	Evelyn Anthony	£2.95
☐ The Heart of the Country	Fay Weldon	£2.50
☐ The Stationmaster's Daughter	Pamela Oldfield	£2.95
☐ Erin's Child	Sheelagh Kelly	£3.99
☐ The Lilac Bus	Maeve Binchy	£2.50

Prices and other details are liable to change

ARROW BOOKS, BOOKSERVICE BY POST, PO BOX 29, DOUGLAS, ISLE OF MAN, BRITISH ISLES

NAME..

ADDRESS..

....

....

Please enclose a cheque or postal order made out to Arrow Books Ltd. for the amount due and allow the following for postage and packing.

U.K. CUSTOMERS: Please allow 22p per book to a maximum of £3.00.

B.F.P.O. & EIRE: Please allow 22p per book to a maximum of £3.00

OVERSEAS CUSTOMERS: Please allow 22p per book.

Whilst every effort is made to keep prices low it is sometimes necessary to increase cover prices at short notice. Arrow Books reserve the right to show new retail prices on covers which may differ from those previously advertised in the text or elsewhere.

Bestselling Thriller/Suspense

☐ Hell is Always Today	Jack Higgins	£2.50
☐ Brought in Dead	Harry Patterson	£1.99
☐ Russian Spring	Dennis Jones	£2.50
☐ Fletch	Gregory Mcdonald	£1.95
☐ Black Ice	Colin Dunne	£2.50
☐ Blind Run	Brian Freemantle	£2.50
☐ The Proteus Operation	James P. Hogan	£3.50
☐ Miami One Way	Mike Winters	£2.50
☐ Skydancer	Geoffrey Archer	£2.50
☐ Hour of the Lily	John Kruse	£3.50
☐ The Tunnel	Stanley Johnson	£2.50
☐ The Albatross Run	Douglas Scott	£2.50
☐ Dragonfire	Andrew Kaplan	£2.99

Prices and other details are liable to change

ARROW BOOKS, BOOKSERVICE BY POST, PO BOX 29, DOUGLAS, ISLE OF MAN, BRITISH ISLES

NAME...

ADDRESS...

....

....

Please enclose a cheque or postal order made out to Arrow Books Ltd. for the amount due and allow the following for postage and packing.

U.K. CUSTOMERS: Please allow 22p per book to a maximum of £3.00.

B.F.P.O. & EIRE: Please allow 22p per book to a maximum of £3.00

OVERSEAS CUSTOMERS: Please allow 22p per book.

Whilst every effort is made to keep prices low it is sometimes necessary to increase cover prices at short notice. Arrow Books reserve the right to show new retail prices on covers which may differ from those previously advertised in the text or elsewhere.